Dedication

I dedicate this book to a very special person who encouraged and supported my endeavor. She is my love and my wife. Thank you for giving gentle words to nudge my curiosity. When my train of thought was derailed, you encouraged me to rely on my intuition and follow that path.

I know writing a book is transforming to its author and I have also learned that supporting the writer is another form of love and transforming in itself. Thank you my love.

Table Of Contents

About Dr. Todd Spinks

Dr. Todd Spinks, Director, Office of Sustainability,
The University of North Texas System

Dr. Spinks joined UNT in 2009, and oversees all sustainability efforts at the university in areas of research, operations, outreach, and teaching students. He has received over $2.2 million in grant monies, to conduct research and implement infrastructure projects in renewable energy. Dr. Spinks serves on, and works with, several UNT research groups, to include the Renewable Energy & Conservation research cluster.

Dr. Spinks travels internationally consulting communities, government leaders, and corporate executives toward developing frameworks for sustainable growth. Prior to joining UNT, Dr. Spinks worked at the U.S. EPA, as the lead social scientist on several regional and national task forces to develop solutions addressing community development, environmental justice, challenges to indigenous communities, intergovernmental relations, and environmental issues around the globe. Dr. Spinks' research and course instruction focus on international sustainable community development, causes of political violence, and comparative politics. Dr. Spinks served in the US Army, stationed in Southeast Asia and the Middle East.

About Raynard O. Kearbey

Raynard O. Kearbey AIA, NCARB, LEED AP BD+C, MSFM
Associate Vice Chancellor for System Facilities
University of North Texas System

Mr. Kearbey joined the University of North Texas System in February 2007. Prior to joining the UNT System, he spent six years in Planning and Construction at Southern Methodist University in Dallas, Texas and twenty-five years in Real Estate, Design and Construction at Southwestern Bell Corporation. Mr. Kearbey received a Bachelor of Architecture from Kansas State University and a Master of Science in Facilities Management from Southern Methodist University. While at KSU Mr. Kearbey was awarded membership in the Tau Sigma Delta Architectural Honorary Society. As the Associate Vice Chancellor for System Facilities, Mr. Kearbey oversees the planning, development and construction of capital projects for the campuses in the UNT System. In addition, he manages the Office of System Facilities, Planning and Construction.

Mr. Kearbey is a member of the American Institute of Architects, the Texas Society of Architects, National Council of Architectural Registration Boards, the Society for College and University Planning, and the International Code Council. A LEED Accredited Professional in Building Design and Construction, in the past seven years he has overseen the construction of multiple LEED certified buildings in higher education – all have achieved a minimum of Gold level certification. The building types and purposes were quite diversified – ranging from an Engineering teaching laboratory, General Academic, Biology Research, Medical Education Training, Business Leadership, a parking garage with central plant and offices, and one LEED Platinum collegiate football stadium.

About Ralph W. Jarvis

Ralph W. Jarvis - Sustainability Author, Senior Consultant
Global MBA - International Finance, MM - MIS,
Executive Certificate in Global CSR, LSS Black Belt

Mr. Jarvis has over 30 years of Business, IT and Sustainability experience. In addition, he has worked with clients and colleagues in Asia, Australia, Europe, North and South America. His engagements, before and during his 10 year career at EDS, includes a variety of Fortune 500 multinational corporations; federal, state, and Indian Nation governments; as well as, not-for-profit organizations.

As a management consultant, he knows that company Owners and Executives are constantly searching for better ways to do business. With hands-on experience in business evolution, he believes Sustainability will be a key centerpiece in every prudent 21st century business strategy and that will yield increased corporate performance, profitability and a competitive advantage. While many Owners and Executives are considering Sustainability projects, very few are clear how to effectively implement a Sustainability initiative. This book provides one path.

This book was designed to answer many of the Sustainability questions why executives would consider making a change to their organization and what are the wastes that should be eliminated from the enterprise. This book provides a step-by-step approach, from Vision to eliminating Waste, in molding the organization into a Sustainable Develop enterprise and finally gaining tangible benefits.

In 2011, Mr. Jarvis published his first book, "Any Questions?", which is a leadership primer to addresses the union of Sustainability and Quality management to optimize profitability, increase performance and reduce waste.

Mr. Jarvis graduated from Texas Tech University with a Bachelors in Business Administration. Shortly after graduation, he began work at Texas Instrument in Lubbock, Texas. There he worked in International Operations and Information Systems.

He successfully completed postgraduate work at Thunderbird Graduate School of Management where he majored in International Finance. He accepted a planning position with NCH Corporation and implemented a planning system that covered over 50 countries. He worked 13 years in that transition, working with different cultures, changing mindsets and integrating many of the concepts promoted by William McDonough and Michael Braungart.

He also attended the University of Dallas where he received his second Masters degree in Management Information Systems. There, he graduated with Highest Honors, was the sole MIS graduate with that distinction and was inducted into the National Honorary Management Fraternity.

He completed and received his capstone Executive Certificate in Global CSR (Corporate Social Responsibility) under the tutelage Dr. Gregory Unruh at Thunderbird in 2011.

Acknowledgements

"No other time in history has Humanity seen future possibilities for Earth and Humanity will be judged by its actions to preserve its biosphere. For Humanity will be defined by how we preserve or exhaust Nature."
~ Ralph Jarvis

Learning is based on desire, effort and understanding. It is a deliberate process of reading, researching and teaching oneself the principles of the subject matter. In a pragmatic sense, it is linking the information and applying it to the real world. We need to seek understanding through careful preparation, study and applying previous experiences that have worked and avoid those that did not. The Sustainability body of knowledge is in its infancy.

Sustainability promotes awareness.
Awareness promotes learning and values.
Learning promotes anticipation for the future.
Imagination triggers ideas of what could be created, and
Innovation creates that future we want to build.

Sustainability is based on a growing body of knowledge, gathered for about 40-50 years. It is still evolving. Some elements are founded on environmental foundations, some are based on economic approaches, and others, still, originate from social disciplines and experiences. This collective intellectual capital will be a catalyst for a Future Renaissance that will meld various disciplines into abundance of solutions for the present and the future.

We are discovering that Business can indeed exist profitably, in tandem, with Nature and will need to successfully accomplish that goal for the remainder of this century. This is a shift in thinking, mindset and effective transformation for humanity and how we use Earth's resources effectively.

We should glean understanding not only from case studies, books, research, but integrate that knowledge with pragmatic experiences of varied professionals. The Future Renaissance will leverage this model to create new and better approaches that will engage millions around the world to better fit humanity into a new model, based on Sustainability and Commerce. For this is a collective process of integrating intelligence into holistic approaches and models that present comprehensive solutions to a very complex problem for survivability, sustainability, restoration and steward-ship of the biosphere.

I wish to thank my friends and mentors who helped me gain a greater un-derstanding of various aspects of disciplines, whether academic or applied knowledge, that enriches and is a segment of Sustainability through dis-cussions surrounding human behavior, business considerations, environ-mental considerations, architecture, energy conservation and construction, sciences, history, astronomy, biology, and especially those friends who shared their environmental concerns and interest in renewable energy and development of other resources that minimize the human impact on our Earth.

I count each of these fine people as friends and colleagues who have shared their body of knowledge. Each have a special view of this planet. Each have given me the insight to say; "For Humanity is defined by how we use Nature." Please accept my deepest thanks for sharing your time and thoughts with me.

- Dr. Todd Spinks, thank you for your time in helping edit this book, especially while starting a new semester. I know the timing of edit-ing this book was not optimal, but your actions demonstrated your commitment to Sustainability with a like-minded ally. Not only am I truly grateful, but your opinion is highly regarded by me and your suggestions helped refine my message. I sincerely thank you for your help and your encouragement. I always look forward to our conversations and never walk away from our discussions without insights to think about.

- Raynard Kearbey, I also want to thank you for your offer to help edit this book. It was truly a gift. Sharing your thoughts around Sustainable Development and applying engineering and construc-tion techniques in making the world energy efficient, water sensi-tive and applying renewable energy, effectively gave me insights and areas for consideration. Like other Sustainability practitioners, your legacy will include "doing the right thing" that will stand the test of time and I know your family will share in that legacy for generations to come. I always look forward to our talks and your encouragement, too.

- Dr. Greg Unruh, thank you for sharing your knowledge and your lecture series that gave me a framework for Sustainability. Your insights continue take me through the Sustainability journey and provide knowledge that validated my studies and assumptions. Maybe one of these days our stars will align and we'll finally have that lunch. Again, thanks for sowing those seeds of Sustainability.

- Dr. Walt Casey, you have been a great help in so many ways. Walt. I was always grateful for your vigilance in catching and emailing germane Sustainability articles for my research and accompanying me to on-site projects. (Yeah, I confess, I often enjoyed our diametrically opposed exchange of ideas, too.).

- Bill Hubeny, your breadth of knowledge has astounded me so many times over the years. Bill, you have often been a good kibitzer, a mentor and source of wonderful forms of information. Thank you for our conversations about history, religion and many areas of science.

- Dr. Greg Bell, thank you for the opportunity to bring my insights to the classroom and planting those Sustainability "seeds" into the minds of a new generation of business professionals.

In a metaphorical sense, we are all linchpins to the success of Sustainability. Each linchpin is connected to another, to another and to others. The result will be a network of connectivity focused on solutions supporting a new business model, Sustainability, like linchpins, when is not connected, our effectiveness will be under utilized and ineffective.

There is real hope for the future. Those who came before us, in various disciplines, prepared the foundation of understanding and imagination for generations to come. We have that ability to keep our economic models. We now have knowledge that also creates significant capabilities for our environment and society. We have the building blocks to create a foundation for future growth and preserve our planet, Earth.

Perhaps Galileo put it in context when he said; "The sun, with all those planets revolving around it and dependent on it, can still ripen a bunch of grapes as if it had nothing else in the universe to do."

Forward: Looking Through A Sustainability Lens

"We have reached a point where the value we do add to our economy is now being outweighed by the value we are removing, not only from future generations in terms of diminished resources, but from ourselves in terms of unlivable cities, deadening jobs, deteriorating health, and rising crime. In biological terms, we have become a parasite and are devouring our host."
~Paul Hawken, The Ecology of Commerce, 1994

This book is written to provide an overview of Sustainability for Owners, Board of Directors, Stakeholders, Executive Officers and Employees. It is designed to present the "whys" of Sustainability Transformation. Its goal is to provide a grasp of the subject matter for anyone who wants a better understanding of the value of Sustainability, its principles and answer many of the "whys" and "hows" of change.

There were several ways of organizing this book by subject matter. Many other researchers have taken the approach of "People, Profits and Planet"; or "Environmental, Economics and Social"; but I thought that would add more value to illustrate a "top-down" approach with employee engagement and empowerment, driven by a keen desire for a company "to do the right thing".

It also discusses Sustainability combined with Quality methodology to compliment the effort to eliminate waste in the organization and its processes and to secure gains by eliminating waste. The combination of these two major concepts, when merged, will provide your organization with a structured approach for organizational maturity and growth. Those principles will also construct the "spine" or "backbone" to add other essential internal and external branches as your enterprise continues to grow and mature.

There are misperceptions that only very large corporations would benefit from Sustainability. That is not entirely correct. Due to their size, their waste may be higher and remediation of those wasteful practices could have significant impact on costs and eliminations of environmental wastes. But waste exists in almost all business enterprises and governments. Savings and efficiency can be extracted by changing the organization and "current practices", regardless of organizational size.

Strongly linked to Sustainability is the concept of "Corporate Social Responsibility". It is often used interchangeably with Corporate Responsibility, Corporate Citizenship, Social Enterprise, Sustainability, Sustainable Development, Triple Bottom Line, Corporate Ethics, and in some cases Corporate Governance. Though these terms are different, they all point to Sustainability and Sustainable Development as primary frameworks for transformation.

In a very general sense, Owners and Executives Officers need to think locally, even though they may be a global enterprise. Fundamentals are discussed, such as the importance of our biosphere, impact on the resources and ultimate tipping the balance of nature. Understanding and becoming aware of how Nature cradles our survival, exposing Humanity's impact on Nature, and discussing megaforces that, if trends continue, will threaten Humanity's existence. Discussions include how the enterprise can be adapted and exploit changes, both internally and externally, to reduce waste and become more Sustainable.

What Did Ray Think?
Ray Anderson, an industrialists and the first modern day American Sustainability pioneer, was asked about transforming the contemporary business mindset. He agreed that many ideas are out of date strongly believed that Sustainability principles would be the new mindset. Anderson said; "I also believe that it doesn't happen quickly ... it happens one mind at a time, one organization at a time, one building, one company, one community, one region, one new, clean technology, one industry, one supply chain at a time ... until the entire industrial system has been transformed into a sustainable system, existing ethically in balance with Earth's natural systems, upon which every living thing is utterly dependent."

1. A Vision For Sustainability[1]

"People only see what they are prepared to see."
~ Ralph Waldo Emerson

Ray Anderson was one of the first pioneers in Sustainability. An American industrial engineer who became a billionaire from his company Interface that produced modular carpet tiles. He recognized that business practices and laws permitting emissions were destroying the country he dearly loved. In his book <u>Mid-Course Correction</u> that was published in 1998, he wrote; "There is not an industrial company on earth, and - I feel pretty safe in saying - not a company or institution of any kind … that is not sustainable. In the sense of meeting its current needs without, in some measure, depriving future generations of the means of meeting their needs. When Earth runs out of finite, exhaustible resources and ecosystems collapse, our descendants will be left holding the empty bag."

He could envision that Sustainability is a mindset and that mindset would ultimately frame those ideas into a methodology for transformation. Mr. Anderson also had the insight and conviction to motivate him to be a pioneer and leader in Sustainability. He passed that baton along to the next generation of proponents of sustainable development. Now it is your turn.

Companies in all sectors need to prepare themselves for a world where raw materials may be in short supply[2]. Within the next five to ten years, resources will be affected and their shortages will impact industries and products delayed to the marketplace. Most significant will be shortage of food and water. These are only examples, but assuming continued population growth and demand for products, the shortages will become much larger and more critical as we move closer to 2050. The future scenarios are topics of repeated studies and reports that provide insight how business "as usual" will need to adapt. Business models that embrace Sustainability will be better prepared and better positioned to survive major disruptions in resources.

"More and more companies are embracing Sustainability as a cornerstone in their strategy to build competitive advantage. There is clearly strategic thinking going on at the highest level in business and government." At the same time, Haugland[3] warns that "there is still a large number of companies that are not acting decisively on Sustainability issues due to the lack of knowledge and organizational capabilities…and ultimately this will lead to winners and losers. Put simply, Sustainability matters to business and those who take it seriously and use it as a source for innovation will prosper in the years ahead[4]." Sustainability is an evolutionary process and builds on previous stages of development:

- First, Sustainability is a new mindset and focuses on awareness how resources are used, wastes created and compliance with regulations.
- Second, understanding leads to elimination of waste. This conviction will be a key driver, encouraging optimization of processes as an underpinning to successful Sustainability, reaping costs savings and increased productivity.
- Third, leverage your Sustainability effort to differentiate your products. Build a closer relationship with existing Customers to address their needs and differentiate new products for new customers.
- Fourth, interleave Sustainability throughout your corporate strategies (Operations, IT, Marketing etc) and create a comprehensive single "Sustainability strategy" for both external and internal communities.
- Fifth, promote and refine your aspirational strategies for philanthropy (e.g., breast cancer, military vet programs, diseases, etc), restoration (e.g., wetlands, reforestations, etc.), other social and environmental issues. For those efforts will reflect on your brand image, but remind yourself that continued optimization is ongoing for a Sustainable enterprise, not a one time goal.

Your Vision also introduces Transparency to all stakeholders. Transparency is more than just a way to comply with legal responsibilities; it's how you attract societal resources to solve them. Sharing information openly with your constituents will open your business for ideas and innovations from every crack and crevice of your organization. By systematically measuring and reporting on your own sustainability, you will engage everyone--from your employees to your customers to your suppliers to your critics--in the process of building a truly sustainable enterprise[5].

Defining Sustainability

Sustainability is a pattern of resource use that aims to meet current human needs while preserving the environment so that those needs can be met not only in the present, but in the indefinite future. The terms originated in the Nixon Administration with the passing of the National Environmental Policy Act (NEPA), which established the EPA, and whose purpose was to "foster and promote the general welfare, to create and maintain conditions under which man and nature can exist in productive harmony and fulfill the social, economic and other requirements of present and future generations."

The National Environmental Policy Act of 1969 articulated a growing interest in understanding the importance of the relationship between humans and the environment. The very language of the act foreshadows ideals soon to be of great significance globally:

"... to declare a national policy which will encourage productive and enjoyable harmony between man and his environment; to promote efforts which will prevent or eliminate damage to the environment and biosphere and stimulate the health and welfare of man."

In 1987, a World Commission on Environment and Development report (UN, 1987) entitled, Our Common Future (also known as the Brundtland report) called for the global adoption of these principles and presented the classic and most quoted definition of sustainable development:

"... development that meets the needs of the present without compromising the ability of future
generations to meet their own needs."

It is clear that a significant transformation of human production and consumption patterns will be needed in order to enable continued economic growth while protecting critical environmental resources[6].

Views about Sustainability are much like a random meeting of 12 different people. They meet, rub their chins, scratch their heads and express their opinions from over heard conversations at the coffee shop and watching Nature videos. There may be disdain, wariness, skepticism, curiosity, or just recognizing "you know that you don't know". If you start a conversation, most will agree what Sustainability is not and what it is. However, keep in mind that Sustainability addresses a humanitarian, as well as, planetary issues, protecting the biosphere:

- Sustainability is not a political issue (i.e., Democratic, Republican, Libertarian).
- Sustainability is not a radical environmental issue, though there is that perception, especially when it hinders profits.
- Sustainability is an effective approach to meet or eliminate emissions, address compliance regulations, remove waste and boost profitability.
- Embracing Sustainability as a corporate philosophy and ethic will promote improvements in brand image, performance and link closer to community constituents.
- But unanimously, after deliberate thought, they would probably agree Sustainability is not "their" problem, it is "our" problem.

Sustainability is constantly evolving as a body of knowledge. Learning from decades of transformation to rectify centuries of lacking knowledge or general awareness of consequences. We now generally understand how we can take ownership and change our behavior to avoid those pitfalls. These components are interlocks to effectively preserve our planet while benefitting society to provide a comprehensive platform for sustainable business strategy and for accelerating best practices and performance.

In the course of examining Corporate Strategies and linking to corresponding Sustainability Strategies, each of these levels will drive the focus of the Transformation Initiative and how a Sustainable Development Transformation will be integrated into your organization. For weaknesses found in each of these questions, an opportunity exists in transforming that weakness into strengths. Earlier, I shared the five most important business questions that should be asked in Business, Sustainability and Quality terms:

- What is our Mission?
- Who is our Customer?
- What does the Customer Value?
- What are our Results?
- What is our Plan[7]?

The business environment is changing, mainly due to population growth and its demands on the biosphere. Sustainability addresses environment, economic and social issues. Businesses foresees over regulation by government and possible fines and increased fees for current and previous emission issues. Business is becoming more competitive and your Customers are more important now than ever before. Sustainability addresses many of those marketplace issues. It is a framework to recognize constraints, highlight opportunities, identify internal weaknesses and build on strengths. In short, Sustainability provides insights that can leverage your strengths and opportunities.

Vision Examples

In general, Vision Statements define the organizations purpose and offer aspirational goals, rather than bottom line measures. It communicates the purpose and values of the enterprise. For employees, it sets expectations to behave, addresses ethics, inspires their employees to "do the right thing" or give their best. Externally, outside stakeholders are given insight to the company's philosophy, best practices, social and community goals, and provides an understanding of why those stakeholder would want to work with the company.

Vision Statements are a reflection of the shift in mindset of the enterprise. Business is no longer just focused on profit, but its role is based on shared value, recognizing that its activities affect the society and environment that thrives in. The following Vision Statements, although individually unique, have Sustainability objectives and values embedded, which helps focus on their core values and aspirations:

Chevron: At the heart of The Chevron Way is our vision ... to be *the* global energy company most admired for its people, partnership and performance. Our vision means we:
- safely provide energy products vital to sustainable economic progress and human development throughout the world;
- are people and an organization with superior capabilities and commitment;
- are the partner of choice;
- earn the admiration of all our stakeholders – investors, customers, host governments, local communities and our employees – not only for the goals we achieve but how we achieve them;
- deliver world-class performance[8].

Herman Miller: At Herman Miller we believe the future quality of human life is dependent on both economic vitality and a healthy, sustainable natural environment. We do not see these goals as mutually exclusive, but inextricably linked. Mankind's future depends on meeting the needs and aspirations of a growing global population, while enhancing and protecting the ecosystem on which all life depends.

In keeping with our pledge to strive for economic, environmental, and social equity, we have launched "Perfect Vision," a broad initiative that sets significant sustainability targets for the year 2020, including:
- Zero landfill
- Zero hazardous waste generation
- Zero air emissions (VOC)
- Zero process water use
- 100 percent green electrical energy use
- Company buildings constructed to a minimum Leadership in Energy and Environmental Design (LEED®) Silver certification
- 100 percent of sales from DfE-approved products

We recognize the challenges inherent in setting such goals, but we believe the exercise of sound strategic thinking across our enterprise, coupled with evolving technologies, will enable us to achieve our objectives[9].

Interface Global: Ray Anderson, was the Sustainability pioneer of Sustainability transformation and began trailblazing the Sustainability journey for the US and perhaps the world.

To be the first company that, by its deeds, shows the entire industrial world what sustainability is in all its dimensions: People, process, product, place and profits — by 2020 — and in doing so we will become restorative through the power of influence[10].

Changing a Vision to Sustainability

Interesting enough, research shows there are at least two paths to Sustainability. Sustainability can be a voluntary, directed and focused initiative designed to transform the mindset and culture within your organization. Often times this is a culmination of a series of transformations that has brought your organization to realize that the next step should be long-term and more stable over time. Sustainability can also be an obligation from the central government to ensure environmental control of emissions that encourages best practices or driven by market or internal forces to survive the changing market landscape.

However, there is another perspective that acknowledges that Sustainability is the evolutionary "next step" of investigating internal and external opportunities. Not every company understands Sustainability, nor embraces CSR to implement it correctly. Understanding starts with recognizing threats and accepting why change is necessary. Here are twelve possible scenarios why a company would choose to be socially responsible:

Reason #1: Urgently Needed Fixes: Often times, Owners and Executives will want to transform their organization, with a since of urgency, for immediate reasons. Many times this is triggered by a crisis or event that forces the need for change. It may be a vacuum in the succession of the business leadership, market valuations, illegal business practices or environmental catastrophes. Owners and Executives, who are forward thinking, will recognize potential impact of their crisis and foresee the consequences and recognize the potential exposure from past practices.

Reason #2: It's just the way it has always been[11]: Succession of leadership is an opportunity for change. This is especially true when the original founders of the Corporation past leadership roles to trusted personnel and family. Taking this transition creates an opportunity for change that could outline a number of reasons why executives would consider Sustainability as the next logical organizational change. The organizational mantra "it's always been this way" should be a signal for leadership to look at areas of waste and applying Sustainability and Quality principles.

Reason #3: CEO interest[12]: A CEO may have a number of interests around Sustainability, but the two most important are based on tangible benefits in mitigation of external risks. Today, more often than not CEOs will rely upon their CFOs expertise and understanding of tangible benefits from Sustainability. From a risk point of view, CEOs must play the leadership role when confronted by NGOs. As Steve Fludder, VP of Ecomagination, GE said; "Let's figure out how to take the world in a different direction and let's all go there together."

Reason #4: Reducing Costs To Stay Competitive: Good leadership will have costs as targets for business success. Would these cost savings have happened anyway without Sustainability? Perhaps. Looking through Sustainability lens, identification and elimination of costs will be seen differently. Here are some examples of how costs could increase performance and profitability in an organization:

- Cut mileage out of transportation routes
- Reduce energy consumption
- Reduce water consumption
- Telecommuting to reduce employee carbon footprint and increase productivity
- Eliminate a variety of waste, internally and externally

Reason #5: Legislative Uncertainty: CSR is a form of corporate self-regulation integrated into a business model. CXOs see a large amount of uncertainty in the private sector that spans social, environmental and economic arenas. From and executive perspective, the CSR model is adopted to address shrinking resources, create a competitive advantage, instill innovation and provide end-to-end control of the business.

Especially in the U.S., CXOs are wary of "anti-business" rhetoric that could cascade into possible legislation that would create barriers and add new costs that will increase government involvement in environmental processes and procedures. In this context, CSR is a mitigation tool against government over regulation of an industry. Further, CSR policy functions as a built-in, self-regulating mechanism; whereby a business monitors and ensures its active compliance with the spirit of the law, ethical standards, and international regulations.

Whether through court decisions, regulations, or legislation; companies and industries can be forced into social and environmentally responsible practices. They are also worried about possible legislation that would penalize previous behavior and increase future litigation and risk to business.

Currently, EPA regulations mostly monitor impact from air, water and land emissions. But increased presidential use of Executive Orders are expanding scope and regulations over business, thus incurring new costs, narrowing profitability and possibly limiting business opportunities.

Reason #6: Overzealous Marketers[13]: "Greenwashing" is recognized as the "yellow journalism" of marketing. It makes claims about a product or company that cannot be substantiated by actual business or environmental actions or records involving the protection of community, habitat or the entire planet. Overzealous marketers are essentially disingenuous story-tellers who are not practicing social responsibility and not transparent. However, prudent leadership caught in "liar, liar, pants on fire" scenario may be compelled to rectify that behavior and improve their brand image through active Sustainability practices.

Reason #7: Third Party Intervention: A financial institution that has supported the business may seek improvements in the business performance to reduce a potential risk to their investment. This may prompt the business leaders to take improvement actions that were previously alien to satisfy the institution and reduce the risk to their own assets that may be held as a guarantee against the investment[14].

Reason #8: **Sales Decline:** There may be a serious decline in sales. Competition, new technologies, a failure to meet the customer needs and expectations, a history of poor product development and introduction or poor marketing may all be contributory factors in reduced sales and be the catalyst for the business owner to change the approach to the business development[15].

Reason #9: **Takeover:** The business is acquired and the policies and practices of the acquiring business are adopted and introduce a proactive approach to the business. This may follow the appointment of new executive directors[16].

Reason #10: **Lack of Internal Skills:** The dearth of management skills within the business may trigger the appointment of an external senior executive who brings new methodologies, planning and enterprise to the business[17].

Reason #11: **Family Business 'Turmoil':** The autocratic control of an owner may at times only be changed through the realization that permanent family divisions are undesirable. It may well be the opportunity for perhaps the 'university educated next generation of family' to demonstrate their abilities in setting and achieving sustainable growth strategies and managing the culture change[18].

Reason #12: Where's The Beef? This a true "loss of face" predicament when your executives have promoted that the company meets or exceeds compliance to Sustainability principles and standards, but either have not fully implemented checks and balance, not completely institutionalized all employees, have not tethered executive incentives to behavior or do not hold Suppliers to the same standards. The most obvious example is British Petroleum [BP]. BP had engage its entire enterprise and committed to Sustainability for years. It was often highlighted as an example of making a carbon based industry leader into a paragon of Sustainability virtue.

However, in 2010, that lofty status was dethroned when BP created the worst environmental disaster in the Gulf of Mexico.

In hindsight, it could be suggested that their Sustainability program was a form of "greenwashing" and not practicing sustainable practices. Other contend that the spill was due to lack of management, sustainable or otherwise, since unpublicized - revealed by media investigations - found that BP had a poor safety record leading up to the oil spill. However, should you go to BP's[19] web site, their Sustainability goals are clearly displayed:

- We strive to be a safety leader in our industry, a world-class operator, a responsible corporate citizen and a good employer.
- We expect all our contractors and their employees to act in a way that is consistent with our code of conduct.
- We are committed to meeting our obligations to the countries and communities in which we do business.

For all enterprises, understanding Sustainability, truly institutionalizing best practices, integrating ethics, recognizing environmental and social issues and making Sustainability a key strategic initiative can mitigate risks to the survival of your corporation. But, not understanding Sustainability and not weaving that responsibility throughout your organization can have significant consequences.

Awareness, Reveals Issues
For the near future, a number of external influencers are identified that would need to be considered in formulating strategies in today's world. The imperative to stretch resources ever further will make Sustainability a central design principle for the winning corporations of the future.

Our planet now supports over 7 billion people and impact from mega-forces, dynamics in technology transfer, will those warning and guidelines in the 1980s are still sound and forewarn where business transformation in the 21st century will be required.

- ***Resource Consumption:*** Given population growth rates, increase in manufacturing output will be needed just to raise developing world to meet consumption of manufactured goods to industrialized world level by 2050.

- ***Emission Technology:*** Industrialized nations have proven that anti-pollution technology is cost-effective in terms of health, property, and environmental damage avoided, and that it has made many industries more profitable by making them more resource-efficient.

- **Technology Transfer:** Many developing countries also need assistance and information from industrialized nations to make the best use of technology. If developed countries resist, African and Asian countries will consider their alternatives. In this scenario, corporations should acknowledge potential increase corporate espionage, corruption and bribery.

- **Potential Legislation from Developed Countries:** With expected export of hazardous industrial and agricultural chemicals to Third World will probably be tightened with new legislation.

- **Potential Future Taxes:** Human needs can be met only through goods and services provided by industry, and the shift to sustainable development must be powered by a continuing flow of wealth from industry.

- **Increased Tariffs or Embargoes:** With increased consumption of rare earths, supplying countries may try to control supplies restricting production of energy efficient or energy producing products in other countries.

Sustainability is rooted in doing more with fewer resources or at least doing more with more recycled resources. Essentially, it is wasting less and making responsible decisions about how to operate more efficiently. However, if your company is focused or dependent on carbon energy, then there are other ways of reducing resource usage while improving performance. In the logistics industry, there's no getting around it: It takes fossil fuels to transport goods.
- At UPS, fuel represents about 5 to 6 percent of our costs.
- Anytime we reduce fuel usage, we reduce costs.
- Anytime we make our global supply chain more efficient, we reduce costs.
- And, in the process, we reduce carbon emissions.
- This is relevant to anyone in the audience whose company ships goods.
- How many of you have shipped something in the last month? …
- An efficient supply chain is a more sustainable supply chain, especially in these days when goods are as likely to come from across the world as across the street[20].

Sustainability and Bottom Line
It is also a time that Humanity has recognized our planet has limited resources to fulfill your needs (but it is not the first time). It is a new time. It is a time for well-managed resources. We cannot pack up and move to virgin territory after mismanaging previous resources. It is a time we need to

control resources and consumption of those resources to benefit the needs of this generation and those that will inherit what resources left for them. It is a pragmatic issue for the 21st Century, that is moving business to a new model, Sustainable Development, recognizing:

↑ Sustainability + ↑ Quality + Continuous Improvement + Secured Gains = Increase Profitability Potential

Sustainability is not a replacement for strategic planning. It is a series of processes that expand and compliment your visibility of your business activity. It provides method to acknowledge new opportunities and threats. It focuses on your cultural organization can be oriented and aligned to your current strategic planning framework. For example, many touch points will be integrated to reflect Sustainability in your enterprise, examples of some of the key points include:

- Create a clear Vision outlining what the organization should be in the Future State.
- Create a Mission Statement, which defines the fundamental purpose of your organization, briefly describes why it exists and what it does to achieve its Vision.
- Bedrock Corporate Values that are shared among the Stakeholders of an organization.
- A set of strategies (sometimes called a roadmap) that is the path determined to apply resources and effort towards the end Vision.
- Determine your Current State and set a baseline where you are.
- Identify what is important and what you need to be successful in the Future State.
- Define what you must achieve in order to survive, bridge the gap between the Current State and the Future State, growth and other steps to achieve to reach those levels.
- Determine who is accountable for achieving objectives, project goals and milestones and recognize joint team efforts.
- Review successes, review issues mitigated, review compliance, review your timeline, review metrics and take action of effective information.
- Always communicate results throughout the organization, setting priorities, setting expectations and empower your employees to take proper actions.

Examples of Industry Usage

Research studies indicate that there are vast differences of acceptance of Sustainability across industries. The differences are based on disparity of perceptions of Sustainability, gaps in levels of integration, and overall trend of Sustainability importance. Accenture and UN Global Compact surveyed 766 CEOs and found 93 percent believed that Sustainability will be "important" or "very important" to the future success of their company.

Closer examination reveals that significant differences appear at the industry level. For instance, 100 % of automotive CEOs, and 100 % of executives heading large consumer goods companies, see Sustainability as critical to their success. While the banking sector has not traditionally focused on Sustainability, banking CEOs see these Sustainability as a strategic priority, with 68 % regarding Sustainability as "very important" to their future success[21].

On the other hand, only 22 % of CEOs in the communications sector perceive Sustainability to be a "very important" factor in shaping their future success, the lowest in any of the seven industries. However, with 70 % of communications CEOs seeing the potential for revenue growth and cost reduction as a primary motivation for taking action on Sustainability (the highest figure across the seven sectors), the research suggests that Sustainability may be growing in importance[22].

Moving towards the future, business executives around the world are faced with the need to change their commercial mindset. What principles for the future will be different from those of previous generations? A sustainable economic arena will be the foundation for sustainable environmental arenas, as well. Understand that all Sustainability solutions are local. Economic, Environmental and Social costs will choose alternatives locally in most cases to offset rising costs, awareness of carbon usage and influences from tax incentives. Owners and Corporate Executives need to think locally and wisely leverage local resources. By definition, the best sustainable solution for a geographically diverse organization will be sourced near the location of each subsidiary, even though your corporation may be a global in scope.

As more companies adopt Sustainability that knowledge is shared with their industry. These industry specific insights make Sustainability more appealing to industry levels. Understanding those challenges and opportunities within each sector, often encourages how leaders are going about creating a new competitive advantage. Industries are taking different approaches to Sustainability. Some of the similarities and the differences among the sectors include:

Automotive: 100% of automotive CEOs believe that Sustainability issues will be critical to the future success of their business. 95% of automotive CEOs believe that Sustainability issues should be fully integrated into the strategy and operations of a company. 86% of automotive CEOs believe that companies should integrate Sustainability through their supply chain; only 57% believe that their company has[23].

Banking: 98% of the banking CEOs surveyed believe that Sustainability issues will be important to the future success of their business. 80% of banking CEOs stated that Sustainability issues are now fully embedded into the strategy and operations of their company[24].

Communications: 81% of communications CEOs believe that Sustainability issues will be 'important' or 'very important' to the future success of their business. 81% of communications CEOs believe that Sustainability issues should be fully integrated into the strategy and operations of a company. 81% of communications CEOs believe that companies should integrate Sustainability through their supply chain; only 48% believe that their company has done so[25].

Consumer Goods: 98% of consumer goods CEOs believe that Sustainability issues will be critical to the future success of their business. 97% of consumer goods CEOs believe that Sustainability issues should be fully integrated into the strategy and operations of a company. 92% of consumer goods CEOs believe that companies should integrate Sustainability through their supply chain; only 59% believe that their company has[26].

Energy: 94% of CEOs in the energy industry believe that Sustainability issues will be critical to the future success of their business. 96% of CEOs in the energy industry believe that Sustainability issues should be fully integrated into the strategy and operations of a company. 94% of CEOs in the energy industry believe that companies should integrate Sustainability through their supply chain; only 57% believe that their company has. 91% of CEOs in the energy industry report that their company will employ new technologies to address Sustainability issues over the next five years[27].

Infrastructure & Transportation (I&T): 89% of I&T CEOs believe that Sustainability issues will be critical to the future success of their business.93% of I&T CEOs believe that Sustainability issues should be fully integrated into the strategy and operations of a company. 84% of I&T CEOs believe that companies should integrate Sustainability through their supply chain; only 50% believe that their company has done so[28].

Utilities: 92% of utilities CEOs believe that Sustainability issues will be important to the future success of their business. 88% of utilities CEOs believe that Sustainability issues should be fully integrated into the strategy and operations of a company. 84% of utilities CEOs believe that companies should integrate Sustainability through their supply chain; only 64% believe that their company has[29].

Extend your Vision and Commitment to a legacy for your company, its employees and their families involved in this journey. That Vision illustrates areas where the road to Sustainability will create opportunities, areas for growth and aligning best practices to become increasingly aware of your impact on the environment and society. We are now working in the most interconnected market place ever known to Humanity.

Trends In Business And Sustainability

Business initiatives are driven by gains, large tangible benefits, competitive advantages, complying with new laws and regulations and answering to Customer needs. Change is always a constant in business. Leading organizations are taking a hard look inside their operations and across their enterprise (e.g., supply chains, building energy usage, formulating a broad Sustainability strategies, fostering product and process innovation, etc.). Adopting Sustainability metrics that more accurately measure their progress and improve their image in the marketplace. Achieving this broad vision provides companies with opportunities to enhance revenue and brand value, engage effectively with key stakeholders, manage risk and reduce costs.

As Sustainability practices continue to mature with understanding, refinement and programs that shifted from the greenwashing of years past toward more pragmatic risk management and environmentally conscious operations. "Greenwashing" efforts traditionally have been motivated by public relations, human resources or marketing programs. Many corporations have missed the real tangible benefits of Sustainability: brand image, growth, profits, performance and elimination of waste by embracing poor "greenwashing" practices. However, Sustainability is driving trends that will promote these benefits and include:

- Moving away from "greenwashing" practices to earnest business Sustainability practices and substance
- Providing greater consensus on indirect emissions accounting
- Employee engagement of best practices
- Major attention to water risks as it becomes in the reality

Today, pressures are coming from other stakeholders more and more often. Each has a concern centered on their point of view. Additionally, Investors and other Financial Resources are recognizing that Sustainability is important to companies' economic viability and provide investment opportunities.

Patti Prairie, who wrote "Biomimicry", a ground breaking environmental book that credits the value of learning from Nature and to work with Nature, sees Sustainability practices maturing and changing. Recent events and trends have set the stage for significant shifts in recent years to include:

- As these measures continue to gain ground, expect corporate Sustainability programs to shift from the public-focused "greenwashing" of years past toward more robust risk management and environmentally conscious operations.[30]

- The new standard signals greater consensus on indirect emissions accounting, and coupled with the sheer magnitude of indirect emissions, paves the way for more widespread management of impacts[31].

- These new employee engagement best practices and industry metrics will unleash people power to deliver change in Sustainability performance.[32]

- Don't expect corporate carbon management to disappear, but do expect a major increase in attention to companies' management of water risks and other aspects of climate adaptation[33].

- As application interoperability and cloud computing become new IT standards, expect Sustainability applications that harness big data by integrating with existing business systems to become commonplace[34].

Shareholder pressure on corporate accountability was the fastest-growing motivator for Sustainability initiatives in Brighter Planet's recent study, up 10 percentage points in 2011 over 2009. Ernst & Young recently found a 40% year-over-year growth rate in Sustainability shareholder resolutions and predicted that fully half of all shareholder resolutions this year will be Sustainability-related[35].

Why Act Now?

Over the last 20 years, the amount of money flowing across borders grew at more than three times the rate of global GDP. International trade and foreign investment more than tripled; trade in natural resources grew six-fold; and internationally traded financial assets such as bank loans, bonds, and portfolio equity soared by a factor of 12[36].

Political and Business leadership, mostly in Europe, and many multinational organizations with revenues exceeding $1 billion annually have already recognized the global need for Sustainability and, in many cases, implemented initiatives to transform to 21st century realities. Major players clearly understand the consequences of their actions, possible scenarios, and the need to manage potential threats or conflicts. The future of current societies will be based on keen understandings of what is required to be efficient, sustainable and promote policies of "zero waste" with long-term commitments from business, governments and citizens.

Market Dynamics: In a broader sense, business leaders see a change in the marketplace. A market landscape that recognizes Sustainability from several facets: Customer demands, product composition, Supplier involvement and long-term leadership commitment to Sustainability. A recent MIT survey reflects current CEO thinking. CEOs were asked what are key questions that you should ask before committing to a Sustainability program. Factors that lead to change in your business model as a result of Sustainability considerations:
- 53% see Customer preference for Sustainability
- 35% see Resources scarcity
- 34% see Legislative or political pressure
- 34% see Competitors increasing their Sustainability
- 30% see Stricter requirements from your value chain partners
- 30% see Owners demands for broader value creation
- 27% see Customers willing to pay a premium for Sustainability offering
- 26% see Competition for new talent[37]

Many organizations are preparing for limitation of resources in the next three to five years. China has already demonstrated restraints on the export of rare earths or other commodities to the West. For this century, we need Sustainability Leadership that effectively orchestrates resources to preserve our planet for this generation and succeeding generation to meet their needs, whether East or West. Protracted trade wars would have little or no advantage to the global economy and could be a catalyst for a second recession.

Comparing the 20th century to the 21st century is a contrast in scenarios and outcomes. In the last century, lines were drawn across ideologies and almost produced a cataclysmic event that would have changed the world permanently, in just a few minutes.

Your Vision Drives A Long-term Commitment
Without a clear, concise and collaborative approach, Sustainability transformation will probably not succeed. It does not replace Strategic Planning, but should be integrated and aligned. It does not replace your ethics and values, but makes you consider other ethical issues and what you could / should do. It highlights current practices (i.e., Accountability, Governance, Incentives, Innovation, Stakeholders, etc.) introduces new concepts (i.e. Externalities, Economical, Environmental, People, Social,

Waste, etc.). It does not replace your Vision, but is a catalyst to refine your Vision for the long-term and provide a path for Commitment to Sustainability that begins with the completion and integration of these key points:

- Gain corporate cultural awareness, define your baseline and identify where sustainability opportunities lie. The first level of scope will begin eliminating waste, internally and externally. Capture the low lying fruit and eliminate the obvious waste, first. Refine your framework in reporting compliance regulations.
- Develop your remediation methodologies (e.g., Lean, Six Sigma) for your organization to remediate risks and explore opportunities through costs savings and productivity, define the second level of scope and empower your organization to take actions. Implement methodologies to govern waste elimination. Sustainable and Quality perspectives provide a complete organizational visibility and systematic elimination of wastes, while retaining gains. Costs are often seen through the lens of Sustainability and Quality.
- Customers will especially provide insight to improving your products and services. Branding products and services as a "differentiation" characteristics wanted by Customers. Begin involvement with externalities and explore stakeholder view points. Define this as the third level of scope.
- Sustainability and should be woven into your current business strategies. Incentivize rewards based on Sustainable, Quality and performance results. Define this as your fourth level of scope.
- Evaluate your buildings energy usage and energy loss. It represents about 35 percent of you energy needs and about 65 of you electrical consumption.
- Evaluate your IT buildings energy usage and energy loss. Not only most corporations have high energy and electrical consumption, but in most cases your data center generates the highest GHGs.
- Interconnect Sustainability into all corporate strategies to align to your Supply Chain objectives.
- This is external facing image that can vary to the environment, energy, social, financial and other areas of promotions. Your aspirational strategies will reflect you corporate values, affect brand image, be recognized in your communities and ultimately be reflected as a player as a potential Sustainability investment. Consider creating energy augmentation projects, depending on your energy needs. Energy intensive enterprises would reduce risk to potential market disruption with wind and solar alternatives. More and more companies are being evaluated and included in sustainable portfolios since they are perceived as better managed, generate returns in terms of market success and effective cost performance. Define this as your fifth level of scope of on going Sustainability.

Be a Visionary

Whether we recognize it or not, we are in fact setting a baseline for Sustainability, person-by-person, company-by-company, state-by-state and country-by-country. John D. Rockefeller said; "Good leadership consists of showing average people how to do the work of superior people." Leading your people by empowering them with skills and knowledge is a critical success factor for Sustainability and Quality transformation. Change your thinking. Mold it into a new way of looking for opportunities, instead of problems.

Your leadership provides the Vision for the future and enlisting employee-led changes to improve procedures, processes and effective innovation for now and the future. Provide training and skills to identify problems, issues and risks. For all employees own the success of Sustainability and Quality. Encourage personal growth and learning to solve complex puzzles. Set high expectations for all employees and encourage innovative thinking. Be open to their opinions and solutions by holding these simple leadership principles:

- Tell the truth.
- Communicate roles and responsibilities.
- Create a workplace culture that values real people relationships.
- Be fair and open.
- Model the behaviors you seek[38].

Local education and practices will be key milestones of every community, government and organization. Bring in new ideas through speakers, workshops, training or outside consultants that could be catalysts for that change. It all begins with a change in mindset.

Individually, each person determines their own development through choices and decisions. So, we are in a dilemma that Humanity has never seen before, right? Understanding every decision we make can and often does impact our future. Isolated choices for our needs often are not the best choices if we don't consider its impact our limited planetary resources.

Historically, there have been civilizations that have declined or disappeared due to climate change, droughts that affected food and water resources, and disease that devastated large populations. What do we need? The wisdom to recognize our changing world, the understanding of the actions we need to make, and knowledge that hesitation will only prolong the consequences of a poorly appreciated and abused resource, Our Earth.

Vision: Carl Jung, a contemporary of Freud, said; "Your vision will become clear only when you can look into your own heart. Who looks outside, dreams; who looks inside, awakes." That awakening is the kernel of knowledge that awakens an owner or an executive to begin questioning whether current business practices are pragmatic or are there better ways of improving their enterprise. From that searching for optimization, benefits will become apparent. From the understanding of benefits, your vision and commitment will lead you to a new journey that recognizes that business is not isolated.

The stakes are high and growing more in the U.S. compared to European counterparts. Given the increasing role of Sustainability and its approach plays in transforming an organization into a more competitive enterprise - from adaptive supply chains to effectively using disruptive technology to meeting the needs of the Customer - the gaps will continue to grow between those who use Sustainability and those who do not.

I believe Jung was correct. Your Vision is based on your sense of what is right, your values, understanding your constraints, understanding where opportunities might be gained, and awakens and engages your employees to take the journey to a more Sustainable Developed company. What needs to be gathered to align those ingredients to build strategies? Build your vision on these standards:
- Follow your "gut" feelings or personal values you have internally can lead the transformation.
- Assumption of changes in resources and areas of Sustainability issues and their impact through 2050.
- Be a realist, but set aspirational goals. Develop strategies on holistic and focused approaches that can clearly be completed for the size of your company of government.
- Leverage your Sustainability and Corporate Values to align to your corporate philosophies and legal constraints.
- Incorporate those values into your entire organization. Utilize your Core Assets to underpin and govern values and strategies.

Build a Future: Assumptions for the future will vary widely, based on the circumstances in geographical areas. If you are a global company, then this will need to be addressed in assumption that preclude your strategic planning efforts. If you are not a global company, then the consequences of the larger corporation may very well impact your business (e.g. Supply chains, logistics, etc.). There will also be particular local challenges in relation to:
- Reducing and ultimately reversing deforestation in countries like Brazil, Indonesia, Canada, the US (in Alaska in particular) and Russia;
- Sustainable use of water in areas like the Middle East, Saharan regions of Africa and northern China;

19

- Improving agricultural yields and access to food in areas with continued relatively rapid population growth, particularly Africa and India; and
- Dealing with the systemic sustainability challenges associated with rapid urbanization across the emerging economies[39].

Build Strategies. Framing it in context to Ceres Principles can facilitate converting your Vision into reality. By using these principles, you can envisage the right combination of Business and Sustainability strategies and their possible outcomes.

In 1989, a major environmental disaster shook public confidence in corporate America—the Exxon Valdez oil spill. Nearly 11 million gallons of oil poured into Alaska's Prince William Sound, devastating one of the world's most pristine habitats. Suddenly, the environmental cost of doing business became painfully clear and it was apparent that companies weren't doing enough to account for the environmental and social impacts of their operations. Six months after the spill, a group of investors launched an organization to tackle the problem: a nonprofit called Ceres[40] was established. Consider using The Ceres Principles[41] in your initial establishment of strategies:

- ***Biosphere Awareness:*** Reducing waste and making continual improvement the norm is an institutionalized approach. Corporate and cultural understanding of how the enterprise coexist with the environment and society can extend to restoration of habitats affected by your operations, protect open spaces, refuges and wildernesses.

- ***Leadership Commitment:*** Whether you are the Owner, Board of Directors and Chief Executive Officer it is the responsibility of leadership to provide oversight and for environmental, economic and social issues. All levels of Governance will need to be fully informed about pertinent Sustainability issues and are fully responsible for its policies.

- ***Natural Resource Usage:*** Use of renewable natural resources, such as water, soils and forests prudently. Ensure that they are utilized many times and can be done so safely to the consumers and the environment. Design and utilize non-renewable natural resources through efficient use, careful planning, and recycle to conserve and extend usage.

- ***Reduction And Elimination Of Wastes:*** Reduce and eliminate waste through product redesign (e.g., source reduction and recycling) with the goal to eliminate landfills and emissions. All waste will be handled and disposed of through safe and responsible methods (i.e., possible waste elimination, source reduction, recycling, etc.).

- **_Conserving Energy:_** When possible, conserve energy and improve the energy efficiency of our internal operations and of the goods produced and services sold. Make every effort to use environmentally safe and renewable energy sources. Install sensors to detect inactivity that will switch off lights, machinery and appliances not needed at night. Investigate peak rates and determine if 24/7 appliances could be recharged only at night when demand is lower (e.g., freezers and refrigerators).

- **_Risk Mitigation:_** Minimize risk associated with environmental, health and wellness, safety to your employees and their communities in which to operate safely and by being prepared for emergencies.

- **_Safe Products And Services:_** Reduce or eliminate the use, manufacture or sale of products and services that use hazardous material that causes environmental damage, impacts health or creates safety hazards. Also, promptly and responsibly inform Customers that corrective actions will be forthcoming due to circumstances that endanger health, safety or the environment.

- **_Environmental Restoration:_** Promptly notify authorities and responsibly correct conditions caused that endanger health, safety or the environment. This may avoid hefty fines and penalties from state and governments, To the extent feasible, redress injuries caused to persons or damages incurred environment. If damage to the environment occurs, acknowledge your responsibility and commit to restoring the environment.

- **_Informing The Public:_** Be Transparent, even if it is sometimes tough to do so. As an ongoing practice, regularly seek advice and counsel through organizations and people in your communities near your facilities. If employees report dangerous incidents or conditions to management or to appropriate authorities, not take any action against them or ignore the problem. In the long run, they may be providing a benefit of reducing business risks.

- **_Audits And Reports:_** Validate your process, products and services, people exposure and involvement, truing needs and best practices that properly record benefits from Sustainability. Conduct an annual self-evaluation of progress in implementing these Principles and ensure Best Practices. Support timely creation of generally accepted Sustainability audit procedures. Incorporate these results with other reports, especially your Transparency/Sustainability Report and Financial Reports, which are made available to the public.

Alignment between Sustainability and corporate strategies is critical and key. Companies can extract more from their original investments if they move one step further, viewing Sustainability and Quality execution and as an integrated business process. That process builds on the solid partnerships between business Leaders, Stakeholders and Shareholders. Today's organizations are rarely structure to take advantage of benefits such a model can deliver.

Core Values and Core Assets: How you mold your Vision is like an artesian taking a lump of clay to create a coffee cup. It can be utilitarian or decorative, it can be symbolic or practical, or even have another purpose entirely. But it is first designed mentally, conceptually. Only when it is created a second time, physically, is the Vision truly socialized, communicated and pledges actions to make real change.

While based on Sustainability and Corporate Values, you should integrate Ceres principles, a company's obligation and accountability for all of its products, operations and activities. Recognize that Sustainability values affect Stakeholders and Shareholders with the aim of achieving sustainable development in the Economic, Social and Environmental dimensions.

Your Core Assets are driven by business Core Values recognizing that Sustainability aligned to the needs of the present without sacrificing resources for future generation's needs. It challenges your ideals beyond your brick and mortar walls and it is a role that legacies are made from. They are composed of five internal segments that include:

- *Corporate Values:* Desire to inspire a shared your Vision with others by creating something that you are proud to tell your grandchildren. Core beliefs and values should be based on legal considerations, as well as, bedrock beliefs in ethics and Sustainability. For these Sustainability Values, if adhered to, will guide your decision-making process from resource management to brand image in a Sustainability context.

- *Innovation:* Constantly innovate to meet or exceed your Customers needs and wants. Innovation will be your catalyst for pragmatic Sustainability. Apply it to your products, services and processes.

- *Products And Services:* Nurture your corporate culture. Push for Continuous Improvement in Sustainability, Quality and Excellence. Never let your Customers down and do not be late to market in new Products and Services.

- *People:* Leaders should lead the organization, communicate the values of the company and share information to acknowledge progress and issues. They are responsible to ensure incentives and direction of their human resources. This persuades employees, who share a common direction, get to where they are going more quickly by leveraging each others experiences, knowledge, skills and trust.

- *Processes:* CSR is about considering the whole picture, from your internal processes to your Customers, taking every step that your business takes during day-to-day operations, to meet the needs of the Customer. CSR can also monitor environmental responsibility, recycling policy, regulatory compliance or accumulating external issues.

Core Values are based on your Corporate values, based on demonstrable ethics, forms your leadership's fundamental assessment and decision-making model. It is a mindset that defines integrity, which is the basis of honest Communication, Ethics, incentives, and visible commitment to Sustainability and Quality. These are your linchpins to address Stakeholder and Shareholder requests, and a push for cost reductions through greater efficiency. Be thoughtful that your corporate Culture will change and core values will be the hub for your transformation.

Overall, this framework must cover seven business components: strategy, people, information, product, IT, property and business operations. These components are common to virtually any enterprise or organization dealing with energy and environment issues.

The principles for ethics can be summed up in one word: Sustainability. For this can ethic can be embedded into you Core Values that drive your Core Assets. Stewardship is an ethic that embodies responsible planning and management of resources. The concept of stewardship has been applied in diverse realms, including with respect to environment, economics, health, property, information, and religion, and is linked to the concept of Sustainability[42].

Business needs a model to integrate strategies with objectives, business integrated with Sustainability, to collaborate internally, listen to external publics, effectively apply effort and resources that produce products and services fulfilling expectations of the customer. It promotes continuous improvement while recognizing Stewardship for the environment, while benefitting the corporation. It is a business philosophy and practice that reaches out to Externalities (organizations outside the brick and mortar boundaries), empowers your Internalities (your core assets: people, processes, products, innovation, values) and creates an awareness that your enterprise does not exist in an isolated setting.

Your Core Assets, when aligned to your Vision, will focus efforts and convert that Vision into reality. The Values, established by the owner, CEO or a consensus of CXOs (C-suite executives), drives what your people should value, how the processes should be used ethically, create products that are not harmful to the environment of society or provide constraints that innovation develops products wanted by your Customers.

Taking Ownership

First, the Owners and CXOs can only see what they are prepared to see. Second, after understanding this new vision, only then can can they take that new vision and apply it to their organization and the outside communities to begin the journey to Sustainability. The key to taking ownership is the first step of wanting to see the possibilities.

- *Intel:* "Intel has an ambitious vision: Create and extend computing technology to connect and enrich the life of every person on Earth. We believe that technology will play a fundamental role in finding solutions to the world's toughest environmental and social challenges, from energy and water to health care and education. Our strategic objectives support this vision, including our objective to "Care for our people, care for the planet, and inspire the next generation." ~ Paul S. Otellini, President and Chief Executive Officer[43]

- *Ingeroll Rand:* "With a focus on sustainability, enabled by passionate employees, Ingersoll Rand is well positioned to grow our business and deliver on our vision of sustainable progress and enduring results. ... Across our global sites, more than 6,700 employees contributed to 450 unique energy saving and waste reduction projects." ~ Michael W. Lamach, Chairman and Chief Executive Officer[44]

- *Anadarko:* "For Anadarko, sustainability lies in the enduring nature of our values and the objectives of our mission. Acting with integrity and respect, protecting the environment, serving our communities, and remaining ever mindful of the safety and health of those around us are essential as we develop energy resources at a competitive cost for the welfare of a global society." ~ R. A. Walker, President and Chief Executive Officer[45]

What Did Erich Think?

"When people can see a vision and simultaneously recognize what can be done step by step in a concrete way to achieve it, they will begin to feel encouragement and enthusiasm instead of fright." ~Erich Fromm, (March 23, 1900 – March 18, 1980) was a German social psychologist, psychoanalyst, sociologist, and humanistic philosopher

---

"A man must know his destiny... if he does not recognize it, then he is lost. By this I mean, once, twice, or at the very most, three times, fate will reach out and tap a man on the shoulder... if he has the imagination, he will turn around and fate will point out to him what fork in the road he should take, if he has the guts, he will take it." ~ George S. Patton

2. Executive Commitment and Vision[46]

"As we look ahead into the next century, leaders will be those who empower others." ~ Bill Gates

---

Transformation is modeled with foundations for better leadership, based on these two lessons: The leanest will be more competitive [Lean Six Sigma - LSS]. The leanest will be better stewards and create a better chance of making the future a success [Sustainability]. All resources are finite, but the journey to pursue excellence is based on optimizing profitability. So, recognizing the definition of Sustainable Develop slightly refocuses our formula for increased Profitability:

↑ Sustainable Development + ↑ Quality + Continuous Improvement + Secured Gains = Optimizing Profitability

Will transformation create opportunities for increased performance, reduced costs, provide for growth of brand and attract quality employees? Research and results indicate it will provide your organization with those opportunities and establish a Continuous Improvement process to refine and meet your future competitive landscape. Your true litmus test is two-fold. First, the results of aligning your Vision, holistically, to integrate Ethics into your organization and philosophy to create a unique Culture that attracts the quality people you want and need. Second, is the true increase in profitability and competitiveness that is an ongoing refinement by fusing Sustainability with an effective Quality effort.

What Executives Discovered In The Great Recession?
The United Nations Global Compact (UNGC) and consulting firm Accenture released findings of a comprehensive survey that addresses every stakeholder in the market. ... The survey was extracted from a population of 766 CEOs from leading global companies. The surveyed CEOs emphasize that the downturn counter-intuitively gave them the opportunity to assess how their Sustainability initiatives "deliver core business value like cost reduction and revenue growth."
- Economic downturn raised importance of Sustainability as an issue for top management: 80%
- Company reduced investment in Sustainability as a result of the downturn: 12% [see note][47]
- The downturn led company to align Sustainability more closely with core business: 74%

While a resounding majority cites brand, trust and reputation as the No. 1 reason (72%), potential for revenue growth (44%) and personal motivation (42%) come in the second and third spots. And 31% cite employee engagement and recruitment as their main motivation[48].

Total Executive Engagement

Organizations evolve and change with their business environment, much like living organisms do with nature. The Owners and CXOs alike should always be aware of that change, understand its impact, and be proactive in managing change to improve performance and extract tangible benefits for his company. But there are different perspective between Owners and CXOs.

Owners adopting Sustainability produce quick, focused and committed programs (e.g., Ray Anderson at Interface). Oftentimes, the Owner may wear all corporate roles of CXOs in its umbrella of responsibility. Additionally, due to this comprehensive role, importance and awareness of potential tangible benefits are obvious to many Owners, earlier.

On the other hand, CXOs have different perspectives, responsibilities and different incentives. The key members in most organizations are usually the CEO, CFO and COO. Their perspectives are specialized and evolving Sustainability roles and considerations include:

The CEO Role: Sustainability has also found its way into controllership and financial risk management, Ernst & Young said, most notably in SEC guidance, which says that a company's CEO and CFO must certify that the company has installed "controls and procedures" allowing it to discharge its climate change disclosure responsibilities. Sustainability activities must now be treated like financial activities, with a controller to monitor and account for them, the report said.

Besides fiduciary responsibilities, CEOs, are recognizing not only risk management, but a variety of other benefits. However, on an average, CEOs reported these results[49]:
* 48% see an improvement to brand reputation
* 31% see an increased competitive advantage
* 28% see innovation of products or services offerings
* 25% see better business models and processes
* 22% see reduced costs due to energy efficiency
* 20% see reduced cost due to the materials or waste efficiencies

The CFO Role: The report listed five actions CFOs can take now to enhance corporate value through Sustainability:

- Actively pursue a Sustainability and reporting program
- Ensure that those responsible for Sustainability matters do not operate in isolation from the rest of the enterprise — especially the finance function
- Enhance dialogue with shareholders and improve disclosure in key areas, particularly those related to social and environmental issues
- Ensure that directors' skills are relevant to the chief areas of stakeholder concern, including risk management tied to social and environmental matters
- Consider using nontraditional performance metrics, including those related to environmental/Sustainability issues. Doing so could help align compensation with risk, Ernst & Young said.

In a report released by McKinsey, 88 percent of 164 CFOs surveyed reported that CEOs expect them to be more active participants in shaping the strategy of their organizations. Half of them also indicated that CEOs counted on them to challenge the company's strategy. Many roles of the CFO, especially concerned with initiatives and tangible benefits, now report[50]:

- 79% of CFOs involved with equity analysts to consider Sustainability performance,
- 65% of CFOs involved in Sustainability initiatives, and
- 39% of CFOs authorize funding of capital investments

Learn how to speak the language of the CFO when you're talking about Sustainability. In fact, I'd like to lay out five reasons that CFOs should care about Sustainability. They are:

- You can cut costs and enhance efficiency.
- You can mitigate risks.
- You can open up new competitive and revenue opportunities.
- You can drive innovation.
- And you can improve employee development and retention[51].

Coincidently, the same five reasons, which are significantly important to CFOs, are also germane to quality methodologies (Lean and Six Sigma). The disciplines approach from Sustainability and LSS provides leadership and visibility of tangible benefits and progression in reforming your enterprise.

The COO Role: Today, one of the five top management practices that reduce operating costs are in the realm of a Chief Operating Officer. A Deloitte study found:

- 46% of COOs engage with suppliers (at any tier level)
- 45% of COOs provide suppliers with monetary rewards for sharing expertise and knowledge around Sustainability

- 41% of COOs provide tools, policies, or processes to suppliers and value chain partners[52]

Sustainability Commitment

So, what is Sustainability Commitment? In simple terms, from a global perspective, it is a pattern of resource use that aims to meet current human needs while preserving the environment so that those needs can be met not only in the present, but in the indefinite future. Sustainability is a long-term strategy to eliminate waste, both externally and internally, while supporting the survivability of the enterprise.

From Ray Anderson's viewpoint; "The five big things, those technologies of the future are: solar energy, close loop recycling, zero waste, harmless emissions, and resource efficient transportation[53]." Commitment to Sustainability, owning that long-term decision for decades, is one of the single most important decisions any Owner or CEO can make. It is a decision to frame the future you want and that journey starts with the decision to transform.

From Jim Collins thinking, "The 20 Mile March" is more than a philosophy. It's about having concrete, clear, intelligent, and rigorously pursued performance mechanisms that keep you on track. The 20 Mile March creates two types of self-imposed discomfort:
- the discomfort of unwavering commitment to high-performance and difficult conditions, and
- the discomfort of holding back in good conditions.

Southwest Airlines, for example, demanded of itself profit every year, even when the entire industry lost money. From 1990 through 2003, the US airline industry as a whole turned a profit of just 6 of 14 years. In the early 1990s, the airline industry lost $13 billion … Despite an almost chronic epidemic of airline troubles, including high-profile bankruptcies of some major carriers, Southwest generated a profit every year for 30 consecutive years[54].

How does Sustainability Commitment define Business Transformation? Brian Goonan set a definition for Business Transformation that includes; "a combination of strategic, process, organizational change, and technology development focused around one clear vision, resulting in a significant change in the organization and substantial financial benefits[55]." Sustainability Transformation focuses the organization's mindset and provides cultural and enterprise indicators that guide and determine the importance to organizational effort.

Collins' ideas meld well with Sustainability Transformation when executives understand that committing to a Sustainability paradigm is not only in their best interests, but a continuous improvement tool to be applied to long term survivability[56]. Defining that Commitment along a long-term timeline will favor your success on four points:

- It provides a long-term Vision and Future you will commit to and design to build.
- It provides a framework of self-control in a chaotic environment.
- It will provide confidence and direction to Core Assets to perform well even in adverse circumstances.
- It reduces risk and anticipates catastrophic situations when hit by turbulent disruption, whether man-made or natural.
- It will focus on reduced waste and cost, increased revenue and better asset utilization.

Aligning that definition with Corporate Sustainability measures must be broadened to include improvements in labor practices, reductions in supply chain toxicity, protection of biodiversity and innovation that leads to cradle to cradle solutions. Sustainability is not simply reducing waste, water and turning out lights and adjusting thermostats.

Most Business Transformational initiatives by definition should end up in creating a sustainable competitive advantage. ... They become aligned to a compelling vision. In most cases they transform themselves into a high performance organization with a clear direction and execution strategy, ultimately benefiting all stakeholders in the value chain. Organizations taking up transformational initiatives tune themselves better to an existing market or create a new market. Internally they promote cross-organizational and functional process improvements by introduction of new processes and automation for optimal performance and operational excellence[57].

Commitment is a 20 Mile March. Corporate Sustainability is a business approach that creates long-term shareholder value by embracing opportunities and managing risks deriving from economic, environmental and social developments. Corporate Sustainability leaders achieve long-term shareholder value by gearing their strategies and management to harness the market's potential for Sustainability products and services while at the same time successfully reducing and avoiding Sustainability costs and risks[58].

Step back for good a look. Much like what we see as economic, environmental, and social models of today; in many cases, do not recognize those megaforce's influence and pressures of today's society. Sustainability reviews those influences, and takes into account their impact into all aspects of social, economic and environmental purviews.

In a sense, Sustainability views or portrays a holistic picture of our bio-sphere. It recognizes that man's impact on this planet addresses every level of the biosphere. It impacts the hydrosphere, it impacts the litho-sphere, it impacts the atmosphere, and impacts the exosphere of our planet. In other words, Humanity impacts the deepest parts of the oceans to outer space that envelops our planet.

Drivers For Sustainable Development

What are the drivers of the Sustainability maturity model? It is based, in part, on the mindset of the executive team. The Sustainability maturity model is a five-stage approach that is a long-term commitment, but some executives will circumvent the model's intent and declare success with near-term milestones. One of the first companies in the US to embrace Sustainability, Interface Corporation, began its transformation in the mid-1980s and continues to improve to this day.

Over the past couple of decades, globalization, e-commerce and informa-tion technology have dramatically impacted businesses, industries and markets. We are living in a time of lower costs, quicker time to market and interconnecting processes to make it all work easier and more efficiently. Over the next twenty years, these and an expanding number of mega-forces, will drive market and industry changes. Companies that recognize this fact and position themselves at the forefront stand to reap sizable competitive advantages. Consider the following emerging realities:

- **Resource Constraints:** Prices for food, water, energy, and other resources are growing increasingly volatile. Companies that have optimized their Sustainability profile and practices will be less ex-posed to these swings and be more resilient.

- **Energy Usage:** As the population grows, consumption increases and so does the demand for energy. While the developed countries have decreased energy consumption in the last decade, developing countries are increasing their usage.

- **Demographic Global Concerns:** Human population on Earth has surpassed 7 billion people. Mega-urbanization and the rise of megacities, increased growth in human populations in Africa and Asia, increased population migration to coastal geographies, in-creased middle-class wealth and demands for consumer products will dramatically impact the biosphere (deforestation, ecosystem decline, etc.).

- **Stakeholder Intervention:** Customers, other Stakeholders and the Government are paying more attention to Sustainability and putting pressure on companies to change. Stakeholders concerns are becoming more apparent relating to economic, environmental and social issues.

- **Future Government Laws And Obligations:** Governments' agendas increasingly advocate for Sustainability. Companies that are proactively pursuing this goal will be less vulnerable to sudden regulatory changes. They will also be better positioned to have a voice in shaping policy—rather than simply reacting to it.

- **Growing Financial Resources:** Capital markets are paying more attention to Sustainability and using it as a gauge to evaluate companies and make investment decisions. Sustainable Developed enterprises are considered better managed and are more sensitive to their customers, quicker to their needs and listen to their externalities.

- **Supply Chain Impact:** Businesses are often defined as a constant for change, and that unique characteristic provides multinational corporations (MNCs) the ability to impose demands on suppliers faster than governments can craft legislation.

Some of these trends and forces are creating new markets and business opportunities; others present strategic risk to business models and markets. A successful global change advisory firm must stay ahead of current thinking and understand the forces that will fundamentally change the world in which business must operate over the next decade.

Become Aware of Current Use

If we want to be sustainable, how can it provide benefits to everyone in society? Are we limited to only Carbon, Hydrogen, Oxygen, Nitrogen, Phosphorus and Sulfur components (they are important elements that facilitate recycling)? Also, these are important key elements, and their compounds, for innovation, end of life and profitability. But applying those causes for changes also generates effects, so transformation provides movement from basic recycling to ultimately more complex endeavors such as restoration. Here are some examples:

- Office buildings use approximately 19 percent of all energy consumed in the US.
- Energy use can account for over 30 percent of a company's operating budget, while adding 20 percent to the nation's total greenhouse gas emissions.
- Heating, ventilating, and air conditioning (HVAC) systems account for between 40 percent to 60 percent of total energy use (all forms of energy) in the commercial sector.

- An American family of four uses up to 260 gallons of water in the home per day. A five minute shower is equal to 20-35 gallons of water versus a full bath is equal to approximately 60 gallons of water. Water efficient fixtures can cut water use by 30%.
- Though accounting for only 5 percent of the world's population, Americans consume 26 percent of the world's energy. America uses about 15 times more energy per person than does the typical developing country[59].

Today's energy mix in the United States is undergoing radical change. Traditional energy sources are declining, while natural gas, renewable energy and energy efficiency are on the rise. The 2013 Factbook, researched and produced by Bloomberg New Energy, highlights include:

- Renewable energy installations hit an all-time record with at least 17 GW of new nameplate capacity added in 2012.
- In April 2012, electricity generation from natural gas equaled that from coal for the first time in US history.
- Policies and approaches for financing energy efficiency continued to make market headway; energy intensity for US commercial buildings has now dropped by more than 40% since 1980 and investments in smart grid topped $4 billion.
- Carbon dioxide (CO_2) emissions from the energy sector were on pace to sink to their lowest level since 1994[60].

Awareness, from a business perspective, is learning how to adopt Sustainability principles to produce a corporation's best practices of resource consumption like carbon, water, and electricity in order to run their businesses in compliance with existing requirements and regulations. Awareness also establishes a common framework that promotes forward thinking to anticipate future usage and potential regulations.

Value Chain

The value chain is a series of processes within department that provides services and functionality to create the products and services that are sold to the Customers to meet their needs. This includes the various groups that interface with suppliers and resources, logistics, operations, marketing and sales services. Another key area is the Core Assets (Corporate Values, Innovation, People, Processes, and the Products and Services). Waste (from a Sustainability viewpoint and Quality viewpoint) is elimination from all products and services.

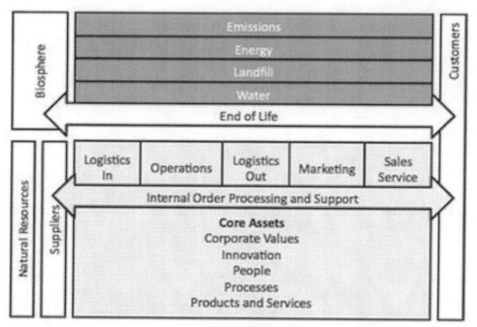

Sources: Jarvis Business Solutions, LLC, Copyright 2008-2013

Internal waste is usually a sign of lack of procedure, management or increase in market demands (composed of material production waste, wait time, overstock, queuing problems in production, etc.). External waste is the by-product of the production process and is a constant target of improvement (elimination of waste in emissions, energy, landfill and water) and prevention of contaminating the biosphere.

Waste has a financial impact to your organization. Waste is a cost to your profit / loss statement. Eliminate that costs, then you add profitability to your bottom line. That is one example of a benefit from your value chain.

Vision and Sustainable Development

If corporate leaders are not prepared for the change, nor considers the appropriate management style that is required to manage transformation, then resistance will be formidable and expect "push back." Sometimes failure simply fails due to lack of proper communication. Change programs fail in that they are seen as just that: "programs" instead of calling it a business translation or initiative. Clearly understand that a rigid management style, a poorly thought through, paying little detail to transformation processes will almost always result in resistance, poor quality and increased costs. Management must recognize that transparency; honest communication, incentives and visible commitment to Quality will be your

your initiative linchpins. Most importantly, Executives will take ownership for their organization's role.

Avoid complexity when implementing a business transformation initiative.
Choose an approach that is suited for your business (and use the KISS
method, when possible). Ensure your methodology is a "cookie-cutter"
approach that promotes a simple model, avoids complexity, encourages
replication and ease of transition. Do not create complexity to your transformation by piling methodology upon methodology, program upon program. For example: an organization that implemented Six Sigma, Balanced Scorecard and IIP [Investment in People] methodologies simultaneously, affected the performance to its enterprise. Their results were dismal.
Apply changes simply in a progressive sequence that leverages milestones
in previous phases.

Use the "Golden thread" to link effort to strategic objectives. All employees are considered equal from the janitor to the CEO. All have a part to
play in the profitability of the company and are an integral part in promoting the corporate culture to their colleagues and the world. The result will
be the "reins" to help control behavior and direct effort in the enterprise.

SWOT for Sustainable Development
SWOT analysis has been used in strategic planning for over fifty years and
most businesses and governments understand how to apply the tool and
extract kernels that impact their strategies. Using it for Sustainability and
Quality is no different. In fact, at times you may need to use it in your
remediation projects to help generate solutions.

Understanding Sustainability is part of the learning curve and external and
internal are key areas for investigation. SWOT analysis is a structured
planning method used to evaluate the Strengths, Weaknesses, Opportunities, and Threats involved in a project or in a business venture. SWOT
analysis is a standard planning tool that can also be applied to Sustainability. A SWOT analysis can be carried out for a product, company, industry
or government. Setting the objective should be done after the SWOT
analysis has been performed. This would allow achievable goals or objectives to be set for the organization.
- *Strengths:* internal characteristics, which I call and internality, of
  the business or project that give it an advantage over others
- *Weaknesses*: are internal characteristics, which I call and internality, that place the team at a disadvantage relative to others
- *Opportunities:* external elements, which I call and externality, that
  the project could exploit to its advantage
- *Threats:* external elements, which I call an externality, in the environment that could cause trouble for the business or project

Setting long-term aspirational objectives are much easier to visualize by working through the SWOT analysis. The analysis identifies internal Strengths and Weaknesses to the organization. Also, the Opportunities and Threats, presented in the SWOT analysis, identifies and highlights external considerations for the organization.

Externalities: There are two definitions for "externalities". Economists commonly use the first definition. Factors whose benefits (called external economies) and costs (called external diseconomies) are not reflected in the market price of goods and services. Externalities arise when firms create social costs that they do not have to bear, such as pollution[61]. Thus, society must impose taxes, regulations, and penalties so that firms "internalize" these externalities—a belief influencing many government policy decisions.

The second definition for externalities is the identification of external groups or areas where influence could impact the internal operations and business practices of the enterprise. Externalities are a loss or gain in the welfare of one party resulting from an activity of another party, without there being any compensation for the losing party[62]. Externalities are an important consideration in cost-benefit analysis. For discussion, we will use the second definition.

The CSR framework addresses the organization's Externalities (those external organizations that can have an influence on your organization in a variety of different ways). The model includes:

- **Customers:** There are two types of Customers. First definition applies to Customers who are external groups of buyers for your products and services. This group has a set of needs expectations and wants that are met in the marketplace. External Customers are those parties that receives or consumes products (goods or services) and has the ability to choose between different products and suppliers.

- The second definition refers to Quality: The second type is an Internal Customer within your organization that usually focuses on waste, effectiveness and performance. A manager within a firm, responsible for establishing requirements of a process (accounting, for example) and receives the output of that process (a financial statement, for example) from one or more internal or external suppliers[63].

- **Suppliers:** Suppliers are Externalities - external to your business- that provides resources or can a party that supplies goods or services. A supplier may be distinguished from a contractor or subcontractor, who commonly adds specialized input to deliverables[64].

- **Competitors:** Any person or entity that is a rival against another. In business, a company in the same industry or a similar industry which offers a similar product or service. The presence of one or more competitors can reduce the prices of goods and services as the companies attempt to gain a larger market share. Competition also requires companies to become more efficient in order to reduce costs[65].

- *Industries*: An industry is an area of economic production that involves large amounts of upfront capital investment before any profit can be realized. The most successful industries in a given sector tend, to be either companies started with a great deal of seed money, or early innovators of some new technology brought first to market, so that a great deal of capital can be quickly raised from sales for further research into technological improvements (e.g., large-scale production: organized economic activity connected with the production, manufacture, or construction of a particular product or range of products).

- *Financial Resources*: Companies often need funding for starting or continuing business operations. Small businesses typically need start-up funds, while medium and larger companies may need funding to expand operations or purchase competitors. Different types of funding are usually available based on the company's size and needs.

- *Human Resources:* Human resources is the set of individuals who make up the workforce of an organization, business sector or an economy. Likewise, other terms sometimes used include "manpower", "talent", "labor", or simply "people".(e.g., employee recruitment and management: the field of business concerned with recruiting and managing employees or personnel: all the people who work in a business or organization, considered as a whole).

- *Natural Resources:* A natural resource is often characterized by amounts of biodiversity and geodiversity existent in various ecosystems. Natural resources are derived from the environment. Some of them are essential for our survival while most are used for satisfying our wants. Natural resources may be further classified in different ways (e.g. the natural wealth of a country, consisting of land, forests, mineral deposits, water, etc.). The central challenge of our age must be to decouple human progress from resource use and environmental deterioration[66].

- **Communities**: Community can refer to a usually small, social unit of any size that shares common values. The term can also refer to the national community or international community. In human communities, intent, belief, resources, preferences, needs, risks, and a number of other conditions may be present and common, affecting the identity of the participants and their degree of cohesiveness (e.g., people in area: a group of people who live in the same area, or the area in which they live people with common background: a group of people with a common background or with shared interests within society).

- **NGOs:** Non-Governmental Organizations [NGO, example: Red Cross] are any non-profit, voluntary citizens' group which is organized on a local, national or international level. They are usually task-oriented and driven by people with a common interest, NGOs perform a variety of service and humanitarian functions, bring citizen concerns to Governments, advocate policies and encourage political participation through monitoring information.

- **Governments**: A government is the political system by which a state or community is governed. From a democratic viewpoint, government is usually based on laws and normally consists of executive, judiciary and legislative bodies with administrators and arbitrators.

- **Regulators**: These are government officials who are responsible for control of a particular activity and makes certain that regulations are met and compliance is enforced to those laws (e.g., an official or agency who controls a particular activity and makes certain that regulations are complied with; EPA, Export/Import, etc.).

- **The Media**: The media reports on and investigates the actions of many companies, particularly large organizations, and most companies accept that they must contend with and effectively "manage" their relationship with the media[67].

Sustainability considerations will take issues into account from touch points that affect Externalities perceptions of your enterprise. Externalities arise when firms create social costs that they do not have to bear, such as pollution. Thus, society must impose taxes, regulations, and penalties so that firms "internalize" these externalities—a belief influencing many government policy decisions.

This perspective has also shaped the strategies of firms themselves, which have largely excluded social and environmental considerations from their economic thinking. Firms have taken the broader context in which they do business as a given and resisted regulatory standards as invariably contrary to their interests. Solving social problems has been ceded to governments and to NGOs. Corporate responsibility programs—a reaction to external pressure—have emerged largely to improve firms' reputations and are treated as a necessary expense. Anything more is seen by many as an irresponsible use of shareholders' money. Governments, for their part, have often regulated in a way that makes shared value more difficult to achieve. Implicitly, each side has assumed that the other is an obstacle to pursuing its goals and acted accordingly[68].

External Issues: Outside influencer, often called externalities, are often the originations of signals for change. These come as different players, each with their unique agenda, who press to be recognized and are often included in assessing your barriers and hindrances into economic, environmental and social sectors:
- Investors: seeking to invest in line with their own values, or in line with an expectation that companies with a CSR approach will be better investments;
- Consumers and others in the supply chain: choosing one product, service or company over another on the basis of their understanding of its environmental or social credentials;
- Public authorities: through a range of mechanisms including promotion and information provision, their own role as purchasers, regulatory and fiscal signals;
- NGOs: monitoring and assessing the environmental and social impact of business and campaigning for improvements;
- Trade unions: seeking to influence company behavior through mechanisms such as collective agreements;
- Other companies, business networks, intermediaries and supply chains: co-operatively through sharing experience, developing a shared understanding of better approaches and expectations, providing external benchmarks and challenging practices in business to business relationships[69].

Internalities: Again, we have a choice of terminology and how it will be utilized throughout the discussions. An internality is a term used in behavioral economics to describe those types of behaviors that impose costs on a person in the long-run that are not taken into account when making decisions in the present. Economics usually analyzes these costs similar to the way that externalities are analyzed.

For our use, we will look internally to provide visibility on the internal working of the enterprise. Internalities are dependent on essential products, processes and services that may behave or contain internal elements or contradictions of Sustainability theory (e.g., toxins, water emissions, air pollution, resource over utilization: deforestation, filling land-fills) or can be defined in terms of branding or reputation.

Internalities (influences both internally and externally that can affect your Sustainability Value Chain), Sustainability initiative that includes external resources that when amalgamated define Sustainability, and Quality initiative that focuses on the improvement, effectiveness and performance of meeting Customers needs in a timely manner.

- *Community Engagement*: In context of Sustainability, is defined as private or corporate initiatives, for public good, focusing on quality of life. This could be applied to a broad range of issues (e.g. inoculations, medical research, habitat restoration, philanthropy, etc.).

- *Shareholder Value*: shareholder value is the sum of all strategic decisions that affect the firm's ability to efficiently increase the amount of free cash flow over time.

- *Business Partner relationships*: A business organization in which two or more individuals manage and operate the business. Both owners are equally and personally liable for the debts from the business.

- *Customer Engagement:* Also known as CE, is the engagement of customers of a company or a brand. The initiative for engagement can be either consumer or company led.

- *Core Assets*: Core Assets are built with key building blocks from your corporation that is something essential to success and distinguishes an advantage. Those building blocks include:
  - Corporate values
  - People
  - Processes
  - Products
  - Innovation

- *Supplier Relationships*: Is the alignment and managing of interactions with third party organizations that supply goods and/or services to an organization in order to create a more collaborative relationships with key suppliers in order to uncover and realize new Sustainability value and reduce risk.

Transformation initiatives are often complex, detailed and targeted series of projects to successfully transform an enterprise. Transforming an enterprise to leverage Sustainability benefits is no exception. Internal review, identification and urgent application of lessons learned reduce business risks, improved quality, and performance of Processes, Products and Services.

Internal Issues: Leadership commitment, in the longer term, is seen to promote business success in a sustainable developed world. It is also argued that when relevant shareholder value is considered, those companies that are contributing deliver better returns from Sustainable Development.
- Protecting or enhancing the resources (environmental or human) on which the business depends;
- Differentiating from, and gaining an edge over, competitors;
- Improving relationships with stakeholders[70].

Value Chain: CEOs reflect on current progress to date, challenges ahead and the impact of the journey toward a sustainable economy. Businesses will increasingly move away from seeing themselves as operating within a separate and distinct parts of a value chain toward taking greater responsibility for an entire system of inputs and outputs (from Resources to Customer to End-of-Life). In this view, ecosystem functions or the importance of water, the early warning indicators may not be material from an economic perspective, but in terms of the functioning of the value chain.

Global CEOs are starting to see the shape of a new era of sustainability coming into view. The global economic downturn might have been expected to weaken the commitment to environmental, social and corporate governance issues. What did happen, in fact, had an opposite effect: 80 percent of CEOs believe that the economic downturn raised the importance of sustainability as an issue for senior leadership.

Companies increasingly recognize that their contributions can be more effective if they align them with core competencies that create products that are sensitive to the environment and social needs. Companies can improve the quality, quantity, cost, and reliability of inputs and distribution while they simultaneously act as a steward for essential natural resources and drive economic and social development.

Understand the Culture
"Company cultures are like country cultures. Never try to change one. Try, instead, to work with what you've got." was the mantra of Peter Drucker.

Organizations not prepared to address the internal culture will meet stiff resistance and 'pushed back' against the change. Understand how communication with employees can be enhanced by empathizing, creating a business case, providing a vision for the future and enlisting employee-led changes to improve procedures and processes. LSS will instill a "measured" culture; one that quantifies a problem, investigates the root cause and applies solutions that should mitigate the problem. One of LSSs goals is to attain process stability and efficiency.

Sustainability is a philosophical magnate for new talent. Most employees want to work with companies who are 'doing the right thing' and being proactive with corporate environmental and social programs. A Global Study of Business Ethics by the American Management Association, one of the top five internal practices for ensuring an ethical corporate culture is developing corporate social responsibility programs. Confirming that study, Adecco, an international HR company, found that 52% of employed adults feel their companies should do more about the environment.

Sustainability and Ethics: Sung-joo Kim, CEO of Sungjoo Group, said; "Sustainability started as a moral obligation, but has now become a key differentiator for consumers." Sustainability has now become a concern of virtually every sector of human society. It enjoys more popular support than environmental resource conservation because it focuses on human needs, but also because it provides a positive vision for the future of the human family. From a motivational perspective, few people are inspired by the notion of "being less bad" in their environmental impact. In contrast, Sustainability provides a framework and markers for making positive change[71]. In recent years business increasingly has been viewed as a major cause of social, environmental, and economic problems. Companies are widely perceived to be prospering at the expense of the broader community.

An ethical approach to Sustainability suggests that society has an obligation to restrain wasteful uses of resources among the affluent, but it also has a special obligation to foster economic development for the poorest of the poor, all while maintaining environmental resource protection. When referring to Sustainable Development, one needs to define what is to be sustained, for whom, and for how long. Sustainability is not an absolute condition, but always partial. Sustainability, like justice, occurs along a continuum, and making progress along this is necessarily incremental. Restraint is its price.[72]

Even worse, the more business has begun to embrace corporate responsibility, the more it has been blamed for society's failures. The legitimacy of business has fallen to levels not seen in recent history. This diminished trust in business leads political leaders to set policies that undermine competitiveness and sap economic growth. Business is caught in a vicious circle[73].

Sustainability and Quality: Quality is an evolutionary journey, based on the teachings presented by Deming, Juran, Smith and Ohno. Today seek out areas of waste and remove it from their processes. Quality methodologies also provide examples that can inspire and encourage your organizations to take the bold and often courageous step in embracing and applying Dr. Deming's theories and teachings.

Quality also focuses your mission on key / critical success factors. LSS will instill a "measured" culture; one that quantifies a problem, investigates the root cause and applies solutions that should mitigate the problem. One of LSS's goals is to attain process stability and efficiency. Lean and Six Sigma have similar roots, but different applications. The following goals are typical examples of each methodology, but when combine, represent a very effective way to eliminate waste while retaining "gains" from previous projects.

One special realization of that change is the award of The Malcolm Baldrige National Quality Award. It recognizes U.S. organizations in business, health care, education, and nonprofit sectors for performance excellence. It is based on these criteria:
- Leadership
- Strategic planning
- Customer and market focus
- Measurement, analysis, and knowledge management
- Workforce focus
- Process management
- Results

As Deming said: "Why wouldn't a company embrace quality? After all, its virtually free. It enhances the products and services that are sold to the public. It improves the brand image of the company [and mitigates warranty costs, safety and quality issues, etc.]. It can save money on removing defects, improving customer satisfaction, improving clarity on goals and objectives, improve delivery of products and services in terms of time to market, enhance your production processes and provides a structure for ongoing improvement that enhances and perpetuates your quality effort, through Continuous Improvement. As Deming pointed out, quality management provides gains in many areas:
- Quality up ...
- Production of good product up ...
- Capacity up ...
- Lower cost per unit of good product ...

- Profit improved …
- Customer happier …
- Everybody happier …

These gains were immediate [within seven weeks]; cost, zero, same work force, same burden, no investment in new machinery. This is an example of gain in productivity accomplished by a change in the system, namely, improvement in definitions, effected by management, to help people work smarter, not harder[74]."

Deming was a strong believer in supporting analysis with concrete facts and quantifiable studies … If you have implemented a quality program, then use that specific jargon to communicate exact needs. Remove misunderstanding, ambiguity or vagueness. People want to win and achieve their goals. Ensure that your thoughts are clear and initiate action to achieve those goals[75].

The intent of any organization's Continuous Improvement efforts is to improve the effectiveness (e.g., reduce defects, variations, and waste) and efficiency (e.g., cost cutting per transaction) of the business processes. What one often does not see as part of the effectiveness definition, however, is the expectation that the newly redesigned or improved business processes need to reflect the stated Sustainability Values and its impact on the Core Assets of the organization. LSS investigates how a current process functions, by products, services and potential waste, and identifies viable areas of Growth, Performance or Savings.

Total Leadership Engagement: Two years into a Six Sigma deployment, one company did a review on its progress to date. The review included interviews with key decision makers throughout the organization. One of the more revealing interviews came from the vice president of product development – a key player in the organization. First, the vice president said, he had not been invited to attend any Six Sigma training, nor had any Champions or Black Belts asked him about his priorities. Second, he and his staff were keenly aware of all the money and effort being devoted to the Black Belts. The vice president and his staff had absolutely no reason to actively support Six Sigma, and instead had grown to view it with some resentment. By ignoring the importance of their commitment and support, the organization missed a prime opportunity to capitalize on all its resources.

In another instance, senior management announced that its strategic direction had change. Their top executives remained aloof and distant, leaving the hands-on and actual change to less motivated and incentivize people. Lack of involvement from senior leadership is a guaranteed formula for failure.

Managers will never fully support any form of transformation if they view it as taking away from their resources rather than adding capability and helping them become more successful in achieving their goals; nor will they actively support it if they think it is eating up vital budgetary allotments rather than setting the stage for significant financial payback. To avoid such pitfalls, a company must involve all key business leaders in helping to design its deployment. By giving them a voice in project selection, priorities and ongoing monitoring, an organization can be assured of their commitment to the effort.

Accountability is required for the transformation of the enterprise. The three levels of accountability are: Executive engagement and ownership, visibility with agreed metrics and data gathering; and embracing and implementing LSS in your entire organization.

When the Leadership makes the commitment to transformation (e.g., Sustainability, Lean Six Sigma, Sustainability and Lean Six Sigma) that CEO most often steps in and focuses on priorities for the company and its future. The CEO is often the catalyst to create Governance roles, often engages with the Board of Directors in overseeing progress, and plays a key role in creating executive accountability for the entire Sustainability Initiative.

After careful review, MetaPlanning recognizes critical sub-initiatives that need attention and execution. It should create a Program Office for the control activities. Distill your action plans into actionable progress reporting units that reflect your planned timeline. This should be accomplished and commentated to all involved process "owners", as well.

A key Sustainability-impassioned leader should be selected, either internally or externally, as a Champion along with a small staff recruited to serve as temporary facilitators and coordinators for the functional units.

Gathering information should be co-sponsored by both the Accounting and IT departments to align with information strategies that currently reside in your enterprise. Sustainability and LSS are disciplines that add value decision-making processes. Visibility over your costs reduction and opportunities for new revenue streams are found in this context.

"Many years ago quality wasn't as formal as it is now. We continue to put more attention, more structure, and more discipline to it," said Diane Seloff, Chief of Staff at Vanderbilt University Medical Center, Nashville, Tennessee. "We have various quality councils that focus on driving and approving the quality goals and plans; they assure the accountability. They make sure that there's transparency in the organization's quality metrics.

We have the ability to push out quality metrics to all the different areas within the organization so they know how they're doing and they work on action plans to improve. Our quality experts are not necessarily trained in any one area – they are trained to solve problems," she said[76].

Roadmap to a Sustainable Vision

Originally business organizations were inundated with complaints and confrontation from externalities (e.g., NGOs, SIGs, Regulators, Governments, etc.) that affected sales and brand image. In the 1990s, Sustainability was seen as the restart button to address those issues. That approach to resolving Sustainable issues was both good and bad. First the good, it was often a short-term solution that had a limited impact.

Second the bad, executives often focused their organization's effort on public relations, marketing campaigns and labeling products as "green" without substance. The result was known as "greening" products that were either unchanged or promoted on elements that did not exist in the products originally. These products were not improved, reformulated or designed to fit better in reducing impact on the environment or society. The lesson from this strategy was that "greening" a product was often considered disingenuous, and many times continued to erode brand image it was designed to enhance.

Lessons learned have help transform a framework to better fit the realities of Sustainability with LSS to establish a structured framework for change. Organizations that truly commit to Sustainability and LSS want to be good corporate citizens and good neighbors. Focusing on emissions, applying energy conservation, eliminating waste through recycling and repurposing, and offering "sustainably developed" products that do not contain toxins. Today, many business leaders view Sustainability holistically and consider it an integral component of their business strategy, identifying opportunities, mitigating risks, enhancing revenue possibilities, and adding brand value.

Additionally, organizations with a broader, more strategic plan for Sustainability will not only drive innovation across their enterprise — including transforming key processes, products and services — but may also influence what their customers want and how their suppliers operate[77]. These are the true ways of taking ownership and shaping your culture to meet the current needs of your Customers without sacrificing the future Customer needs. These are the element to your Sustainability roadmap.

Taking Ownership

Executive Commitment to the Sustainability Vision will determine whether their company will truly adhere to a long-term, long march to the top of Mt. Sustainability. Mt. Sustainability was the metaphor Ray Anderson used to communicate the potential opportunities and elimination of waste that could be extracted by a Sustainability approach. Sustainability is not a short-term approach.

- *PG&E:* "Because PG&E provides natural gas and electricity to 15 million people in Northern and Central California, our customers depend on us to be there for them not just today, but over the long run, planning and preparing for a sustainable, secure energy future. … Other recent examples of our commitment include:
    - Delivering some of the nation's cleanest energy with more than half our electricity coming from greenhouse gas-free resources;
    - Spending more than $1 billion over three years to help customers save energy and money through industry-leading energy efficiency initiatives;
    - Empowering customers through smart technology, such as the "Green Button," which offers an easy-to-use way to access and analyze energy usage data online;
    - Building career pathways for veterans and others through our pioneering PowerPathway™ workforce development program; and
    - Achieving our highest-ever supplier diversity goals and earning a top 10 ranking for supplier diversity nationwide from DiversityInc." ~ Anthony F. Earley, Jr., Chairman of the Board, Chief Executive Officer and President[78]

- *Walmart:* "We welcome the world's high expectations of Walmart, and we embrace the opportunity to make a difference for our customers, our company and the communities we serve." ~ Mike Duke, President and CEO[79]

What Did Ben Think?

Benjamin Franklin (January 17, 1706 – April 17, 1790) was one of the Founding Fathers of the United States. A noted polymath, Franklin was a leading author, printer, political theorist, politician, postmaster, scientist, musician, inventor, satirist, civic activist, statesman, and diplomat. He was also proud of his working-class heritage. Franklin's father, Josiah Franklin was a tallow chandler, a soap-maker and a candle-maker. A man of many facets and a genius of many, he was a visionary in his own right and said; "All human situations have their inconveniences. We feel those of the present but neither see nor feel those of the future; and hence we often make troublesome changes without amendment, and frequently for the worse."

"I was seldom able to see an opportunity until it had ceased to be one"
~Mark Twain

3. Corporate Social Responsibility[80]

"Management is efficiency in climbing the ladder of success; leadership determines whether the ladder is leaning against the right wall."
~ Stephen F. Covey

Corporate Social Responsibility (CSR) is a framework and encompasses not only what companies do with their profits, but also how they make them, ethically and effectively. It does not replace your Strategic Planning system, rather it should be integrated into your existing one to address new business opportunities. It goes beyond philanthropy and compliance and addresses how companies manage their economic, social, and environmental ramifications. CSR also addresses relationships in all key spheres of influence: corporate values, the workplace, the marketplace, the supply chain, the community, and the public policy realm.

CSR is a coordinated and structured approach for business, government and non-profit transformation. It is not a marketing campaign on a "green" product. It is not a facility's managers duty, process or procedure. It is not a Public Relations, Human Resource or Procurement job. It is not about philanthropy for non-profit organizations. It is not about community involvement like building a playground for your local park. Rather it is a framework that focuses a lens on the tangible benefits that can be garnered from Sustainability and how company's work within the sphere of the community. Businesses responsibilities and their roles, throughout the industrialized world, have seen a sharp escalation in the social roles corporations are expected to play.

CSR is also a long-term commitment based on an honest strategic effort, results, best practices and driven by transparency to the public. It is interwoven with business strategies and engages with external organizations. It is about measurable transformation, internally and externally, that extracts tangible benefits. Sustainability is more than platitudes and recycling efforts, for recycling is a beginning. It should be able to show financial benefits directly relating to waste reduction, conservation, improvement of internal processes and engagement with externalities (i.e., NGOs, Governments, Customers, Suppliers, etc.).

Century of Change
The 21st Century will be a Century of Change, transformation, new ideas and innovation, and discoveries that will enrich our society. We have entered a new industrial revolution. An industrial change that acknowledges our environment, our current generation's needs, our need to revisit best

practices, our business need to transform and prepare our legacy to meet the needs for succeeding generations.

We currently have, in place, a budding Sustainability industry that will continue to grow, mature and expand in the next 20 years. This is not a siloed approach, but an integrated solution approach that is tailored to fit each organization's needs.

Ideas will come from Humanity combined with Nature will show us the path. We will see a dance between Technology and Science that will build our economies as nothing before. Technological arrays will focus on issues resolution through the use of technology. All biological sciences will focus on how to restore our environment. It will continue to build on array and matrix foundations, which will holistically support industries, countries and the world in the transformation to a sustainable planet. Technological arrays will interconnect technologies for remediation of Sustainability issues (i.e., transportation, traffic, internet, water purification, etc.). Environmental matrices will produce biological and "natural" views will make solutions for converting waste to bio-nutrients for the purpose of environmental restoration. This is a long-term mending and nurturing strategy to restore our planet while benefiting from that change.

Adopting Corporate Social Responsibility

Defining CSR is evolving. Currently, CSR recognizes a company's accountability is linked to its community. CSR is not only what companies do with their profits, but also how they make them. It goes beyond philanthropy, compliance, ethics and it addresses how companies manage their economic, social, and environmental impacts, as well as their relationships in all key spheres of influence: the workplace, the marketplace, the supply chain, the community, and the public policy realm. Often times, linking social issues with business are interdependent and create a shared value for mutual success.

CSR is also a leadership opportunity for the transforming the enterprise. There may be numerous reasons for transforming your organization; however, CSR is a self-regulating and integrating approach based on a structured business model that recognizes the potential exposure to past practices or products that polluted the environment or caused harm to the population. Also, CSR policies function as self-regulating mechanism that monitors active compliance with laws, regulations, ethical standards and international regulations.

Traditionally, companies adopted Sustainability strategies in order to comply with government regulations and avoid fines. In many cases, corporations are adopting Sustainability in order to be a part of the conversation on environmental policy. Corporations deal with a wide variety of social, economic and environmental issues and problems, some directly related to their operations, some not. Here are some of the common contemporary issues:

- Environmental issues
- Global issues
- Food and Water Security issues
- Social issues
- Technological issues

But perhaps most important: nearly 50 percent of companies have changed their business models as a result of Sustainability opportunities — a 20 percent jump over last year. As we will explore in detail, business-model innovation is the crux of Sustainability profits. Companies reporting that it adds to their bottom lines leverage these innovations to translate Sustainability opportunities and pressures into profits[81].

A Model For CSR: Business and Governmental Sustainability Transformation is serious business and should be built with the clear understanding of client driven objectives, transformation tasks, attention to the mitigation of risks, employee training, and your culture's need during the transition. The architecture for this transformation is centered on the transformation paradigm. This model addresses the four stages of change based on the scope of an initiative. A key determination is the selection of how you want your initiative applied: do you need to create a Sustainability and Quality initiative, or do you need to only create a Sustainability initiative, or do you need to create only a quality initiative?

Although Corporate Social Responsibility (CSR) is commonly discussed, existed for over for over 30 years, but is rarely understood. CSR is defined through long-term strategy(s) that incorporate not only what companies do with their profits, but reflect as to how ethics make them beneficial for society. In a sense, it is a mirror that shows how companies manage their economic, social, and environmental consequences, as well as their relationships in key areas of influence: the workplace, the marketplace, the supply chain, the community, and other public policy arenas.

There is a global awareness as to how businesses behave, produce goods and services, and have disregard for people and the environment (e.g., Hooker Chemical and Love Canal). Customers, Governments, and deteriorating resources are pressuring Businesses and Industries to be accountable not only to Shareholders, but also to Stakeholders such as Customers, Employees, Communities, Regulators and Suppliers.

European Union's Interpretation: Corporate social responsibility is by definition is a multi-stakeholder concept. Facilitating dialogue between stakeholders is an important part of the Commission's policy on CSR[82].

- Commitment from key people (e.g. owners, senior managers);

- Ensuring that the values and vision of the CSR approach are integrated into the business and its culture;

- Integrating the CSR approach and any associated practices and tools, with the C. strategy, core business, mainstream management processes and policies, and everyday operational practice. This might mean adapting existing systems, or adopting or developing new ones;

- Setting appropriate goals or targets, related to the core business, developing a staged plan for achieving them (including some quick wins), evaluating progress towards them, and communicating this appropriately;

- Communicating about the approach, strategy, aims or activities in a transparent and meaningful way. Such communication is also a way of helping to magnify the benefits associated with drivers of CSR practice, for example through aiding learning and innovation, as well as building credibility and helping to improve relationships with stakeholders.

- Openness to learning, improvement and innovation;

- Engagement with external stakeholders - including local stakeholders in non-EU countries – understanding their views and expectations, being open to learning from them, communicating well with them about issues, goals and progress, being open about areas of agreement and disagreement and thus building a trusting relationship, where the company and its stakeholders are willing to co-operate in good faith in efforts to achieve its CSR goals, including to the extent of working in partnership together;

- Involving employees and their representatives in developing and implementing CSR, programs, activities and initiatives;

- Sharing experience, learning from and with peers, in a multi-stakeholder initiatives or through networks, good practice examples, initiatives and benchmarking, and being willing to solve problems, innovate and improve as a result of this learning;

- The availability of easily accessible and specific advice, and appropriate, effective and credible tools and initiatives which the company can learn from when developing its own approach, use, or join in with, which are suitable to its circumstances or are flexible enough to be enable the company to learn over time, innovate and respond to circumstances.

- Particularly for developing countries, the existence of an appropriate legal environment which reinforces compliance with fundamental standards, and the presence of strong civil society organizations such as trade unions and NGOs as stakeholders and potential partners;

- A high level of awareness among consumers and investors, of the issues and companies' options in responding to them[83].

Why Is CSR Important?

A strategic approach to CSR is increasingly important to a company's competitiveness. It can bring benefits in terms of risk management, cost savings, access to capital, customer relationships, human resource management, and innovation capacity. It also encourages more social and environmental responsibility from the corporate sector at a time when the crisis has damaged consumer confidence and the levels of trust in business.

- Through CSR, enterprises can significantly contribute to the European Union's treaty objectives of sustainable development and a highly competitive social market economy. CSR underpins the objectives of the Europe 2020 strategy for smart, sustainable and inclusive growth, including the 75% employment target. Responsible business conduct is especially important when private sector operators provide public services.

- CSR requires engagement with internal and external stakeholders so it enables enterprises to anticipate better and take advantage of fast-changing expectations in society as well as operating conditions. This means it can also act as a driver for the development of new markets and create real opportunities for growth.

- By addressing their social responsibility, enterprises can build long-term employee, consumer and citizen trust as a basis for sustainable business models. This in turn helps to create an environment in which enterprises can innovate and grow. The economic crisis and its social consequences have to some extent damaged levels of trust in business, and have focused public attention on the social and ethical performance of enterprises, including on issues such as bonuses and executive pay.

- Helping to mitigate the social effects of the crisis, including job losses, is part of the social responsibility of enterprises. In the longer term, CSR offers a set of values on which to build a more cohesive society and on which to base the transition to a sustainable economic system.

- By renewing efforts to promote CSR now, the Commission aims to create conditions favorable to sustainable growth, responsible business behavior and lasting job creation for the medium and long-term[84].

What Policy Actions Should CSR Cover?

The effectiveness and evolution of CSR will churn decade after decade. Changes in the biosphere, business and government strategies, national and international laws, availability of resources, disruptive technology and other key variable will continue to blend policy requirements to meet actionable and Sustainability needs. Currently, we have two major approaches to a CSR framework, one obligatory the other voluntary and more flexible, namely the European Union and U.S. Policies and Practices:

European Union: I n the European Union it is a different approach. On 25 October 2011, the European Commission delivered a new CSR policy that outlined an action agenda for the period 2011-2014 covering 8 areas:
- Enhancing the visibility of CSR and disseminating good practices
- Improving and tracking levels of trust in business
- Improving self- and co-regulation processes
- Enhancing market reward for CSR for responsible business conduct
- Improving company disclosure of social and environmental information
- Integrating CSR into education, training and research
- Emphasizing the importance of national and sub-national CSR policies
- Better aligning European and global approaches to CSR[85]

U.S. Policies and Practices: In the U.S., this is an ambiguous area at best. CSR, Sustainability Transformation and Transparency reporting are all voluntary, not obligated action areas for compliance. With adaptation to change, organizations often go through growth stages and leave other elements aside during organizational acceleration. Here are risk areas and scenarios that may usher the need for Sustainability change and policy action areas:
- *External Risk Mitigation:* Smart leadership will recognize their organization has limited knowledge that may not bridge the needs for Transformation. Experience in enterprise transformation in information technology, business systems and a pragmatic application of Sustainability principles are key linchpins.

- *Systems Integration:* Before, during and after Transformation initiatives are executed and implemented, integration provides linkage to groups in your organization, based on your new business paradigm to apply their new knowledge, approach and information support to its Employees, Stakeholders and the Sustainability Vision.

- **Optimization:** This is not your "low hanging fruit", but it is an area of great potential. Organizations often use this increased awareness to optimize their processes, compelled by financial benefits through cost savings and increased productivity. This is a long-term commitment and usually rewards organizations that have been built through levels of maturity.

- **Internal Transformation:** Experience in enterprise transformation in information technology, business systems and a pragmatic application of Sustainability is key. This is your "low hanging fruit". They simple in the early stages and can often be applied with minimum costs. Depending on your company or government size, the results can be huge.

- **Brand Image:** Promoting differentiation in your products and services that are unique and possess intrinsic values for your Customers are significant in attracting "niche" markets or creating entirely new markets. Building brand value through setting, keeping, and communicating Sustainability promises to stakeholders will appeal to your Customer base.

- **Strategies:** Creating an isolated Sustainability strategy will promote failure from the onset. Sustainability strategies must be woven into overall corporate strategies, like Quality management strategies, to reap true tangible benefits. CSR is a framework to link Sustainability with current business strategies and ensure ownership is clearly understood through the enterprise. If you have planning issues, then Sustainability Transformation will highlight those inconsistencies.

- **Transparency:** Build brand value through setting, keeping, and communicating Sustainability promises to all Stakeholders, especially Customers. Integrity based results communicated to show tangible and visible commitment to Sustainability and Quality will be your linchpins to address Stakeholder and Shareholder requests, and a push for cost reductions through greater efficiency, increase brand awareness and improve environmental issues. However, it must be real and verifiable. These reputational improvements will be short-lived if the companies don't back up claims with real action and measurable improvements.

- **Resource Restrictions:** If you are and MNC (multinational corporation) your organization has probably experience resource shortages in the past and currently may have shortages on a day-to-day basis. Poorly constructed infrastructure, inefficient logistics, resource quality issues and limited resource availability are "normal" risks in many countries today. But general business and government environments will be affected too. Even in developed countries, resource restrictions will appear. Consider the trends in extended use of those resources, and compound limits on food and water now, then resources will be problematic in the very near future (3-7 years).

- *Energy Consumption:* As population grows, so does the demand for energy. Thirty years ago energy was "cheap" by today's pricing. Those trends will continue for the upcoming decades and business and government have recognized that impact. Thirty years ago we were primarily a carbon-based energy market (coal, natural gas and oil) with small contribution from water generated electricity. Today, that market has diversified. We still have a large percentage of carbon based energy, hydro-generated electricity, but we now have new technologies that have introduce renewable energy alternatives (photovoltaic, geo-thermal, biomass, as well as wind and ocean generated electricity). Costs are becoming more competitive to meet increasing demand.

- *Zero Waste and Benign Emissions:* Some people say the cost of zero waste strategy would be costly to implement. But one needs to be suspicious of the assumptions that support that statement. From a Sustainability point of view, zero waste includes the policy, processes, people and their training, and product design to eliminate waste, zero waste. Benign Emissions can be apart of that process (e.g., water, water vapor, clean air, etc.). Zero Waste Goal is to reduce the amount of waste sent to the landfill.

By applying these critical factors, the European Community has leap-frogged efforts in their geographic region. These critical factors should link to your Sustainability strategies and those goals and targets you want to attain in your fiscal year.

Building A Business Case

Your business case begins to set expectations. Without a clear business case, Sustainability transformation will probably be less likely to succeed. It does not replace your Vision, however it does model it into aspirations, objectives and possible results. It is a tool and a catalyst to refine your Vision for the long-term. Your business case does not replace Strategic Planning, but should be aligned to it. It does not replace your ethics and values, but makes you consider other ethical issues and what you could / should do. It highlights current practices (i.e., Accountability, Governance, Incentives, Innovation, Stakeholders, etc.) introduces new concepts (i.e. Externalities, Economical, Environmental, People, Social, Waste, etc.).

Organizational complexity will affect your modeling, business assumptions and Sustainability outcomes in each developed scenario. Ascending to higher levels, rung by rung in the ladder, is based on a clear business case criteria and its implication to your organization. Only those who have a business case, show deep advantages regardless of organization sizes:

- Have a business case for Sustainability: 59% and have added profit
- Have tried to make a business case, but it was too difficult to develop: 25% and have added profit
- Have not made a business case for Sustainability: 15% have added profit[86]

Renewable energy increases operational efficiencies: SC Johnson is a privately held cleaning products company and maker of Windex and other brands has become more aggressive in investing in clean energy projects. Renewable projects are nothing new; SC Johnson's managers are locking up long term contracts with renewable energy providers to keep fuel prices more stable. Currently 40 percent of the company's energy needs come from renewables; this is set to increase to 44 percent by 2016.

Encourage employees to behave more sustainably: Your culture could affect your employee's life-style too. SAP realized its employees were commuting enough miles to drive from earth to the moon, back to earth . . . and back to the moon again. Within just one year, SAP employees in Germany generated more than 22,500 carpools, avoided more than 311,000 miles (500,000 km) of driving, created an additional 1400 days of networking and saved 47 tons of greenhouse gas emissions. SAP has estimated the value through cost savings, networking and emission reduction generated during its first year at $3 million (€ 2.3 million).

Be water efficient: See how water can be better utilized. Campbell Soup Company's business operations are typical of food processing companies— of all the water the iconic company consumes, only two percent of it ends up in actual products. Partnerships with agricultural suppliers to adopt drip irrigation; the retrofit of systems now allowing factories to use heat from hot water for both heating and cooling facilities; and smarter washing of vegetables and other ingredients all added up to savings. Campbell has estimated water efficiency projects resulted in a 15 to 20 percent internal return on investment for the company. Simply using a practice of using water more than once will also yield benefits. Design and apply best practices that capture run away water or reuse water:

- Utilize rain water, usually captured in cisterns or ponds, for reuse in landscapes, urinals and flush toilets.

- Utilize and capture "storm water" from your roofs, garage tops, paved areas and streets that can be channeled to "swales" (a low-lying or depressed and often wet stretch of land).
- Use only what your people, products and processes need.
- Monitor your usage. If consumption does not rise and billed usage shows an increase, check for leaks.
- Utilize "grey water"; water coming from domestic equipment other than toilets (e.g., bathtubs, showers, sinks, washing machines). Grey water can be used to clean and reuse in urinals and flush toilets. Grey water is preferred to be kept separate from black water.
- Utilize "black water", it is untreated with chemicals, and can be used to water landscape and ensure it does not leave your site.

Sustainability can revive brands and sales: Unilever launched its Sustainable Living Plan in 2010 after a decade of sluggish performance. The company's programs from promoting hand washing to a shift towards fair trade tea to selling safer cook stoves. While the company is not ready to link this shift towards sustainability to performance, the correlation is definitely there: sales went up 6.5 percent between 2010 and 2011; and then jumped 6.9 percent in 2012.

Small companies can benefit: Setton Farms is a small pistachio grower in California's San Joaquin Valley. Two years ago the company launched the largest solar power project in the region; the 2.6 million megawatt facility creates enough energy to fuel its processing facility and Setton sells energy back to the local grid. Over 25 years the company expects to save $14 million in energy costs[87].

General Guidelines: Whether you are a Sustainability consultant or internal manager, professionals often find themselves caught in a vicious circle: Information is power and relinquishing that information is often seen test of wills. Leverage your Champion and resolve the barrier to gain access to the information and advise your Champion of the additional costs (as it may impact your transformation budget).

- Your business case is a part of a wider change program. There will be studied and scrutinized by CXOs, Owners, or the Broad of Directors. That means that information must be based on accurate and verifiable information and that you know who are the internal stakeholders you need to influence, especially in the finance function.

- Go to the finance department with a safe pilot. Unless someone in your C-suite has an epiphany, you will need to start with a small and safe pilot. Identify an initiative, project, decision or process where the business case can be investigated without requiring too much resource.

- Use the pilot to build credibility and awareness. Wherever possible get the finance department themselves to investigate the business case. They will find their own results the most credible. You can use the pilot to learn how to speak their accounting language better, and to help them understand Sustainability too.

- More important is demonstrating, first, that you are searching for how Sustainability can create profits, and, second, that there probably is a business case for the company, even if not with what was piloted.

- Throughout the process, continue to build permission to investigate more of the business case, and use the results to get the next round of permission. Along the way you will want to build the capacity of individuals to understand and act on Sustainability.

Keep creating a "permission and results" cycle. Hopefully, by this stage you have some credibility and interest from the finance function. You can use that to address larger and more important areas. How can you bring Sustainability into capital expenditure decisions? Do Sustainability related risks get valued correctly in the risk register? Do people in strategy planning understand the size of Sustainability related opportunities?

-

Preparing the Business Case: The following guidelines are just that, guidelines. Sustainability is evolving, Sustainable Development is also developing, but as a business professional must recognize standard measures and tools of analyzing for developing a business case. From a business perspective, your efforts need to pragmatic and include cost reduction approaches. Your financial and accounting experts may have other components in developing your company business case, use their expertise and accept their perspectives in creating a case.

However, one caveat is how they capture data elements to link to the business case. This is a case of implementing a Lean or Sustainability accounting system. If you cannot leverage current databases to gather data, then it must be gather manually. Beware, you could get push back, but this will open the door for better reporting and augmenting the existing system to meet Sustainability reporting. This is a multi-year quest and one that requires alliance in the financial and accounting community.

Introduction to the business case should also include these five points. You want to show how the business case will fit, internally and externally, while at the same time, recognize how the business case will reflect upon strategies based on Sustainability. Build a matrix on each task, obtain buy-in from each owner, and leverage common metrics as well as unique metrics to measure success of each task. Find agreement on reviews (usually monthly and quarterly) that compares progress and milestones.

- Business Drivers are US and Global reflect sustainability business trends and the current economic, environmental and social arenas. A descriptive rationale, ideally measurable, used to support a business vision or project to clarify why a change or completely new direction is necessary.

- Champion who will designate as the leader to help nurture and break up log jams in the transformation or project implementation. Any corporation around the world interested in tackling the challenges of performance, innovation, growth and Sustainability.

- Scope is the depth and breadth of project. Is it a pilot or test project for proof of concept or is it a project that will address or continue to face legal, social, and ethical issues brought on by the increasing globalization or other constraints in business?

- Stakeholders are those individual organizations, also called externalities, that can build brand value through setting, keeping, and communicating Sustainability promises to all stakeholders, including customers and suppliers. Keen use of Transparency. Is an effective communication to, open to your stakeholders, indicating progress of your Sustainability strategies, objectives, progress through issue resolution.

- Merging Financial and Sustainability metrics as measures of success and improvement based on revenue, costs, assets and performance. An example would be applied in incentives. Example: 80 percent of the bonus plan is tied to traditional financial metrics, 20 percent is reserved for non-financial goals including safety, diversity, and environmental health, as indicated by reducing CO_2 emissions by 400,000 tons (weighted 5 percent).

Pilot Business Case: Analysis of the business case, especially pilots, is a "best guess" of what will be accomplished given that all comments have been correctly and completely identified. It also assumes that all data is gathered to fairly compare to indicate the success or failure of the pilot. It is a foundation of understanding the "gaps" and "complexity" of the environment. Essentially it is a comparative exercise for "lessons learned". If you find it unfavorable, look into the methodology of comparing expected returns versus what your pilot actually presented. If it is significantly over stated results, then the same exercise should be engaged to verify the assessment. Review these elements in you pilot:

- Assumptions: List and recognize business stakeholders, environmental and social implications.
- Strategic Options: Identify how this business case could drive strategies, whether internally or externally.
- Other Benefits: Include other benefits that might be considered, but not listed in assumptions or other areas of analysis.
- Opportunity Costs: Identify opportunity costs if this business case is implemented or not.
- Cash Flow Statement: Cash flow statements have three distinct sections, each of which relates to a particular component - operations, investing and financing of a company's business activities.
- NPV = Net Present Value, prepare a NPV of the business case. Net present value analysis eliminates the time element in comparing alternative investments. The NPV method usually provides better decisions than other methods when making capital investments.

  - The Net Present Value Formula for a single investment is: NPV = PV less I

  - Where:

  - PV = Present Value

  - I = Investment
- Cost Reduction: 54 percent of projects are focused on costs[88].
- Build Reputation: 30 percent are focused on reputation[89].
- Manage Risks: 12 percent are focused on Business and Sustainability risks[90].
- Drives Revenue: 8 percent are focused on driving revenue[91].

CSR Business Case Review

The fourth annual study, which is based on a survey of 2,600 executives and managers from companies around the world, also revealed that nearly half of the companies surveyed changed their business models as a result of Sustainability opportunities — marking a 20 percent rise from the previous year. The report calls these companies "Sustainability-Driven Innovators."

A company's Sustainability efforts refer to incorporating Sustainability thinking into all its areas of discipline — supply chain, marketing, finance and product development — as well as devising new business models and strategy grounded in Sustainability. The study found that companies in emerging markets — nations in the process of rapid growth and industrialization — change their business models as a result of Sustainability at a far higher rate than those based in North America, which has the lowest rate of Sustainability-driven, business-model innovation and the fewest business-model innovators[92].

"The research suggests that business-model innovation, top-management support, collaboration with customers, and having a business case are all critical to creating economic value from Sustainability activities and decisions," says Knut Haanæs, a BCG partner who leads the firm's strategy practice and co-author of the report. "Executives need to view Sustainability as both a business necessity and an opportunity. Even moderate changes to company business models can reap significant financial rewards."

Sustainable Development Objectives: "Change is a constant!" How many times have heard that mantra? In fact, business is really based on change. There are changes in resource costs, there are changes in processes, there are changes in improved logistics, there are changes in Customer demands and all of this change is concentrated on your business. In general, companies need to set objectives aligned with these Sustainability Metrics, as a quarterly update of:
- Carbon emissions
- Water and energy use
- Wastes generated
- Safety data

The Walmart Example: It was simple, to the point, easily communicated across the enterprise and focused on key issues to generate results. All Stakeholder would be see the results. As the world's largest retailer, their actions had the potential to save their Customers money and help ensure a better world for future generations. Their three aspirational Sustainability goals were:
- To be supplied 100% by renewable energy
- To create zero waste
- To sell products that sustain people and the environment

Walmart is exemplar and we will be discussing in detail their results in transforming their organization that was driven by the three key objectives addressed above.

Potential Revenue Drivers[93]: Always verify assumptions that would generate revenue, where it would be generated, how it would be related to Sustainability or Quality and track your analysis to validate those assumptions.
- How will changes in customer demand patterns affect pricing?
- What percentage of climate-related costs (alternate energy, emission reduction, etc.) will we be able to pass through to customers?

- How can we generate streams of revenue from new low-carbon products?
- What new forms of income (for example, carbon credits) will become available?
- What threats do we face from low-carbon substitute products?
- What will be the impact of weather patterns (flooding, logistic restrictions, etc.) on revenue?

Potential Cost Drivers[94]: Costs should be evaluated and confirmed in a logical fashion similar to your revenue assumptions. Understanding the assumptions will better prepare your "lessons learned" after the end of the project, final year or initiative cycle timeframes.

- How will regulatory policy affect our costs? (Will we need to purchase emissions allowances, such as carbon credits?)
- Is there a chance that emissions will also, or alternatively, be taxed?
- What capital expenditures do we face as a result of emissions-reduction plans? Will new equipment be required or can updates be made to existing systems?
- How much will our raw materials costs escalate? How much will those of our Suppliers escalate? Will your Suppliers be able to provide alternatives and expertise?
- How much will our energy costs rise? Does it matter whether energy is only furnished from utilities or should the enterprise consider generating its energy?
- How will our risk profile affect our insurance premiums? Are other areas at risk due to prior business practices?

Taking Ownership

Stephen Covey was right he said; "leadership determines whether the ladder is leaning against the right wall." A CSR framework establishes the direction that ladder leans. It combines the business orientation and the sustainability orientation to optimize opportunities and eliminate wastes. Here are two examples:

- *Dow:* "We need to put a price on these things every time we put something in the ground. Because the long-term cost of ownership and our right to operate should be the mindset that not only this generation of leaders leads by, but also future generations as well." ~ Andrew N. Liveris, Chairman and Chief Executive Officer[95]

- *First Solar:* "Our sustainability mindset enables us to achieve long-term growth and lower energy costs while upholding social contracts with communities and partners and following environmentally responsible practices." ~ James Hughes, CEO[96]

What Did Ray Think?

Ray C. Anderson (July 28, 1934 – August 8, 2011) was founder and chairman of Interface Inc., one of the world's largest manufacturers of modular carpet for commercial and residential applications and a leading producer of commercial broadloom and commercial fabrics. He was "known in environmental circles for his advanced and progressive stance on industrial ecology and sustainability." He was truly a pioneer for Sustainability and said; "I believe that a sustainable society depends totally and absolutely on a new mindset to deeply embrace ethical values. Values that, along with an enlightened self-interest, drive us to make new and better decisions."

In the summer of 1994, carpet-tile mogul he made a sobering discovery: Although his billion-dollar business was the biggest of its kind in the world, everything about it was wrong. That realization came after reading "The Ecology of Commerce" by Paul Hawken. "It was an epiphanic spear in my heart, a life-changing moment," he recalled in a 2006 interview with the Guardian of London. "I realized I was a plunderer and it was not a legacy I wanted to leave behind."

The book led Anderson to reexamine his business model through the lens of environmentalism. His Georgia-based company, Interface, made carpet tiles from petroleum products. The nylon in the carpets came from oil. The electricity that ran its plants came from fossil fuels. The finished tiles were transported on diesel-powered trucks. The entire enterprise, he would later say, was so oil-dependent that "you could think of it as an extension of the petrochemical industry."

Every enterprise has the wherewithal to regroup, refocus and realign to Sustainability principles. Your question is: does your enterprise leadership have the will?

4. Corporate Planning and CSR[97]

"When planning for a year, plant corn. When planning for a decade,
plant trees. When planning for life, train and educate people."
~ Chinese Proverb

20th Century Strategic Planning and Quality

You might call the this century of quantitative and qualitative ideas, understanding and control, and flirting with innovation as tool to improve products. During this period, major ideas developed into frameworks that directly developed corporate planning and developed the methodologies for quality management.

Driving Theory: In the 1960s-70s, economist Milton Friedman argued against CSR (at that time it was called social responsibility). He believed that management is to make as much money as possible within the limits of the law and ethical customs. He argued that the primary responsibility of business is to make a profit for its owners, albeit while complying with the law. According to Friedman, an agency theory perspective implies that CSR was a misuse of corporate resources that would be better spent on valued-added internal projects or returned to shareholders. It also suggested that CSR was an executive perk, in the sense that managers use CSR to advance their careers or other personal agendas[98]. If the operation of the free market cannot solve a social problem, it becomes the responsibility of government, not business, to address the issue[99].

Mindset: Many corporations who adopted strategic planning and / or quality management executed these approaches focused on short-term results. Often management applied these tools and focus on short-term results (e.g., monthly, quarterly) to meet and satisfy market analysts.

How Mobil Implemented Strategies

In 1998, I was engaged with Mobil Oil's Y2K effort. As a consultant arriving on site, my experience detected and identified queues in Mobil's organization. One quickly ascertains behaviors and employee's actions that reflect the culture of their enterprise. You witness the enterprise's approach in day-to-day operations. Mobil, as a forward looking corporation, was a cutting edge organization in applying state-of-the-art practices for business, petroleum engineering, information technology, production and operations, and logistics. Mobil had an impeccable business reputation and was selected as a case study in Kaplan and Norton's book entitled <u>The Strategy-Focused Organization</u>, that applied the Balanced Scorecard (BSC).

If organizations that understood a systems approach, benefitted. Organizations, like Mobil, were early adopters of the Balanced Scorecard (BSC) have shown impressive results to date. Consider the following case study:

Mobil Oil (U.S. Marketing & Refining Group) - The BSC was introduced in 1993 to help manage Mobil's transformation from a highly centralized, production-driven oil company to a decentralized, customer-driven retail organization. The results were rapid and dramatic. By 1995, Mobil had moved from last place to first in industry profitability. It maintained this No. 1 position for five consecutive years, through its merger with Exxon in October 1999. From a negative cash flow of $500 million (all currency in U.S. dollars) in 1992, Mobil USM&R recorded a positive cash flow of $900 million in 1998[100].

Our continuing research has revealed a set of five principles that permit organizations to become strategy-focused, enabling them to execute their strategies rapidly and effectively[101].

Principle 1 - Translate the Strategy to Operational Terms: Use the "golden thread" to show objectives and accountability: Processes are your company's linchpins to the "golden thread". Ensure they are efficient and effective. They must work in to ensure success for new possibilities in the present and in the future. It will require thinking through how those objectives and goals will impact internal and external environments, but the time invested will be well spent. Mobil implemented to measure their success:
• Strategy maps
• Balanced Scorecard

Principle 2 - Align the Organization to the Strategy: For organizational performance to become more than the sum of its parts, individual strategies must be linked and integrated[102]. Breaking down silos is the first step for real transformation. These functional silos have their own body of knowledge, vocabulary and specialties needed for the enterprise. However, Sustainability, in many cases become a common area to eliminate waste and improve communication. Mobil implemented to measure their success:
• Corporate Role
• Business Unit synergies
• Shared Service synergies

Principle 3 - Make Strategy Everyone's Everyday Job: Strategy-focused organizations require all employees understand the strategy and conduct their day-to-day business in a way that contributes to the success of that strategy[103]. Provide awareness and make ownership personal by impacting individual paychecks. Mobil implemented to measure their success:

- Strategic Awareness
- Personal Scorecards
- Balanced Paychecks

Principle 4 - Make Strategy a Continual Process: Is it any wonder that strategies fail to be implemented when strategies don't even appear on the executive agenda and calendar? Strategy-focused organizations use a different approach[104]. Provide linkages of plans to budgets, drive the need for analytics that are based on those linkages and extract lessons learned from that strategic experience. Mobil implemented to measure their success:
- Link Budgets to Strategies
- Analytics and Information Systems
- Strategic Learning

Principle 5 - Mobilize Change through Executive Leadership: Experience has repeatedly shown that the single most important condition for success is the ownership and active involvement of the executive team. Strategy requires change from virtually every part of the organization, Strategy requires teamwork to coordinate these changes[105]. Mobil integrated these principles from the top-down and infused them into the corporate culture. Executives were engaged in the review and decision-making process, either daily or quarterly to meet their objectives. Mobil implemented to measure their success:
- Mobilization (of all employees)
- Governance Processes
- Strategic Management System

Critical Success Factors: Critical success factors (within BSC) follow a business approach that enhances relationships and communication with all its stakeholders. Once the Critical Success Factors are identified they are rearranged in accordance with the following four perspectives:
- ***Financial Perspectives*** – Financial strength, support efforts aimed at growth, profitability and risk from the perspective of the owners/shareholders/stakeholders
- ***Customer Perspective*** – Customer satisfaction and meeting Customer needs, support efforts for creating value and differentiation from the perspective of the customer
- ***Internal Perspective*** – Operational excellence, establishes priorities for various business or operational processes that are critical in creating customer and shareholder/stakeholder satisfaction and optimizing performance and productivity while eliminating waste
- ***Growth & Learning Perspective*** – Safe, engaged, and effective employees, guided by Corporate Values focus on activities that create a climate supportive of change, innovation and growth

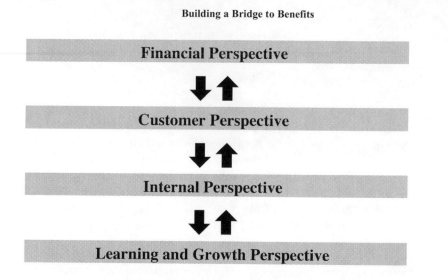

As the saying goes, "when one and one equals three, you don't have the whole picture." Kaplan and Norton were focused on their solutions for effective strategic execution. They were right in so many ways, but ignored the benefits (both tangible and intangible) from Quality frameworks that have benefited government and business for over 100 years by eliminating internal waste. Also, Kaplan and Norton ignored the very substantial gains from Sustainability. Again, be eliminating external waste (e.g., water, energy, emissions, etc.).

21st Century Strategic Planning and Quality

Many management thinkers argue that it is no longer enough to do well financially; companies also need to improve the well-being of (or at least not harm) the communities in which they operate, the environment, and their employees[106]. Sustainability began in the 20th late century and recognized that previous practices did not consider environmental or social issues. Pioneers, like Anderson, were creating an approach that created a competitive advantage, based on elimination of waste, internally and externally, while developing a new philosophy of preserving the planet. That journey started a revolution that has been embraced globally and continues to gain momentum.

Mindset: Sustainability is a long-term commitment. CSR takes a longer term approach to eliminate waste, externally and internally, through methodology, design and practice that should be incorporated as a facet of strategic planning. It will require thinking outside the box and that includes thinking outside the "brick and mortar" box of the corporation. Be open to news ideas. Be open to making things that make you more sustainable, efficient, effective and strive for insight.

Customer and Innovation Focus: These two key concepts, Creating Shared Value and Disruptive Technology, will be the foundation for developing solutions for the 21st century. Not only will they lead to meeting market demands (e.g., product differentiation, improving emission solutions, meeting or exceeding regulatory compliance, eliminating waste by design, etc), they will also be utilized in creating improved solutions with other Externalities (e.g. Natural, Human, Financial Resources, etc.).

Market Acceptance: As more businesses watch their competitors become more competitive by adopting Sustainability, the accumulated effect will be a rush to transforming their businesses. That movement and acceptance is called the "tipping point" and many researchers consider that time is close for a transformation of American and Canadian commerce.

Sustainability Models: What are the elements of Sustainability strategies that creates awareness, identifies direction and should be integrated into business strategies to focus on business, environmental and social opportunities. Currently, two major guideline exist: first is Ceres that was established by investors after Alaskan Valdez oil spill and the second is the United Nations Global Compact.

New Mindset: Interview with Jeff Bezos[107] of Amazon

Bezos discusses that Sustainability is a shift in traditional business models. The mindset recognizes that opportunities exist looking through a Sustainability business lens that might be over looked otherwise. It is long-term execution approach. It does not target short-term performance. It is Customer focused and makes them the highest priority. Stakeholders, as well as, shareholders are aligned and communicated with.

Bezos is representative of the contemporary executive that understands that new business models need to embrace globalization and Sustainability. New companies leverage affordable and ubiquitous technology to build a web presence that extends beyond the "brick and mortar" business paradigm. This contemporary model also reconsiders the purpose of the value chain that includes the tangible benefits from Sustainability. Read what he discovered:

> *What does it mean from the perspective of a CEO to think long-term?* If you're long-term oriented, customer interests and shareholder interests are aligned. In the short term, that's not always the case. We have other stakeholders, too—our employees, our vendors. We take it as an article of faith that if we put customers first, other stakeholders will also benefit, as long as they're willing to take the long-term view. And a long-term approach is essential for

invention, because you're going to have a lot of failures along the way.

You've said that you like to plant seeds that may take seven years to bear fruit. Doesn't that mean you'll lose some battles to companies that have a more conventional, two- or three-year outlook? Maybe so, but if we had always needed to see significant financial results in two or three years, then some of the most meaningful things we've done would never have been started—like Kindle, Amazon Web Services, Amazon Prime.

How much do you care about your share price? I care very much about our shareowners, so I care very much about our long-term share price. I do not follow the stock on a daily basis, because I don't think there's any information in it. The economist Benjamin Graham once said, "In the short term, the stock market is a voting machine. In the long term, it's a weighing machine." We try to build a company that wants to be weighed, not voted on.

Does it make sense for Amazon to stay in the hardware business, which is a low-margin, low-profit area for you? Our approach is to sell our hardware—our Kindle devices—at near break-even. Then we have an ongoing relationship with customers who buy content from us: digital books, music, movies, TV shows, games, apps. We aren't trying to make $100 every time we sell a Kindle Fire, so we don't have to get you on the upgrade treadmill.

You have said that you would be interested, if you had the right concept and approach, in creating a physical Amazon retail experience. Why even consider that? We like to build innovative things, but only if we can put our own unique twist on them. If we could find something differentiated that we thought customers would like, it would be super fun.

Would developing a phone fall into that innovative category? Yeah, absolutely.

Who do you fear is your biggest challenger? We don't get up every morning wondering, "Who are the top three companies that are going to try to kill us?" I know of companies that do that in their annual planning processes, and the competitive zeal motivates them. We do pay attention, but it's not where we get our energy from.

Disruption is a rough business. Do you have any personal regrets about the pain your success has caused traditional retailers? I'm as sentimental as the next person. I have lots of childhood memories of physical books and things like that. But our job at Amazon is to build the best customer experience we can and let customers choose where they shop.

At what point will the goal change from lowering margins and building market share to making a bigger profit? Percentage margins are not something we seek to optimize. We want to maximize the absolute-dollar free cash flow per share. If we can do that by lowering margins, we will. Free cash flow is something investors can spend. They can't spend percentage margins.

Amazon has done a great job of self-cannibalizing its revenue streams—going from Amazon Store to Amazon Marketplace, from print to e-books, and so on. In most companies, moves like those would be hard to execute without organizational turmoil. How have you managed the transitions? When things get complicated, we simplify them by asking, "What's best for the customer?" We believe that if we do that, things will work out in the long term. We can never prove that. In fact, sometimes we do price-elasticity studies, and the answer is always that we should raise prices. But we don't, because we believe that by keeping our prices very low, we earn trust with customers, and that this will maximize free cash flow over the long term.

What have you learned about leadership from running what has become a very big company? If you're inventing and pioneering, you have to be willing to be misunderstood for long periods of time. One early example is customer reviews. A book publisher told me, "You don't understand your business. You make money when you sell things. Why do you allow negative reviews?" And I thought, "We don't make money when we sell things; we make money when we help customers make purchase decisions."

How do you institutionalize the ability to come up with these good, misunderstood ideas? First, there are stories we tell ourselves internally about persistence and patience, long-term thinking, staying focused on the customer. Second, we select people who, when they wake up in the morning, are thinking about how to invent on behalf of the customer. If you like a more competitively focused culture, you might find us dull. We find our culture intensely fun. We have an explorer mentality, not a conqueror mentality.

Driving Theory: Competition's Market Entry

In the 21st Century, business will be the true catalyst for pragmatic Sustainability transformation. This is a systematic approach of eliminating waste, improve efficiency, addressing customer needs, and recognizing corporate social responsibilities will be a model of increased competitive advantage in the marketplace. Sustainability is a systemic framework to address economic, environmental, social and technological issues, to create a sustainable world and avoid declining ecosystems. The business community has begun to implement Sustainability and has proven that change can indeed be profitable and promote performance.

Who will be the winners in this transition? Geoffrey Moore published a landmark book in 1991, entitled "Crossing the Chasm". The theme of the book focused on marketing and selling technical and disruptive products to mainstream customers. In a very real sense, his perception of disruptive products being brought into the marketplace is aligned with similar efforts a company would go through implementing Sustainability principles. He included these categories:

- *Innovators* – Typical characteristics include they are from larger firms, are more educated, more prosperous and more risk-oriented. Innovators pursue new technology aggressively[108].

- *Early Adopters* – Typical characteristics include they are younger, more educated and tend to be community leaders. Early Adopters, like Innovators, buy into new product concepts very earlier in their life cycle, not unlike Innovators, they are not technologists[109].

- *Early Majority* – Typical characteristics include they are more conservative but open to new ideas, active in community and influence to neighbors. The Early Majority shares some of the Early Adopters ability to relate to technology, but ultimately they are driven by a strong sense of practicality[110].

- *Late Majority* – Typical characteristics include they are older, less educated, fairly conservative and less socially active. The Late Majority shares all of the concerns of the Early Majority, plus one additional one: Whereas people in the Early Majority are comfortable with their ability to handle a technology product, should they finally decide to purchase it, members of the Late Majority are not[111].

- *Laggards* – Typical characteristics include they are very conservative, have small firms and capital, oldest and least educated. These people don't want anything to do with new technology, for any of a variety of reasons, some personal and some economic[112].

Everyone who includes and aligns principles of Sustainability into their strategic planning and business model will have performance and profitability consequences. Regarding Sustainability, "Innovators" and "Early Adopters" are clear winners in the marketplace by refining their processes, eliminating waste in their production and products and engaging Customer and Suppliers who also are like-minded. From Moore's book, technical companies considered "Early Majority" businesses were also rewarded.

Why are major corporations engaging in Sustainability and Corporate Social Responsibility? What do they see that other corporations do not? These are leadership segments that Geoffrey Moore called the "Innovators" and "Early Adopters". Their leadership differentiates their companies and products through Sustainability. They are the industry leaders and by being first, permit them to mold their industry. They are the companies who have quickly recognized the value of Sustainability. These leaders find it easy to understand the concepts, appreciate the benefits, and relate benefits to other opportunities. These leaders recognize that pragmatic Sustainability "makes good business sense" and "is the right thing to do".

Those who are considered "Late Majority" and "Laggards" will be the followers and miss the first wave of benefits. They might even miss out on the unique moniker of being a sustainable product. These examples will obliged these two groups to change their business in an effort to survive their competition's deployment of Sustainability strategies. Those executives should ask them selves if their strategies and approaches to Sustainability is leading their company down a road towards missed opportunities or possible failure.

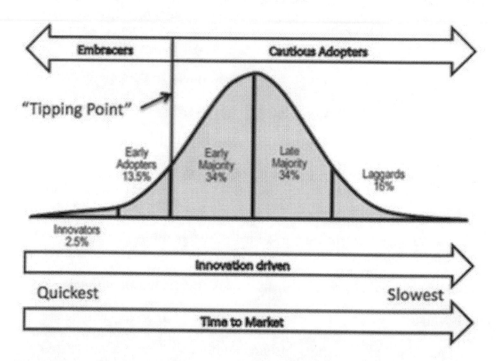

Combined Sources: Geoffrey A. Moore, Crossing the Chasm, 1999, New York, Retrieved: 7 Oct 2013; Embracers and Cautious Adopters: MIT Sloan: Sustainability & Innovation Global Executive Study, MIT Sloan Management Review and The Boston Consulting Group, 2010

Understanding Sustainability also affects special groups within the business sector and how they accept the new ideas and concepts pertaining to Sustainability. It's often the quick wit that will say; "now that's interesting!" and embrace a new journey in terms of creating new revenue streams, reducing costs and increasing quality. In contrast, there were always be that group that is reluctant to make any changes unless forced to (usually by market forces). But there is an undeniable ripple affect that continues today.

Sustainability spending has survived the downturn, with almost 60% of companies saying that their investments increased in 2010. Companies are committing to sustainability but investment levels vary, with companies dividing into embracers and cautious adopters. Embracer companies are implementing sustainability-driven strategies widely in their organizations and have largely succeeded in making robust business cases for their investments[113].

That brings us to a recent study that has reviewed these two camps. The second annual Sustainability & Innovation Global survey reveals two distinct camps of companies: "embracers" — those who place Sustainability high on their agenda — and "cautious adopters," who have yet to focus on more than energy cost savings, material efficiency, and risk mitigation[114].

Companies across all industries agree that acting on sustainability is essential to remaining competitive. Embracers are more aggressive in their sustainability spending, but the cautious adopters are catching up and increasing their commitments at a faster rate than the embracers. They plan to increase their investments by 24% in 2011, while the commitments of embracers (already high) remain static[115].

The report identifies specific practices exhibited by embracer companies, which together begin to define Sustainability-driven management. These include the need to move early, even if you don't have complete information; to be authentic and transparent both internally and with the external stakeholders; and to work aggressively to "de-silo" Sustainability, integrating it throughout company operations. Findings included:

- Improved brand reputation is perceived as the biggest benefit of addressing Sustainability.
- Automotive is seen as the industry for which Sustainability is most critical now.
- The commitment of the cautious adopters to Sustainability is increasing at a far faster rate than that of the embracers.
- Most companies — whether currently embracers or not — are looking toward a world where Sustainability is becoming a mainstream, if not required, part of the business strategy[116].

So, which camp does your organization fall into, "embracers" or "cautious adopters"? Are your markets pushing your organization with their "invisible hand" and oblige her organization to leverage Sustainability? If you are the former, then you are saving money and improving your organization. If you are the latter, then your approach is costing your corporation with missed sales, increased costs and missed opportunities.

The percentage of companies reporting a profit from their Sustainability efforts rose 23 percent last year, to 37 percent, according to a most recent global study[117]. This year, the trend towards profit continued: key measures bumped up and showed that Sustainability is paying off for a growing number of companies. Overall, the portion of respondents reporting profit from Sustainability went up 23 percent to 37 percent of the total. The number of respondents saying their organizations had created a business case for Sustainability went up similarly.

Driving Theory: Creating Disruptive Technologies

Another Harvard professor, Clayton Christensen, author of "The Innovator's Dilemma" and who coined the term "disruptive technology," is also pushing back against the business-as-usual mindset of "measure what you manage and manage what you measure". Christensen has said "[T]he way they designed the world, data is only about the past. And when we teach people that they should be data-driven and fact-based and analytical as they look into the future, in many ways we condemn them to take action when the game is over."

As Christensen once observed, "The only way you can look into the future -- there's no data -- so you have to have a good theory. We don't think about it but every time we take an action it is predicated upon a theory. And so by teaching managers to look through the lens of the theory into the future, you can actually see the future very clearly. I think that's what the theory of disruption has done[118]."

In layman terms, disruptive innovation can be defined as an improvement or advancement that enhances a service or a product in a manner that has never been expected by the market. The basic features of disruptive innovation are as follows:

- The disruptive innovation aims at meeting the needs of the upcoming customers in the market. When the concept is first introduced, this may not be appreciated by the mainstream market but would see a gradual commendation by the budding users of the service, or product who would value the change that has been brought about in the product or service.

- The adaptation of the innovation would gradually result in increase of the performance of the product or service that has undergone the innovation. This increase in the performance would steadily result in going beyond the imagination of the mainstream market of the product.

- The responsiveness of the innovation is seen when there is an influencing change perception of the mainstream market about the value of the innovation. With time, the mainstream market would also acknowledge the superiority of the innovation.

- This change in the perception of the mainstream market will result in replacing and disrupting the existing market of the service or the product[119].

Disruptive technology provides platforms for innovation that will change the marketplace for years to come. Historically, one ubiquitous example of disruptive technology is often attributed to increased productivity and transforming new name markets with new options and growth opportunities. In the not too distant past, it began in the wireless technology market and fundamentally altered the telecommunications industry. First, it provided mobility and eventually replace the "land line". Next, the consumer electronic industry was pulled into the mobile phone with integrated functional of playing songs on the phone. Then it continued to converge and merge with other technologies, the PC, begetting the smartphone category. Last, the smartphone was no long a wireless phone or wireless phone that played music - it has now cascaded into an internet appliance that facilitates communication, plays media (music and video), it has high pixel led photography, uses common software applications for desktop use and web browser capabilities.

Driving Theory: What is Shared Value?

Business is at a crossroad. Embedding your Vision into a Corporate Social Responsibility (CSR) framework will provide your employees with a roadmap and set milestones to achieve the future you want to build. Your existing Vision probably considers your competitive landscape, product and service advantages, financial and operating strategies and objectives. CSR does not replace your business planning effort, it augments it, it broadens your view of the world and how it can impact your organization. It expands your Vision to include Environmental, Economic, Social and Technological considerations that might otherwise be ignored or discounted.

But renown business thought leaders (e.g., Michael Porter, Mark Kramer) are finding that Friedman's approach ignores business activity on the environment and society. Their premise is based on: "Societal needs, not just conventional economic needs, define markets, and social harms can create internal costs for firms[120]." They maintain:

> The best companies once took on a broad range of roles in meeting the needs of workers, communities, and supporting businesses. As other social institutions appeared on the scene, however, these roles fell away or were delegated. Shortening investor time horizons began to narrow thinking about appropriate investments. As the vertically integrated firm gave way to greater reliance on outside vendors, outsourcing and offshoring weakened the connection between firms and their communities. As firms moved disparate activities to more and more locations, they often lost touch with any location. Indeed, many companies no longer recognize a home—but see themselves as "global" companies[121].

The solution lies in the principle of shared value, which involves creating economic value in a way that *also* creates value for society by addressing its needs and challenges. Businesses must reconnect company success with social progress. Shared value is not social responsibility, philanthropy, or even sustainability, but a new way to achieve economic success. It is not on the margin of what companies do but at the center. We believe that it can give rise to the next major transformation of business thinking[122].

Capitalism is an unparalleled vehicle for meeting human needs, improving efficiency, creating jobs, and building wealth. But a narrow conception of capitalism has prevented business from harnessing its full potential to meet society's broader challenges. The opportunities have been there all along but have been overlooked. Businesses acting as businesses, not as charitable donors, are the most powerful force for addressing the pressing issues we face. The moment for a new conception of capitalism is now; society's needs are large and growing, while customers, employees, and a new generation of young people are asking business to step up[123].

Shared Value Impact: Since the 1960s, we watched radical environmentalists confront business and government, to promote environmental and social issues. From the scientific community, environmental and social issues have been studied and shown that indeed our world is changing. Public skepticism has been a byproduct of radical self-promotion and scientific bias. Public opinion is concerned about improved economic conditions, while it also has a growing concern over the environment.

Adopting the concept of creating shared value is a journey companies need to embark on. Such companies seek to create "shared value" — incorporating social issues into their core business strategies to benefit both society and their own long-term competitiveness. Shared value is built on three areas:
- Creating Social Value: Investments that address social and environmental objectives
- Creating Shared Value: Investments in long-term business competitiveness that simultaneously address social and environmental objectives
- Creating Business Value: Investments in long-term competitiveness[124]

Also, we are seeing the expansion of sustainable infrastructure into new areas, destined to build and restore our environment. Successes are often cited in articles about Sustainability initiatives improving business, education, government and the military. Measuring tangible results are posted by a variety of sources: the Business Roundtable, individual company Sustainability Reports and financial market indices. Sustainability is embraced as a smart choice for future, but it is not a quick fix, and will be a long-term commitment.

Creating Shared Value
One guru, Michael Porter, is a contemporary of Kaplan and Norton. He not only recognizes Sustainability's impact, but has begun to rethink his marketing strategies to encapsulate those new ideas with his colleague Mark Kramer. According to Porter, capital markets are part of larger framework for thinking about business strategy than what Porter calls "Creating Shared Value". Michael Porter, once called the father of competitive strategy, is now asking questions about sharing? What changed in the business landscape?

Creating shared value represents a broader conception of Adam Smith's invisible hand. It opens the doors of the pin factory to a wider set of influences. It is not philanthropy but self-interested behavior to create economic value by creating societal value. If all companies individually pursued shared value connected to their particular businesses, society's overall interests would be served. And companies would acquire legitimacy in the eyes of the communities in which they operated, which would allow democracy to work as governments set policies that fostered and supported business. Survival of the fittest would still prevail, but market competition would benefit society in ways we have lost[125].

Translating the idea of creating shared value into action requires a comprehensive effort and that effort, in turn, extends across a company and throughout external business relationships. Firms can do this in three distinct ways: by reconceiving products and markets, redefining productivity in the value chain, and building supportive industry clusters at the company's locations.

A number of companies known for their hard-nosed approach to business—including GE, Walmart, Nestlé, Johnson & Johnson, and Unilever—have already embarked on important initiatives in these areas. Nestlé, for example, redesigned its coffee procurement processes, working intensively with small farmers in impoverished areas who were trapped in a cycle of low productivity, poor quality, and environmental degradation. Nestlé provided advice on farming practices; helped growers secure plant stock, fertilizers, and pesticides; and began directly paying them a premium for better beans. Higher yields and quality increased the growers' incomes, the environmental impact of farms shrank, and Nestlé's reliable supply of good coffee grew significantly. Shared value was created.

Corporate Image and Statements: Sustainability and critical success factors are often based on stewardship for the environment, customers, communities and shareowners. Critical success factors are those factors required for success. What activities are critical? What "must" we do to exist? In a reverse view: What things, if left undone, could cause us to be shut down? Linked to these are your company's vision that is grounded in

values, policies, and standards that cover all aspects of sustainable operations.
- Vision: To be regarded as an exceptional enterprise that produces sustainable products and services; while considering the impact on environment and society.
- Mission: Growth by providing reliable, responsible, fair-priced products and services today and in the future.
- Values: Integrity, safety, respect and Core Values.

Sustainability Image and Statements: Your Sustainability Plan should be developed to emphasize the following:
- Balanced and responsible management
- Operational excellence
- Environmental stewardship
- Engaged and empowered workforce
- Strong community partnerships

Sustainability comprises of representation from a wide variety of departments and work areas. Working with the internal sustainability team, the council developed a definition of sustainability that applies to the business operations of the company, as well as, mission and vision statements.
- Definition: Sustainability is a long-term commitment that is sound and enduring financial, environmental and is based on social stewardship.
- Mission: Promote and support exceptional financial, environmental, and social stewardship across our business practices that eliminate wastes to do not generate emissions.
- Vision: Sustainability becomes a corporate value system and ethic.

A lot changed, the collapse of the credit markets in 2008, the poor record of job creation and middle-class income growth in the last decade, the expanding concentration of wealth, the lack of U.S. leadership on global issues like climate change and in new sectors like clean energy, and the never-ending federal budget morass[126].

What Porter is asking: "what is the shared value being created by business." He goes so far as to say that the benefits of the capitalist system are not being seen by greater society. It's not that profit is inconsistent with society's needs, but rather it is seen as coming at the expense of society rather than to its benefit. If the 20th century model for capitalism was "What's good for business is good for society," Porter sees the 21st-century model as the converse: "What's good for society is good for business[127]."

Shared value could reshape capitalism and its relationship to society. It could also drive the next wave of innovation and productivity growth in the global economy as it opens managers' eyes to immense human needs that must be met, large new markets to be served, and the internal costs of social deficits—as well as the competitive advantages available from addressing them. But our understanding of shared value is still in its genesis. Attaining it will require managers to develop new skills and knowledge and governments to learn how to regulate in ways that enable shared value, rather than work against it.

So, if we redefine business, is Capitalism at risk? The purpose of the corporation must be redefined as creating shared value, not just profit per se. This will drive the next wave of innovation and productivity growth in the global economy. It will also reshape capitalism and its relationship to society. Perhaps most important of all, learning how to create shared value is our best chance to legitimize business again[128]. The capitalist system is under siege, as defined by Milton Friedman. In recent years business increasingly has been viewed as a major cause of social, environmental, and economic problems. Perhaps Porter and Kramer have made a discovery that needs careful consideration. Companies are widely perceived to be prospering at the expense of the broader community.

The solution lies in the principle of shared value, which involves creating economic value in a way that also creates value for society by addressing its needs and challenges. Businesses must reconnect company success with social progress. Shared value is not social responsibility, philanthropy, or even Sustainability, but a new way to achieve economic success. It is not on the margin of what companies do but at the center. We believe that it can give rise to the next major transformation of business thinking[129].

The purpose of the corporation must be redefined as creating shared value, not just profit per se. This will drive the next wave of innovation and productivity growth in the global economy. It will also reshape capitalism and its relationship to society. Perhaps most important of all, learning how to create shared value is our best chance to legitimize business again[130].

The concept of shared value, in contrast, recognizes that societal needs, not just conventional economic needs, define markets. It also recognizes that social harms or weaknesses frequently create internal costs for firms—such as wasted energy or raw materials, costly accidents, and the need for remedial training to compensate for inadequacies in education. And addressing societal harms and constraints does not necessarily raise costs for firms, because they can innovate through using new technologies, operating methods, and management approaches—and as a result, increase their productivity and expand their markets[131].

A number of companies known for their hard-nosed approach to business—including GE, Walmart, Nestlé, Johnson & Johnson, and Unilever—have already embarked on important initiatives in these areas. Nestlé, for example, redesigned its coffee procurement processes, working intensively with small farmers in impoverished areas who were trapped in a cycle of low productivity, poor quality, and environmental degradation. Nestlé provided advice on farming practices; helped growers secure plant stock, fertilizers, and pesticides; and began directly paying them a premium for better beans. Higher yields and quality increased the growers' incomes, the environmental impact of farms shrank, and Nestlé's reliable supply of good coffee grew significantly. Shared value was created[132].

Moreover, companies and investors that integrate Sustainability into their business practices are finding that it enhances profitability over the longer term. Experience and research show that embracing sustainable capitalism yields four kinds of important benefits for companies:
- Developing sustainable products and services can increase a company's profits, enhance its brand, and improve its competitive positioning, as the market increasingly rewards this behavior.
- Sustainable capitalism can also help companies save money by reducing waste and increasing energy efficiency in the supply chain, and by improving human-capital practices so that retention rates rise and the costs of training new employees decline.
- Third, focusing on environmental, social and governance (ESG) metrics allows companies to achieve higher compliance standards and better manage risk since they have a more holistic understanding of the material issues affecting their business.
- Researchers ... have found that sustainable businesses realize financial benefits such as lower cost of debt and lower capital constraints[133].

Sustainable capitalism is also important for investors. Mr. Serafeim and his colleague Robert G. Eccles have shown that sustainable companies outperform their unsustainable peers in the long term. Therefore, investors who identify companies that embed Sustainability into their strategies can earn substantial returns, while experiencing low volatility[134].

Sustainability Strategies by Ceres
Converting your Vision into reality can be facilitated by framing it in context to Ceres. You can bring outside consultants companies with their models for change (e.g., KPMG, Accenture, etc.) and universities (e.g., MIT, Harvard, etc.) that may have similar, but different nomenclature that address these key drivers like:
- Competition for Resources
- Climate Change

- Economic Globalization
- Connectivity and Communications

Ceres sees four key drivers to Sustainability that leverages its model as a "strategic vision and practical framework for sustainable corporations in the 21st century economy." When developing strategies consider what affect Sustainability will have on your enterprise and how it can be improved:

- Governance
- Stakeholder Engagement
- Disclosure (Transparency and Financial Reporting)
- Performance

Ceres is an eight-point code of environmental conduct that is publicly and voluntarily endorsed by companies as an environmental mission statement or ethic. Formed in 1989, shortly after the Valdez oil spill - Ceres is a partnership among environmental groups, labor unions, and institutional investors devoted to using shareholder power to move companies to more sustainable practices.

Governance for Sustainability[135]: Ceres Roadmap Vision: Companies will embed sustainability from the boardroom to the copy room and will manage their entire value chain from a sustainability perspective.

- G1: Board Oversight for Sustainability
- G2: Management Accountability
- G3: Executive Compensation tied to ESG Performance
- G4: Corporate Policies and Management Systems
- G5: Public Policy

Stakeholder Engagement[136]: Ceres Roadmap Vision: Companies will regularly engage in robust dialogue with stakeholders across the whole value chain, and will integrate stakeholder feedback into strategic planning and operational decision-making.

- S1: Focus Engagement Activity
- S2: Substantive Stakeholder Dialogue
- S3: Investor Engagement
- S4: C-Level Engagement

Disclosure[137]: Ceres Roadmap Vision: Companies will report regularly on their sustainability strategy and performance, disclosure will include credible, standardized, independently verified metrics encompassing all material stakeholder concerns, and detail goals and plans for future action.

- D1: Standards for Disclosure
- D2: Disclosure in Financial Filings
- D3: Scope and Content
- D4: Vehicles for Disclosure

- D5: Product Transparency
- D6: Verification and Assurance

Performance: Operations[138]: Ceres Roadmap Vision: Companies will invest the necessary resources to achieve environmental neutrality and to demonstrate respect for human rights in their operations. Companies will measure and improve performance related to GHG emissions, energy efficiency, facilities and buildings, water, waste, and human rights.
- P1.1: GHG Emissions and Energy Efficiency
- P1.2: Facilities and Buildings
- P1.3: Water Management
- P1.4: Eliminate Waste
- P1.5: Human Rights

Performance: Supply Chain[139]: Ceres Roadmap Vision: Companies will require their suppliers to meet the same environmental and social standards as the company has established for itself. Companies will establish sustainable procurement criteria, catalyze improved supplier performance, and facilitate disclosure of suppliers' sustainability information.
- P2.1: Policies and Codes
- P2.2: Align Procurement Practices
- P2.3: Engaging Suppliers
- P2.4: Measurement and Disclosure

Performance: Transportation and Logistics[140]: Ceres Roadmap Vision: Companies will systematically minimize their sustainability impact by enhancing the resiliency of their logistics, companies will prioritize low impact transportation systems and modes, and address business travel and commuting.
- P3.1: Transportation Management
- P3.2: Transportation Modes
- P3.3: Business Travel and Commuting

Performance: Products and Services[141]: Ceres Roadmap Vision: Companies will design and deliver products and services that are aligned with sustainability goals by innovating business models, allocating R&D spend, designing for sustainability, communicating the impacts of products and services, reviewing marketing practices and advancing strategic collaborations.
- P4.1: Business Model Innovation
- P4.2: R&D and Capital Investment
- P4.3: Design for Sustainability
- P4.4: Marketing Practices
- P4.5: Strategic Collaborations

Performance: Employees[142]: Ceres Roadmap Vision: Companies will make sustainability considerations a core part of recruitment, compensation, and training, and will encourage sustainable lifestyle choices.
- P5.1: Recruitment and Retention
- P5.2: Training and Support
- P5.3: Promoting Sustainable Lifestyles

Taking Ownership

First, engaging all of your employees means a change in mindset. It is also a change in purpose. But most of all, it is a change of culture and leadership thinking. Second, this is a long-term approach that recognizes the existing frameworks (planning, supply chains management, operations, marketing, etc.) and integrates CSR, shared value to gather externally issues / opportunities, distributive technology for innovation and active engagement with key externalities. Combining Corporate Planning with CSR is redefining your purpose and resetting your journey, sustainably.

- *Campbell's:* Campbell's integration of corporate responsibility and business strategy ensures our efforts create value for our business and society and provides us with a framework for better business decisions.

  "While we are proud of our past, we are focused on our future. Campbell's Corporate Imperative CSR 2020 Agenda is anchored in our core competencies, fueled by our employees' innovation and driven by four key destination goals:
  - Continue to provide consumers with nutrition and wellness choices in our product portfolio;
  - Measurably improve the health of young people on our hometown communities;
  - Leverage corporate social responsibility and sustainability as key drivers of employee engagement in our culture; and
  - Cut the environmental footprint of our product portfolio in half." ~Denise Morrison, President and CEO[143]

- *Ernst & Young:* "Executive engagement has a profound impact. If the C-suite and the board are indeed on board and promote sustainability, then that message manifests itself throughout the organization. … It's apparent in the news and supported by the numbers. A recent survey of corporate sustainability professionals conducted by Ernst & Young and GreenBiz Group revealed some convincing data. We found that when the CEO drives sustainability and reports progress to the board, 86 percent of companies embed sustainability into strategic planning and capital budgeting. They also weave social and environmental issues into their mission statements (70 percent) and regularly discuss risks and opportunities with investors and other stakeholders (68 percent)." ~ James S. Turley, Chairman and CEO[144]

What Did Jim Think?
James C. "Jim" Collins, III (born 1958, Boulder, Colorado) is an American business consultant, author, teacher and lecturer on the subject of company sustainability and growth.

In 1995, he founded a management laboratory in Boulder, Colorado, where he now conducts research and consults with executives from the corporate and social sectors. He holds degrees in business administration and mathematical sciences from Stanford University, and honorary doctoral degrees from the University of Colorado and the Peter F. Drucker Graduate School of Management at Claremont Graduate University.

He asked this question: Suppose we ask you to catalog everything in your world that's changing. How long a list would you need? Just consider a few categories:
How is the economy changing?
How are the markets changing?
How are fashions changing?
How is technology changing?
How is the political landscape changing?
How are laws and regulations changing?
How are societal norms changing?
How is your line of work changing[145]?

"I would rather have a good plan today than a perfect plan two weeks from now." ~ George S. Patton

5. Sustainability's Engagement Strategy[146]

"Coming together is a beginning. Keeping together is progress.
Working together is success." ~ Henry Ford

Learning how to adopt Sustainability principles to produce a corporation's awareness of resource consumption like carbon, water, and electricity in order to run their businesses in compliance with existing laws and regulations based on "lessons learned". So, …

Sustainability promotes awareness.
Awareness promotes learning and values.
Learning promotes forward thinking to anticipate the future.
Imagination triggers ideas of what could be created, and
Innovation creates that future we want to build.

If trends continue, Sustainability will be the new competitive tool for business in the 21st Century. It is an internal, external, and a forward facing conviction that embeds and integrates disruptive business practices and technology. Internally, it coordinates your Core Assets that are based on common values. Externally, it addresses externalities and builds outside relationships with those entities. Sustainability is dynamic and always interacts within your environmental, economic and social environs. Last, but critical to success, is the evolution of innovation that is designed to fit your business needs. It should continue to adapt and provide services and produce products wanted by your customers and address marketplace opportunities based on Sustainability.

If ethical decision-making is not part of your due diligence analysis, it should be. For it can be the bridge from your corporate values to the actual "go no-go" decision-making processes for a variety of projects and initiatives. It can help steer efforts into avenues that could otherwise be overlooked. Addressing Sustainability and Stewardship in context of approving funding would help ensure your strategic directions are met and align with other business constraints (i.e., ROI, cost reduction, new product development, etc.).

Understanding ethical standards, consequences in violating standards, and the impact on your Core Assets can have a positive effect on whether your corporate culture and should be implemented and enforced prudently. Disregarding those values, can have an underlying perception that those values are not genuine. Regular discussion, execution for ethical issues in applying those issues and business cases are helpful in ensuring sustainable development and stewardship.

Sustainability's Value

Changing before you have to is a matter of perspective: If you are looking through a lens that asks - "How is business affecting Sustainability?" Then you are not asking the right questions. Rather, look through a lens that asks; "How could Sustainability affect the business?" They are two separate approaches that provide two very different sets of answers. If you are considering changing before you have to, the wise executive will use the second approach.

In addition, it is important to realize that while some of these behaviors are dependent on each other, they are mutually exclusive and won't necessarily happen in chronological order.

- Leadership using social technologies to communicate internally and externally
- Leadership encouraging teams to collaborate across the ecosystem (job functions, product teams, channels)
- Social behaviors become a part of employees' everyday workflow and job process
- Internal teams are sharing plans, best practices and knowledge
- Cross functional, interdisciplinary teams and customers innovating products and processes together
- Sustainability business initiatives becomes a consistent line item in marketing, operations and IT budgets
- Human resources adds social behaviors into employees' job descriptions and they are excited about it

Drivers and Barriers

Has your company been contacted by Customers, NGOs, Partners, or other Stakeholders that have addressed these issues? Are they unhappy about toxins in your products, your labor practices in third-world countries or have issues between your Partners or Investors festered due to Sustainability related events or concerns? Then, this is a set of issues that should be on your list to resolve. What have you seen in your organization that indicates this evolution to social business[147]?

New Mindset: Interview with Steve Bishop at IDEO

One of the major benefits of Sustainability is addressing the unmet needs of your Customers. But many companies may not know their market customers, have mainstream customers they don't want to alienate, or have a "green niche" that is hard to expand from. The following interview gives additional insight how Sustainability not only affects the mindset of the employees, but acknowledges that the consumers can also be affected in different ways.

STEVE BISHOP: The problem with that is that big companies really fear alienating their base, their mainstream consumers, who often don't have the same values as that green niche. Mainstream consumers, they want to solve their personal needs first, before they consider those of the planet. The green niche is just the opposite. So there's kind of a mismatch there.

Smaller companies have a slightly different problem. They are very successful at connecting with that green niche, but then have problems extending into mainstream consumers, for the very same reason. They've really associated themselves with the same extreme values of that green niche that just do not jive with mainstream consumers. And so extending that market has been a real problem. ...

We should cater to the green consumer, but in a different way. I think we need to cater to all consumers. And the question about whether we should focus on a green consumer may be not the right way to attack that question, or the way to connect to sustainability. We should really be focused on connecting with all consumers, consumers that are becoming more and more aware of the impact that they're having on the planet, and really find out what it is that matters to them. What values do they have when they reach for sustainability? What is it that they aspire to do, and how do they want to change what it is that they're doing for the better? ...

So we talked to extreme users. We talked to Prius drivers. We talked to people who have never driven a hybrid before. ...

And one story sticks out. And that is of a guy who got in an accident about 17 years ago, and decided, all right, that's it. I'm never speeding again. Speeding is why I got in the accident. I'm never going over 55. ...

And he picked up one trick after another, and understood that he was getting really, really good gas mileage. ... But he's getting 48 miles to the gallon. He's doing this in 17 year old car. And that car is a Ford Escort. There's no technology on board that's helping him there. It is all based solely on behavior.

And that's one of the points, I think, that is most important, is to stop focusing on the green things. Stop focusing on the features that are in those things, and start focusing on the green behaviors that people aspire to.

Another example where this is successful is with the Prius. So drivers who drive a Prius, they have all this technology on board. They have regenerative brakes. They have batteries. They have high-efficiency gas motor, all of these things that help them be more efficient in their driving. ...

And what they're doing is, they're not so much trying to drive efficiently, but they're trying to get high score. And they're playing the game. And that's a behavior that has just never existed in cars before[148].

Sustainable Marketing: Today most managers agree that achieving sustainable profit growth requires having a clear, relevant customer promise; delivering on that promise; improving it; innovating; and supporting all of that with an organization that's open to new ideas and market feedback. However, achieving all of this is difficult[149].

Philip Kotler has been the guru of marketing for over four decades. The following principles are from his Marketing 3.0: The 10 Credos. Much has evolved over those decades and along with that change is the approach to effective marketing. Kotler is still providing good advice and you will see the tendency to swing towards ethics, brand perception and focusing on the Customer's needs:

1. Love your customer, respect your competitors - win their loyalty by giving them great value and connecting with them emotionally.
2. Be sensitive to change, be ready to transform - business landscape is changing and competitors are getting smarter along with customers.
3. Guard your name, be clear about who you are - brand reputation is everything thus ensure you communicate your positioning and differentiation to your target market.
4. Customers are drivers, go first to those who can benefit from you - simple principle of segmentation but you can not and should not try and be all things to everyone.
5. Always offer a good package at a fair price - price and product must match customers expectations not yours.
6. Always make yourself available, spread the good news - don't make it hard for customers to find you.
7. Get customers, keep them, grow them - get to know your customers one on one so you have a complete picture of their needs, preferences and behavior.
8. Whatever your business, it's service business now - you must have the spirit of wanting to serve your customers.
9. Always refine your business process - it's never ending process, exceed your promises to customers and suppliers.

10. Gather relevant information. But use wisdom in making decisions - keep learning and use your accumulated knowledge and experience to make decisions. Consider more than the financial impact of a decision[150].

Sustainable Products: "Sustainable" has become synonymous "green", referring to products and manufacturing techniques that ensure current needs and stability for future generations needs. The fundamental objective is to lower or eliminate waste from the products and services. This is best done by first designing the waste out of those products and services.

- Energy Efficiency: These products not only cut down on consumer energy consumption, but also alleviate utility production. The Energy Star program, sponsored by the US federal government, promotes energy efficient consumer goods, appliances, as well as. encouraging installation of energy-saving solar and wind generators at home.
- Environmentally Friendly: These are products whose ingredients do no contain ozone-depleting substances and are produced without toxic by-products.
- Recyclable: These are products that can be easily reused or can be recycled through a closed-loop recyclable process. Wastes and / or by-products can be reused in the production of other products.
- Renewables: Renewables are non-carbon resources that cannot be depleted, such as sunshine, water or wind.

Defining A Sustainability Vision

First, remove any and all misconceptions. It is not only about compliance reporting. It is not a replacement for existing planning systems. It is not an environmental plan to minimize business profitability. It is not a socialistic reformulation of capitalism. It is not only for very large multinational corporations, it is for small ones too. It is not exorbitantly costly to implement. It does not oblige remaking your business model, but does show areas of vulnerabilities. Sustainability will quite frankly be adopted globally by all business and if you do not adapt, you will probably loose business opportunities.

Often times, executives will want to transform their organization for other reasons. Sustainability is a form of corporate self-regulation integrated into a business model. Informed executives sometimes recognize the potential exposure to past practices or products that polluted the environment or caused harm to the population. In this context, a Sustainability initiative is a mitigation tool against government over regulation of an industry.

Sustainability policy and procedures also function as a built-in, self-regulating mechanism whereby a business monitors and ensures its active compliance with the spirit of the law, ethical standards, and international regulations. That belief reframes a company's purpose and should take into account the social, ethical, and environmental effects of its activities on its staff and the residing community. For society to thrive, profitable and competitive businesses must be developed and supported to create income, wealth, tax revenues, and develop opportunities for philanthropy. CEO Vision, Strategy and Long-term Commitment should be shared with your organization.

External & Internal Transformation Talent: External leadership who bring new methodologies and enterprise planning to the business can visualize end-to-end organizational improvements, from Suppliers to Customers, provide strategies that are sensitive to the environment, enrich brand image, engage with the business community and are focused to reap tangible benefits.

Differentiation: Promoting products and services that are unique and possess intrinsic values for your Customers are significant in attracting "niche" markets.

Innovation: Innovation is assembled from creativity, ideas, strategies, processes, and most important the right human elements and a spirit of entrepreneurship. Innovation can be applied to your existing business environment to increase customer satisfaction, increase profitability, decrease waste and become more in tune with the marketplace.

Integration: After Transformation initiatives are executed and implemented, a leader recognizes that seamlessness may not be apparent in the controlled change. So, integration links groups in organizations, based on your new business paradigm and avoiding relapses to "old ways", to apply their new knowledge in the "new" system with support to its stakeholders and the vision.

Sustainability & Quality: Transformation is modeled with foundations for better leadership, based on these two lessons: The leanest will be more competitive [LSS]. Deming was a strong believer in supporting analysis with concrete facts and quantifiable studies. If you have implemented a quality program, then use that specific jargon to communicate exact needs. Remove misunderstanding, ambiguity or vagueness. People want to win and achieve their goals. Ensure that your thoughts are clear and initiate action to achieve those goals[151].

Lean and Mean: The leanest will be better stewards and create a better chance of making the future a Sustainability success. All resources are finite, but the journey to pursue excellence is based on optimizing profitability:

↑Sustainable Development + ↑Quality + Continuous Improvement + Secured Gains = Optimizing Profitability

Could transformation create opportunities for increased performance, reduced costs, provide for growth of brand and attract quality employees? The results indicate it will provide your organization with those opportunities and establish a Continuous Improvement process to refine and meet your future competitive landscape. Don't be surprised by the results.

Applying Transparency: Good Sustainability reporting builds on core values and sets out decision-making principles that are consistent with these values. Sustainability reporting frameworks can provide a broader context for linking priorities rather than viewing them as competing objectives. [152]Examples of Sustainability decision-making principles used in the reports include:

- Maximizing shareholder value while improving environmental performance;
- Contributions and relationships to the local community and other externalities;
- Life cycle and Innovation analysis;
- Total cost assessment based on Lean and Sustainability accounting; and
- CERES and GRI principles[153].

Internally, those values should be well documented, communicated, understood and applied in the every day business of the enterprise. They should include collaboration and communication. Your brand will reflect the value of the products and services, but additionally reflect the core value of your corporation. Also, rising out of economic, environmental and social needs is the ethics of Sustainability. It is helping mold those values into a matrix that addresses the needs of today with those in the future. By using these lenses, in a comprehensive manner, it provides understanding between resource conservation and resource demand.

Be Transparent, for it displays your integrity, for both stakeholders and shareholders. Let them know when and why actions will be executed. Collaborate with them to ensure communication and be willing to recognize opportunities, should they arise.

Environmental Stewardship: Define environmental stewardship as the responsibility for environmental quality shared by all those whose actions affect the environment. This sense of responsibility is a value that can be reflected through the choices of individuals, companies, communities, and government organizations, and shaped by unique environmental, social, and economic interests. It is also a behavior, one demonstrated through continuous improvement of environmental performance, and a commitment to efficient use of natural resources, protection of ecosystems, and, where applicable, ensuring a baseline of compliance with environmental requirements.

Environmental stewardship is not a new phenomenon. In fact, it has deep and diverse roots in our country. From farming to hunting, from conservation practices to spiritual beliefs, one can find an appreciation for natural resources and the valuable services they provide in many diverse settings.[154]

Stewardship is an ethic that embodies responsible planning and management of resources. The concept of stewardship has been applied in diverse realms, including with respect to environment, economics, health, property, information, religion and is linked to the concept of Sustainability.[155]

Who is the "good steward" you are striving to develop with your program? What characteristics does he or she have? As part of your program "outcomes" and "impacts," develop a list of characteristics a good steward would have. Make this part of your aspirational objectives. Some examples are listed below, although your list may be different[156]. Here are some qualities of a good steward:

- Has knowledge of basic ecological concepts.
- Has knowledge of pertinent problems and issues.
- Feels a personal connection to natural resources.
- Has skill in employing systems thinking and a systems-based approach to identifying, analyzing, investigating, and evaluating problems and solutions (thinks of the world as a system of interconnected, interacting parts; while considers how affecting a part affects the whole).
- Seeks to understand all aspects of an issue (e.g., environmental, scientific, social, political, historical, and economic).
- Has acquired a knowledge of and demonstrated skill in using action strategies essential to sound stewardship.
- Reflects a sense of obligation to future generations and the earth.
- Recognizes the difference between intention and consequence (does the action truly have the desired effect?).
- Has an internal "locus of control" (the belief and/or feeling that working alone or with others, an individual can influence or bring about desired outcomes through his/hers actions) and takes personal responsibility.
- Acts in an informed and responsible manner.
- Is willing and able to pass stewardship concepts on to peers and others[157].

Avoid Pitfalls: John P. Kotter is renowned for his work on leading organizational change. In 1995, when this article was first published, he had just completed a 10-year study of more than 100 companies that attempted such a transformation. Here he shares the results of his observations, outlining the eight largest errors that can doom these efforts and explaining the general lessons that encourage success. *Unsuccessful transitions almost always founder during at least one of the following phases: generating a sense of urgency, establishing a powerful guiding coalition, developing a vision, communicating the vision clearly and often, removing obstacles, planning for and creating short-term wins, avoiding premature declarations of victory, and embedding changes in the corporate culture.* Realizing that change usually takes a long time, says Kotter, can improve the chances of success[158].

Sustainability Lens

Dr. Herman E. Daly, an American ecological economist and professor at the School of Public Policy of University of Maryland, once said; "The economy is a wholly owned subsidiary of the environment, not the reverse." In today's world, we find ourselves in this predicament:

> There is a disparity between assumed and actual drivers of Sustainability initiatives. Companies expect that business in general will be driven by three key external factors: investment pressure, regulations and customer expectations. In reality, however, the top motivations are a genuine concern for the environment and society (cited by 53 percent) and reducing energy and material costs (50 percent). Also important are customer expectations (47 percent) and an opportunity for higher margins and business growth (45 percent).

> Cost is the most significant barrier to Sustainability initiatives, with 43 percent of respondents identifying it. Other key barriers include the inability to measure Sustainability initiatives (31 percent), the lack of government/local government incentives (30 percent) and the belief that one company can't make a difference to global warming (29 percent).

> "It's clear that Sustainability is no longer merely a matter of compliance, but a proactive way to energize commercial strategy," said Bruno Berthon. "Measuring Sustainability performance and results is the first practical step business leaders need to make, but requires new skills and proven methodologies. Get it right and Sustainability champions can form a business case, galvanize internal support and actively secure shareholder support."

Transparency is a lens to examine the core values of an organization. It is insight to corporate mores. Are there barriers and reluctance to publicly share and be transparent? Is it corruption, is it ashamed of poor business practices, or does it have a poor business reputation in the community? In contrast, is it open, is it responsible, is it engaged with the community and clearly listens to its constituents? What transparency should be:

- Executive Commitment is a long-term journey with Transparency, Sustainability and Corporate Social Responsibility. It is a leadership role and resolves redefinition of their organization to create an environment that weaves new principles into their corporate culture.

- Accountability is ownership of responsibility, including a sense of fairness. It also requires capturing data, whether independently designed or leverages Lean and Sustainability accounting.

- Ethics is doing the right thing for the right reason. There are many definitions as to what ethics encompasses: the discipline dealing with what is good and bad and with moral duty and obligation; decisions, choices, and actions we make that reflect and enact our values; a set of moral principles or values; a theory or system of moral values; and/or a guiding philosophy[159].

Align Transformation Strategies to Maturity Models

We are in a new discovery process, unearthing the future relationship between Humanity and Nature. Testing whether this world will survive the impact of Humanity or whether this world will survive because of taking the right actions to ensure proper Stewardship of the planet. To ensure your Sustainability journey is fruitful, accurately measured for effectiveness of your strategies. For they provide the underpinnings, but remember these check points:

Be Committed for the Long-Term: Be committed to Profitability, Sustainability and Quality and especially a long-term Commitment. Do not take it lightly. For Sustainability will continue to provide opportunities for growth, profitability and manifest your values into your products.

Use the "Golden Thread" to show Objectives and Accountability: Processes are your company's linchpins to the "golden thread". Ensure they are efficient and effective. They must work in harmony with the marketplace to ensure success for new possibilities in the present and in the future.

Serve your Customers, for they are the Driving Force: Products and services are created to serve their Customer's needs. Shared value opens up many new needs to meet, new products to offer, new customers to serve, and new ways to configure the value chain[160]. The solution lies in the principle of shared value, which involves creating economic value in a way that also creates value for society by addressing its needs and challenges[161].

Build strong Relationships with Externalities: Engage with your externalities to ensure your efforts are aligned to the "outside" world, resources and organizations that directly affect your enterprise. Incorporate their concerns when they could affect your business. Listen to them, for they may be pointing to a business opportunity despised as a an environmental or social conflict.

Collaborate with Internalities and Empower their Efforts: Make all employees accountable, from the janitor to the CEO. Give your employees responsibility through ownership and recognize their actions and results. Establish visibility to monitor and reinforce behavior through incentives and rewards. In many ways, your employees know more than top management, and empowering them will often disclose other opportunities.

Understand your Carbon Footprint and Reduce It: Eliminate waste, both internally and externally. Be aware of the environmental, economic and social impact of your enterprise. Eliminate your footprint, if possible, and set an example in how you approach Sustainability business.

Verify Results and Lessons Learned: Take your experiences and transform those activities to better serve your Customer, build better relations with other stakeholders, and evolve your enterprise through Continuous Improvement. Engage your auditors and listen to their improvements to resolve issues. Improve systems to capture information. Implement systems like Lean Accounting, Sustainability Accounting and align IT efforts to capture your data elements.

Innovate to Meet and Beat the Competition: Products must meet the cadence of the marketplace within the constraints of responsible Sustainability. When the collective footprint of all the nations exceeds the area of all of the Earth, something will have to give. We must get either another planet or a new model. The current western model that exploits Earth won't do, and we don't have much time to fix it. How do we begin? Taking that critical next step, in what direction shall we move? Toward what end? What shall we use as a map, as a compass[162]?

Institutionalize Sustainability
Peter Drucker once said: "Wherever you see a successful business, someone once made a courageous decision." Organizational change should address expectations for every employee in the enterprise, from the top of

the ladder to the first rung. "Company cultures are like country cultures. Never try to change one. Try, instead, to work with what you've got." was the mantra of Drucker. Recognize organizations not prepared to address the internal culture issues will meet stiff resistance and 'pushed back' against the change. Listen carefully and be engaged.

Leadership Obliged to be Engaged: An engaged culture evolves through innovation, technology and commitment from leadership. It is fueled and inspired by leadership that is actively involved and informed about the realities of the business. For CEOs, organizational openness offers tremendous upside potential— empowered employees, free-flowing ideas, more creativity and innovation, happier customers, better results.[163] They genuinely care about the company's role in the world and are passionately engaged. They are great communicators and motivators who set out a clearly communicated vision, mission, values, and goals and create an environment for them to come alive. What do CEOs believe what matters:
- **61** percent believe in Customer obsession
- **60** percent believe in Inspirational leadership
- **58** percent believe in Leadership teaming[164]

Leadership should not only anticipate day-to-day, month-to-month and year-to-year activities. It should also include anticipating the future. Will resources be lacking in international subsidiaries due to shortages of food, water and natural resources? Will logistic cost increase due to decrease in energy supplies? Practice future scenario planning and be prepared to expect the unexpected.

All Employees should be living Values: It's one thing to have beliefs and values spelled out in a frame in the conference room. It's another thing to have genuine and memorable beliefs that are directional, alive and modeled throughout the organization daily. It's important that departments and individuals are motivated and measured against the way they model the values. And, if you want a values-driven culture, hire people using the values as a filter. If you want your company to embody the culture, empower people and ensure every department understands what's expected. Don't just list your company's values as platitudes; bring meaning to them for people, products, spaces, at events, and in communication.

Instill Corporate Values: Corporate beliefs and values reflect the corporate culture that leadership wants and needs. It focuses on the ability of those in the enterprise to collaborate based on a common commitment of shared values. It promotes profitability through elimination of waste which translates into greater retention. Business decisions are made based on clearly defined corporate values that are communicated clearly and frequently to employees, customers and other stakeholders. All employees, from the lowest rung of the ladder to the top, play a part in making the enterprise profitable and promoting the culture to their colleagues, friends and family.

Collaboration, Responsibility and accountability: Strong cultures empower their people, they recognize their talents, and give them a very clear role with responsibilities they're accountable for. It's amazing how basic this is, but how absent the principle is in many businesses.

Celebrate Success and Failure: Most companies that run at high speed often forget to celebrate their victories both big and small, and they rarely have time or the humility to acknowledge and learn from their failures. Celebrate both your victories and failures in your own unique way, but share them and share them often.

Celebrate everything that aligns with your values. Celebration encourages creativity, creates a mini vacation, transcends routines, leads to unconventional thoughts, raises self-esteem, motivates, creates memories and bonds team relationships. But celebration alone does not address your expectations from employees. Give people empowerment through ownership, responsibility and supporting the outcome. Encourage and reward people for being themselves and making the right decisions.

Communication and Transparency are Essential: All decisions are made based on clearly defined corporate values that are communicated clearly and frequently to Employees and Customers. Being honest and consistent in communication and ensure that Employees always come first.

Be Committed to Profitability, Sustainability and Quality: Commitment is a 20 Mile March. Do not take it lightly. For Sustainability will continue to provide opportunities for growth, profitability and manifest your values into your products, services and organization.

Sprouting Your Vision
It is amazing how major corporations make strategies without regard to the customer's needs, wants and to whether their Customer's satisfaction is met. Look for effectiveness of each strategy and determine its success through tangible benefits. These are areas of improvement linked to strategies with key processes. This is the only true way of measuring the success of your strategies.

There is a wide variety of examples that show tangible benefits that can impact the bottom line of any corporation. As a lens to better understand what can be gained from transformation; operations can be improved by efficiency, productivity and eliminating waste. There are ten specific touch points that most companies move through as they use Sustainability and Quality principles.

What are some examples of tangible benefits from Sustainability initiatives of the corporations? Smart leadership recognizes that Sustainability is a catalyst for improvement. Executive Commitment renders ten touch points for comparison and evaluation:

- *Branding:* Branding considerations are better seen through a Sustainability lens and provide new product and service "differentiation". Beware of empty "greenwashing" and understanding true branding, then a clear picture shows how differentiation and new markets could develop. This strategy focuses on Customer's needs, promotes Renewable Resources, promotes Innovation for Products, Processes and Services and promotes Brand Image & Public Appeal. Rebranding your products should also consider the new opportunities of untapped markets and new revenue implications.

  - As a leading provider of labeling and packaging materials and retail branding and information solutions, Avery Dennison views sustainability as a key dimension of everything we do. For us, sustainability is an opportunity to collaborate with our customers and suppliers to enhance their brands, create shared value and advance our market leadership[165].

  - In 2009, we initiated a five-year plan to identify and improve our environmental and social impacts. This included adopting a broad sustainability policy for our business centered on understanding not only the needs of our patients and customers, but also environmental, employee and community needs.

  - We take the time to educate our employees and our customers on how sustainability can enhance business results, and we provide them the tools to create this success[166].

- *Customer Perspective:* Meeting the needs of the Customer is the common goal of your enterprise. Customers are demanding environmentally safe products and services, while simultaneously providing value. An egged sustainability strategy must be clearly understood and supported by all employees to meet the needs of those Customers.

  Alcoa's Approach: As the world changes around us, we continually challenge ourselves with the hard questions. how do our products and processes save money and add value for our Customers? Are we conducting ourselves and our business with the highest ethical standards? Always, we ask: How can we do better? As we continue to set the bar higher in our business and in our approach to sustainability and aluminum, I believe we are doing better every day[167].

Boeing aspires to deliver sustained, world-class business performance through innovation fueled by disciplined execution and productivity. We invest in new technologies such as the fuel- efficient 737 MAX and the Phantom Eye, a high-altitude unmanned aircraft powered by clean- burning hydrogen. These new products meet our customers' demand for precision performance coupled with game-changing environmental improvements[168].

- **Compliance and Regulations:** Sustainability gains recognition through addressing compliance and regulations (i.e. Carbon usage, GHG emissions, water, etc.). Here are some benefits and objectives: it promotes Brand Image and Public Appeal, reduces or mitigates Business Risk to the Environmental and Social spheres, reduces Business Costs and eliminates Waste, seen and unseen.

- **Employee Engagement:** Employee engagement is the first step on the journey of Sustainability Transformation. It is a team approach to scale a mountain, together. It will take communication, effort for clear attainable goals. It is taking your culture, clarifying your philosophy and values, educating your organization, emphasizing ownership and responsibility of every employee (without exemptions).

- **Financial Impact and Costs:** Sustainability, when promoted through Transparency and true Sustainability principles have demonstrated increased Shareholder Value. Companies are already seeing Sustainability investments generate returns in terms of market success and cost performance. Also companies are already seeing Sustainability investments generate returns in terms of market success and cost performance.

  In addition, expenses and where they are used can be seen through the lens of Sustainability (i.e. carbon, water, energy). Here are some benefits and objectives: it reduces Business Risk to Economic, Environmental and Social spheres, reduces Business Costs and eliminates cost associated with Waste.

- **Mitigate Risks:** Sustainability gives your executives another tool to mitigate risks with externalities (i.e., resources, governments, NGOs, etc.). Your executives have concerns now. On the horizon, they will tell you there are more issues coming: government environmental regulations are likely to increase, legal retribution for misuse of toxic waste or improper waste disposal, possible future environmental and social litigation with severe fines to control US industries, industrial obligation for reporting and legal compliance (like the UK and EU).

- ***Product End of Life:*** Corporations with more mature Sustainability practices, End of Life cycles should be embedded in your product life cycle . Again this strategy needs be woven into your current business strategies. This "Closing The Loop" strategy eliminates waste sent to landfills, incinerators or exported to third world nations, it reduces your production costs, and leverages knowledge from your Suppliers to better compete in the marketplace.

At AKSteel, we manufacture flat-rolled steel products that create benefits for our customers and society. Steel is the most recycled material on earth, and our products promote sustainability in several important ways. For example, our high-efficiency electrical steels reduce energy loss in power transmission and distribution equipment around the world. And, our advanced high- strength steel products help automotive customers design lighter vehicles that maintain superior strength upon impact[169].

- ***Sustainability and Quality:*** Long-term commitment comes into focus. Fusing Sustainability and Quality methodologies offer a complete enterprise tool. Quality management furnishes a framework to ensure, identify and retain of expense reductions while also raising the bar on Efficiencies, Performance and Productivity.

ABBs success includes: Our greatest contribution to making the world a better place lies in what we do for our customers. Following are just a few examples:
  - high-efficiency electric motors that exceed recently enacted standards in the United States.
  - Drives (motor controls) that save the equivalent of the energy used by more than 50 million homes every year and more than 180 million tons of carbon dioxide.
  - Information technology systems that enable "virtual power plants" made up of distributed energy resources, storage devices and demand response programs.
  - Marine solutions that allow ships to avoid running their engines while in port, use efficient DC power systems on

board and improve fuel economy by up to 20 percent while at sea[170].

- **Supplier Perspective:** Suppliers were once measured on availability of products and services, costs and delivery time. In a Sustainability sense, today's suppliers are often resources of improved efficiency and effectiveness. Their expertise is becoming more widely acknowledged and applied to supply chain instances. In many case, these practices can add to profitability as well.

   At Bayer, our business practices, we attach special importance to the areas of compliance, human resources, product stewardship, employees' health, safety and supplier management. For us, sustainable corporate practices also include open dialogue with all stakeholders and social commitment[171].

- **Zero Waste:** Develop a Zero Waste strategy that sets levels and expectations. Zero Waste, like Zero Defects of the 1980s, is unattainable and costly if pursued 100 percent of the time. However, when measuring the emission in terms of "benign" versus "toxic" emissions, the objectives is rational and achievable.

   Zero Waste in a Sustainability context is eliminating all emissions; which is doable. Qualify your strategy with costs and benefits at various levels (i.e., start at 90 percent levels until your goals are reached, then reset your objectives to 95 percent, etc.). This strategy should align your other strategies on Stewardship based on Customers, Community and the Environment.

Taking Ownership

First, ownership begins with engaging the whole organization for transformation. In this case Sustainability transformation. FMC accepted that challenge and took ownership through their business lens: science, technology, engineering and mathematics. Medtronic embraced Sustainability as a driver reflecting their global market reputation. Ownership is an internal and external act of change.

- **FMC:** "We know that a stronger, more sustainable future needs better science. We search for and support programs and projects that focus on science, technology, engineering and mathematics to foster the next generation of innovators." ~ Pierre Brondeau, President, CEO and Chairman of the Board[172]

- **Medtronic:** "Medtronic recognizes that responsible management of our economic, environmental and social impacts will be important to our company's reputation and success in the global markets we serve. Our corporate citizenship strategy is structured around five pillars that advance issues critical to our business, as well as to stakeholders globally. These include:

- Global Leadership in Addressing Chronic Disease
- Collaborative Culture of Innovation
- Responsibility in the Marketplace
- Total Employee Engagement
- Progressive Environmental Stewardship" ~ Omar Ishrak, Chairman and Chief Executive Officer[173]

What Did Walt Think?

Former Chief Executive Officer of ProLogis, Walt Rakowich, recognized Sustainability's value and committed to transforming his organization. He said; "Sustainability is an increasingly important concept in building construction, not only in the U.S. but in all of the regions we operate in around the world. We're pleased that we've been able to incorporate so many cutting-edge technologies and systems into our new facility, which will deliver long-term benefits to the company, our employees and the environment." Many decades earlier Mark Twain, who did not have an impeccable business sense, said; "I was seldom able to see an opportunity until it had ceased to be one".

So, do you want to leave a legacy based on Growth, Performance and Savings or will you elect to wait? Again, the choice is yours …

"These guys have a big, compelling vision for what the company is going to do. They think very hard about the long term." ~ John Hennessy

6. All Employees Own The Vision[174]

"Business as usual is dead. Green growth is the answer
to both our climate and economic problems."
~ Danish Prime Minister Anders Fogh Rasmussen

Engagement is critical in transforming your organization into a Sustainability enterprise, albeit, it will take time, patience and learning from experiences from your people. Engage your employees and make all of your employees accountable. Strong cultures empower their people, they recognize their talents, and give them a very clear role with responsibilities they're accountable for. General George S. Patton Jr. was interviewed and shared this thought; "Don't tell people how to do things, tell them what to do and let them surprise you with their results." When these positive changes have been observed, its important to keep the momentum going and celebrate by:

- Publicly recognizing their work or promotions
- Monetary rewards (bonus, promotion, trips, etc.)
- Team exercises or just saying "thank you" also goes a long way

But, employee engagement is more than praise and recognition. It is enriching what your culture already possesses and builds on employee experience, education and personal responsibilities for the environment and social sectors. A social business model influenced by economic, environmental, social issues, and swayed by generational mores will drive Sustainability's future.

Changing the Current State

Generally, business has been given a bad name from bad apples (Enron, BP Gulf Oil spill, and almost the entire Global Financial Industry) have contributed to the citizens perspective with suspicion and disrespect of business practices. Various polling groups have found that in today's world, Americans generally believe their employers are honest; people have long been ambivalent about regulation, believing on the one hand that it is necessary and that it frequently does more harm than good; and a solid majority still believes that the strength of this country today is mostly based on the success of American business. However, as an Owner or Executive who believes Sustainability is the right course for their business, what are the top three issues to address?

Executive Commitment on Customers and Stakeholders: Marillyn Hewson began work as a new supervisor nearly 30 years ago and as Lockheed Martin. Over that time, she rose through the ranks making trust building a top priority. So, when she was selected as Chief Executive Officer and

President, she decide to visit her Customers, meet with Investors and hold Town Halls with her Employees. She believes these are the first things a new leader should do to build trust:

- **Affirm Your Values:** She take every opportunity to reiterate Lockheed Martin's values and what they mean to us. Trust starts with values. She said; "Our values are 1) Do what's right, 2) Respect others, and 3) Perform with excellence[175]."
- **Share Your Vision and Strategy:** When you share your strategy for success, you acknowledge your trust in employees who determine that success. I've learned that when you show someone that you trust them, they work hard to show that your trust is well placed[176].
- **Be Open, Honest and Transparent:** She finds that one of the most powerful tools for building trust is simply being open. This is especially true when times are tough. Leaders have to fight the urge to circle the wagons during times of pressure or crisis[177].
- **Demonstrate the Power of the Handshake:** The good leader knows the importance to communicate. There is power in a handshake. There is power in a warm, in-person greeting. There is power in a smile from across the room. Personal contact builds trust[178].
- **Offer Sincere and Genuine Thanks:** She feels it is very important to recognize each employees contribution. To paraphrase the famous quote, your employees may not remember everything you say, but they'll never forget how you made them feel. Sincere gratitude goes a long way toward building trust[179].

Trust: Witnessing historic calamities that have impact economic, environmental and social areas, people simply do not trust business. They increasingly see companies as irresponsible, greedy and inhuman. Climate change and economic downturn have accelerated that view, especially concerning new economic expectations.

Engagement: Businesses can no longer afford to work in isolation of the community, for it is an integral part of society and can be a tremendous change agent for Sustainability. It needs to reengage people, to understand their new priorities, rethink their role and value propositions, work in new ways, and enable people to do more themselves and their communities.

We must recognize that business thrives in a social setting, producing goods and services to meet the demands of individuals, businesses and governments. Therefore, a company's purpose should take into account the environmental, ethical and social impact to its community. Companies depend on the resources in the community (financial, human & natural). Benefits for society are linked to the profitability and competitiveness of those companies in society. For companies, it is a reciprocal arrangement;

where they are drivers to create income, wealth, tax revenues, investments and opportunities for philanthropy.

An ethical framework is based on the four phase approach embedded in the Transformation Paradigm for Stewardship (Commitment & Vision, Strategy & Planning, Ethical Transformation, Realization), can help transform and align objectives with other areas of transformation.

Transparency: Expanding business transparency to external stakeholders, especially your Customers, is a new concept for many businesses; while this approach was originally designed to engage only shareholders. The consequences resolve many paradoxes faced by customers who want the best things but also to do "the right thing", suppliers who also want to use "best practices" and business leaders who want to grow but in more responsible ways.

From a business perspective, the externalities that are addressed in Sustainability were excluded intentionally or ignored. Are we overlooking true values of the company that could be incorporated into value proposition? Recognizing the value chain of any product, illustrates the components required to extract the material, creates the product and delivers the product to the customer. A number of books have been published that address efficiency, performance, and total elimination of "waste " within the enterprise. But, are you truly being accountable for the waste and how it should be dispose? However, most business models do not reflect environmental, economic, and social considerations; or their consequences to our biosphere.

The future is our's to create. Sustainability is the holistic business model for the 21st century. From a business perspective, it is a long-term strategy that eliminates waste, both externally and internally, while supporting the survivability of the enterprise.

Communicate From The Beginning: Communicate the reasons for change. Show that your leadership is engaged with all employees and all employees will be engaged in the transformation. Share the Vision, report on the progress and identify the issues. Share on the milestone progress, savings, risks and new ideas that have been generated in the process.

Regular communication about how the changes are impacting the organization will help ensure success. Communication is very important and rewarding desired team or individual behaviors are needed to support Sustainability values and actions. When team members feel informed and supported when they have questions and adopt changes more readily. Discuss and promote how your teams have impacted the bottom line and achieved goals. Encourage and reward employees for sharing their own experiences. Always celebrate accomplishments for individuals and teams.

Your long-term litmus test will be looking for results. Will transformation create opportunities for increased performance, reduced costs, provide for growth of brand and attract quality employees? The results will indicate your organization's ability to transform opportunities into benefits and establish a Continuous Improvement process to refine and meet your future competitive landscape.

Recognize Your Culture's Impact

Get on a Southwest flight to anywhere, buy shoes from Zappos.com, pants from Nordstrom, groceries from Whole Foods, anything from Costco, a Starbucks espresso, or a Double-Double from In N' Out, and you'll get a taste of these brands' vibrant cultures.

Culture is a balanced blend of human psychology; attitudes, actions, and beliefs that combined create either pleasure or pain, serious momentum or miserable stagnation. A strong culture flourishes with a clear set of values and norms that actively guide the way a company operates. Employees are actively and passionately engaged in the business, operating from a sense of confidence and empowerment rather than navigating their days through miserably extensive procedures and mind-numbing bureaucracy. Performance-oriented cultures possess statistically better financial growth, with high employee involvement, strong internal communication, and an acceptance of a healthy level of risk-taking in order to achieve new levels of innovation[180].

Culture cannot be manufactured. It has to be genuinely nurtured by everyone from the CEO down. Ignoring the health of your culture is like letting aquarium water get dirty. If there's any doubt about the value of investing time in culture, there are significant benefits that come from a vibrant and alive culture:

- Focus: Aligns the entire company towards achieving its vision, mission, and goals.
- Motivation: Builds higher employee motivation and loyalty.
- Connection: Builds team cohesiveness among the company's various departments and divisions.
- Cohesion: Builds consistency and encourages coordination and control within the company.
- Spirit: Shapes employee behavior at work, enabling the organization to be more efficient and alive[181].

A sustainable culture is based on cooperation and collaboration for the values of the enterprise, the brand image, and doing the right thing from the social and environmental perspective. Sustainability is a great perspective in differentiating your brand image in the products it represents. This cultivation and nurturing of a corporate culture, based on Sustainability values, evolve, invigorate, and strengthen the organization's functional culture.

Do you manage from a model of simplicity or one of complexity? Are you a micro manager or do you "train the trainers" and push the responsibility to the lowest possible rung of the organization? Do you see the value of transparency and communicate openly to internal and external audiences or are you one who holds the information tightly and "close to your vest"? Your leadership style aligns to the performance issues of assets that drive the nucleus of your enterprise. Using an equestrian example, if you pull the reigns too tight, the horse will either stop or if pulled tighter - back up. Only when the reigns are given slack, will the horse understand that it should move forward. Your Core Assets are the reigns to your enterprise.

Your Core Assets control, manage and shape your Corporate Culture and foster those behaviors into what you want to reach in your Vision for Sustainability. It's important to understand what is driving your corporate culture. Human values with a blend of psychology, attitudes, and beliefs on what are "right or wrong" for your company and environment. A strong Core Asset group flourishes with a clear set of values and norms that actively guide the way a company operates. Employees are actively and passionately engaged in the business, operating from a sense of confidence and empowerment rather than navigating through extensive procedures, bureaucracy and layers of complexity. Additionally, a performance-oriented culture possess statistically better financial growth, with high employee involvement, strong internal communication, and an acceptance of a healthy level of risk-taking in order to achieve new levels of innovation and growth.

Communicate Objectives For Your Engagement Strategy

Why do you need a strategy for your employees? Simple, it is fostered by uncertainty, globalization and recent legislation regarding healthcare. Change is often difficult for most employees and there is an underlying fear of loosing a job and its benefits, as well. There are concerns that their role will be changed so much that their new responsibilities will require re-education and the new learning curve will be difficult to be productive again. There are also concerns that the business may not be as stable as it had been in the past. Executives need to be ahead of these issues and have the forethought to mitigate their effects before cascading across the enterprise.

Lead With A Vision: Leadership should share the Vision of the Sustainably Developed organization, provide Sustainability education, provide direction for that Sustainability journey, close gaps and build on new competencies for the employees, create opportunities for current employees, and motivate and empower your teams to tackle the transformation with fervor. Be clear about where you want to go. Apply your Vision to your timeline and set expectations across your Stakeholders.

- Use Existing Frameworks - Leverage planning knowledge and expertise and incorporate CSR into your business planning paradigm.
- Set A Timeline - What do you want your team to accomplish in 2 – 5 years?
- Understand Your Maturity Level - Reflect on the enterprise capabilities and its level of Sustainability maturity. Collaborate and coordinate activities that are cross-functional.
- Talent - Identify gaps in your workforce or retrain people to fit those needs (their knowledge of the business can be significant when addressing issues through another position in your organization).
- Suppliers - Technology vendors (communities, social CRM, online monitoring) are selected, contract signed and deployment schedule finalized.

Share that Vision: How do you know when a trip is finished? What are components of the Vision for the transformation? Leadership needs to take ownership of this change throughout the organization and clearly articulate the Sustainability Vision. Everyone must understand their importance and how they need to support its implementation. Share thoughts regarding brand image, benefits, savings and potential revenue growth.

Provide Direction: Leadership should acknowledge that Sustainability is a long-term march to reach the top of the summit. Executive communications along all organizations should indicate progress, barriers and resolution of issues is essential. Discussions should also include future actions and how the organization will adjust to those changes.

Set Attainable Objectives: Refrain from sinking your boat with aggressive or unrealistic goals and objectives. Employee motivation is important, especially when implementing a large-scale transformation, employees may initially be overwhelmed by the magnitude of the shift. Remember, your first year is comparing to a baseline for probably the first time. Learn from the process. Set realistic, attainable goals, such as 10 percent reduction in paper use per quarter as a reasonable "first-step" for your business. This will help to maintain employee motivation and keep the project momentum on track.

Sustainability Education: Not everyone will understand about Sustainability, why it helps the business and understand importance to external stakeholders. Provide education and training on Sustainability as it relates to technical and business skills, including collaboration, innovation and project management. Leadership needs to communicate progress, share issues and compliment best practices are part of this educational process, too. Here are a few examples:

- How will it improve the bottom line?
- How can it reduce customer service time and improve satisfaction levels?
- How can it support compliance and disaster recovery processes?
- How can it reduce or eliminate emissions?
- How can it improve Quality of Products and Services?

Build Competencies: Most likely your organization has gaps in roles and competencies. A Sustainability transformation provides your Human Resource department an opportunity to re-examine what the new organization will need, how those requirements can be fulfilled with your experienced employees and identify new areas where new talent will need to be acquired.

Create Opportunities: Leaders should share how education will align their backgrounds to future opportunities in the organization and instill a sense of empathy for their employees. However, leaders should also recognize the wealth of experience their current staff can bring to the process. Engage employees and encourage ownership of these transformation tasks:

- Sustainability planning and implementation, from business case development to reporting results and continuous improvement.
- Establish informal cross functional teams to provide education and help brainstorm issues, solutions, new ideas or innovations. Leverage brainstorming sessions and ensure that time is not interrupted.
- Establish a Continuous Improvement program to review processes, environmental and quality issues, and prioritize new Sustainability projects.
- Establish a Center of Excellence in Sustainability or a Community of Practice to share and develop best practices.
- Provide necessary resources to support engagement (e.g., education and training budget, time, information, backfilling).

Recycle as much waste as possible: This may seem obvious. However, there are companies, governments and building maintenance crews who do not recycle. Establish processes for recycling to ensure that paper, plastic, and metal waste are recycled. Waste reduction through recycling one ton of paper saves almost 700 gallons of oil, 7,000 gallons of water, and 3.3 cubic yards of landfill space a year! If enough volume is present in your business processes, then costs from saving water, paper, cardboard and plastic translate in eliminating expenses and can provide a revenue stream.

Motivate And Empowerment: When an organization is empowered to make change happen, you will be surprised of the results. Leader should inspire employees to commit to the strategy. Show how its benefits and illustrate the importance of their contributions. Encourage solicitation for information and address questions and concerns that are barriers to progress and understanding.

Core Assets Founded on Bedrock Beliefs
John R. Strangfeld, Chairman and CEO, Prudential Financial, recognizes that; "Building talent and culture will have the most significant, longest-lasting impact on an organization — more so than any other activity a CEO can do." Building an organization around Sustainability principles is one example of a long-lasting impact. Sustainable leadership is always looking for opportunities, evaluating new markets, creating new products, and going after the most innovative people. At a high level, these organizations are defined by common characteristics:
- Company has a genuine commitment to Sustainability by executive leadership, with Sustainability principles present in core values and business strategies.
- Sustainability strategies are aligned and integrated with business strategies that are cascaded down through management and are incorporated into organizational and individual performance goals.
- Company has an ongoing interchange with key stakeholders on Sustainability issues, including Customers, to understand how Sustainability issues relate to different market segments.
- A Supply Chain Management strategy that aligns company and Supplier performance targets to deliver a sustainable supply and stimulate product innovation.
- Business risks and opportunities associated with Sustainable Development are well-understood and communicated to key Stakeholders, especially Investors.
- Engage stakeholders and recognize the business impact on these externalities. Defining the behavior, direction and actions of the enterprise impacts the environment and society, for they are interwoven.

Core Assets Defined: As we discussed previously, Core Assets are driven by your moral compass and enterprise principles that affect decision-making. Your ethics and values will drive other assets in this group. They are also the determining constituents that drive corporate values, along with effort, throughout your organization to meet those Sustainability objectives. So, be thoughtful and be careful what you plant now; it will determine what you will reap later. Core Assets are built with key building blocks from your corporation that is something essential to success and distinguishes an advantage. Those building blocks include:

- Corporate values are ethical and legal standards that can drive your decision-making processes.
- People are the most important resource your company needs. They provide service to Customers, new ideas, management and create innovate approaches and products to meet marketplace demands.
- Processes, when automated and focused on Sustainability and Quality principles, provide the value to your Customers.
- Products are your brand image in a visual, tactile and other sensory existence in a bodily or visual form. What the Customer gleans from the product, its services and experiences are a reflection of Quality and Sustainability.
- Innovation is the application of disruptive technology and sets your products apart and ahead of your competition's market segments.
-

Corporate Values: Openness in sharing Corporate Values and especially in recent years these values have become more important to Customers, Investors, Employees and Suppliers primarily due to Corporate Social Responsibility and Sustainability principles. To communicate what those Values are, Transparency is a tool to share Brand Differentiation, Core Values, Integrated Strategies, New Talent, Recognizing the Commons, Risk Mitigation and other issues.

Transparency provides reporting on Sustainability progress, concepts and sensitive issues, with both positive and negative results. Core beliefs and values have many of these common guidelines for ideas and beliefs:

- Supporting beliefs like "doing the right thing".
- Creating something that you are proud to tell your grand children you are part of a legacy.
- Nurturing the corporate culture of liberty and freedom.
- Desiring to inspire a shared vision with others - espirit de corp.
- Good enough is never good enough - strive for perfection.
- Dare to be different - promote out-of-box thinking that enhances change.
- People who share a common direction get to where they are going more quickly by using each others trust.

Innovation: Your innovative mindset should include these four critical characteristics: curiosity, willingness to experiment, engagement with stakeholders and "out-of-the-box thinking". Innovation is a change tool that is controlled by your organization to stay competitive, address new markets, resolve inherent issues with product and services and provide differentiation to the marketplace. Innovation, as well as, other defined

Sustainability strategies needs to align and ensure Business Sustainability initiatives by adding value both to the community and to the business.

Innovation is fundamental to the continued success of your products and services. In any modern corporation, innovation is a key tool to improve position in the marketplace, this is especially true in terms of sustainable development in providing products that consume less resources. Again, ethical considerations and analysis would be prudent in anticipating various issues and problems in introducing new products to landscape.

It should address the Customer's needs and satisfy those needs as clearly as possible. Innovation is also a change tool that is controlled by your organization to stay competitive, address new markets, resolve inherent issues with product and services and provide differentiation.

Resource leadership, in contrast, entails thinking strategically about natural resources from the moment they are pulled from the earth through to their end use. This form of leadership is rare in all too many industries. It involves the ability to see the complex interdependencies of the natural resources system; to engage key stakeholders upstream, downstream, and across sectors; and to promote innovation with economic and ecological benefits within the resource system. Resource leadership thus represents a shift from short-term thinking to stewarding resources for the long term.[182]

Business leaders have often tried to adopt this way of thinking, but they have largely found they cannot do it alone. A resource leadership approach can be implemented only through intensive attention not just throughout a company, but throughout its network of producers, suppliers, regulators, and customers. Such a consortium vastly increases the margin for creative alternatives and innovation, and it distributes the costs of research and development. This is where the importance of government policymakers comes into play.[183]

People: Human Resources are often rated as a commodity by age, education, skills, experience, knowledge and ability to "get the job done". However, your people are tremendous assets often overlooked. Ensure employees are informed, motivated, trained and actively engaged in the company's Sustainability program. Leverage their experiences and empower them to make decisions within your framework of expectations. You will be surprised.

Human resources have always been a critical success factor for business. Decisions regarding people could affect their (wages, healthcare benefits, retirement policies, etc.) motivation, loyalty, and perceived alignment with the employees needs. In a corporate setting, it is one thing to have beliefs and values spelled out in a frame in the conference room. It is another thing to have genuine beliefs that are directional, alive and modeled throughout the organization daily.

Human resources are often rated by age, education, skills, experience and knowledge. In recent generations, other values such as Sustainability, add other dimensions to your organization. In this context, Sustainability is an attraction to people who are concerned about their environment and wish to contribute directly through a company's value based strategies.

Talent management encompasses the entire spectrum of sourcing, attracting, developing, retaining, and measuring the performance of organizational talent. ... So what do current and prospective employee's want?[184]
* Employees want rewarding and meaningful work
* Employees want to make a difference
* Employees want growth and development opportunities

Processes: Processes provide linkages within an organization that delivers products, services, information, maintain customer relations, supplier relations or management control. The effectiveness of your systems of processes should and must be measured and monitored. Ensure that Key Performance Indicators (KPIs) for Sustainability are fully integrated into the business processes, corporate performance, and employee recognition.

Processes, similar to other facets of business, range from ad hoc to very complex. Their purpose is to provide linkages within and organization that deliver products, services, information, maintain customer relations, supplier relations or management control. These are high visibility processes that affect Sales, Assets and Expenses.

Process ownership and improvement are key assets to the effectiveness in most corporations. Lessons learned from the 1990s, when processes were sacrificed for cost savings, increased business risk and lost corporate control of Core Assets. Prudent managers retain their processes, consider ethical considerations for their company's actions and works within an infrastructure that monitors performance.

For external needs, processes are often utilized for compliance, logistics, financial information, or establishing relationships with externalities (NGOs, Suppliers, Media, etc.). Their system availability, performance and visibility are critical to delivering reliable and accurate information to top level decision-making and governance processes.

A business process is a collection of interrelated tasks, which accomplish a particular goal. Essentially, there are three major types of business processes:

- Management processes, those processes that govern the operation of an enterprise. Typical management processes include "Corporate Governance" and "Strategic Management" systems.
- Operational processes, are those processes that constitute internal core business and create the primary value stream. Typical operational processes are Logistics, Purchasing, Manufacturing, Marketing and Sales.
- Supporting processes facilitate the core processes and include examples like Accounting, Recruitment, and IT-support.

Products and Services: The value offered to the community and those unique benefits each provide to satisfy the Customer's needs. Consumers are more sophisticated today and demand sustainable products and services. Enterprises need to build that relationship and track Customer Satisfaction. In addition, product and service stewardship needs to be integrated into the development process, with production and procurement decision-making support for more sustainable choices. Serve your Customers, for they are the driving force for survivability.

Products and Services represent the value offered to the community and those unique benefits each provide to satisfy the Customer's needs. Regular consumption of products and services generate the company's revenue. In another aspect, they represent intellectual capital (ideas), Capital Investments (patents or perceived benefits targeted to a specific market, provide a gateway to new markets via differentiation, and creates other potential opportunities such as building new sustainable market segments.

In the marketplace, attention given to Sustainability is a consideration for all end-users in purchasing products or services. Ethical consideration and implementation of Sustainability are factors that would help ensure those qualities looked for by the customer, whether needs are being met, and would their availability be constrained by limited resources.

Generally, companies often leverage Sustainability principles to differentiate their products and services to the market. These companies often acknowledge sustainable features or components in their products and services, but "greenwashing" for superficial business practices will cause a customer backlash. Always consider your brand image and whether you truly engage in sustainable business practices.

Expectations and Targets
Leadership focuses on Core Assets that validate your Value's impact on the enterprise. Guard what is precious to your Core Assets, for they are the foundation of your culture and promote business integrity. Change them only with extreme caution and communicate any changes with compli-

mentary actions to changing behavior. Remember these simple guidelines for your Core Asset associates:
- Serve your Customers, for they are the driving force.
- Eliminate Waste, both internally and externally.
- Collaboration is true communication.
- Focus on your Core Assets.
- Be Transparent to your Stakeholders.
- Verify your Tangible Benefits.

Leadership's focus on Core Assets validate your effort's impact on the enterprise. Intentionally require all of your key leaders to convey strategic principles not just by asserting them but by explaining them - by generating discussion, understanding and expectations. Guard what is precious to your Core Assets, for they are the foundation of your culture and promote business integrity. Change them only with extreme caution and communicate any changes with complimentary actions to changing behavior. Remember, use these simple guidelines for your Core Asset associates:

Serve your Customers, for they are the driving force: Products and services are created to serve their Customer's needs. Shared value opens up many new needs to meet, new products to offer, new customers to serve, and new ways to configure the value chain[185]. The solution lies in the principle of shared value, which involves creating economic value in a way that also creates value for society by addressing its needs and challenges[186].

Eliminate waste, both internally and externally: Be aware of the environmental, economic and social impact of your enterprise. Understand your energy usage and reduce it. Eliminate your carbon footprint, if possible, and set an example in how your approach favorably impacts Sustainability business.

Collaborate and empower your people: Make all employees accountable, from the janitor to the CEO. Give your employees responsibility through ownership and recognize their actions and results. Establish visibility to monitor and reinforce behavior through incentives and rewards.

Be Transparent to your Stakeholders: Build strong relationships with Externalities: Share with your stakeholders. Engage with your Externalities to ensure your efforts are aligned to the "outside" world, resources and organizations that directly affect your enterprise. Let them know when and why actions will be executed. Collaborate with them to ensure communication and be willing to recognize opportunities, should they arise.

Verify Results and Lessons Learned: Take your experiences and transform those activities to better serve your Customer, build better relations with other stakeholders, and evolve your enterprise through Continuous Improvement. Engage your auditors and listen to their improvements to resolve issues. Improve systems to capture information. Implement systems like Lean Accounting, Sustainability Accounting and align IT efforts to capture your data elements.

Innovate to beat the Competition: Products must meet the cadence of the marketplace within the constraints of responsible Sustainability. When the collective footprint of all the nations exceeds the area of all of the Earth, something will have to give. We must get either another planet or a new model. The current western model that exploits Earth won't do, and we don't have much time to fix it. How do we begin? Taking that critical next step, in what direction shall we move? Toward what end? What shall we use as a map, as a compass[187]?

Taking Ownership
Shared value has successfully been implemented by a variety of corporations in dissimilar industries. It is an integrated approach that reinforces each component. In order to create social and business value, shared value should leverage five ingredients: social purpose, a defined need, measurement, the right innovation structure, and forming the basis for trusted relationships. See how these corporations have gained from shared value:

- ***Dow Chemical:*** Removed 600 million tons of trans fats and saturated fats from the U.S. diet and created a major business with its Nexera sunflower and canola seeds

- ***Nestlé:*** Helped millions of malnourished families in India and other countries by providing inexpensive micronutrient-reinforced spices, which are a fast-growing, profitable business

- ***Novartis:*** Provided essential medicines and health services to 42 million people in 33,000 rural villages in India through a social business model that became profitable after 31 months

- ***Mars:*** Catalyzed a cross-sector coalition to transform farms and surrounding communities in Ivory Coast with the aim of avoiding looming cocoa shortages

- ***Intel:*** Trained more than 10 million teachers in the use of technology to improve educational outcomes, turning education into a profitable business for the company

- ***Becton Dickinson:*** Protected millions of health workers by creating needleless injection systems, which are now a $2 billion business for BD, accounting for 25% of the company's revenue

- ***Vodafone:*** Extended mobile banking services to 14 million people in East Africa through M-Pesa, one of the company's most important offerings[188]

What Did Stephen Think?

Stephen R. Covey (October 24, 1932 – July 16, 2012) was an American author, businessman, educator and keynote speaker. His is best known for his most popular books: The Seven Habits of Highly Effective People, The 8th Habit, and The Leader In Me. He was asked about core values and is quoted to have said; "People can't live with change if there's not a changeless core inside them. The key to the ability to change is a changeless sense of who you are, what you are about and what you value."

"Even the most rational approach to ethics is defenseless if there isn't the will to do what is right" ~ Alexander Solzhenitsyn

7. Ethics And Stewardship[189]

*"Optimism is a good characteristic, but if carried to an excess,
it becomes foolishness. We are prone to speak of the resources of this
country as in-exhaustible; this is not so." ~Theodore Roosevelt,
Seventh Annual Message to Congress, December 3, 1907*

Ethics and Stewardship are the fundamental moral principles that drive and mold your Core Assets. Your internalized ethics and commitment to Stewardship establishes a basis for your corporate culture. That culture provides the corporate guidance, direction and boundaries for acceptable behavior and limits decisions that are consider unethical, irresponsible or illegal in the communities which you operate. As previously discussed, Core Assets are interlinked with your culture and transform those values into actions and results throughout your organization.

Create a Vision, understand the elements and principles of Sustainability and how that would apply to your business. Your business is unique. It may be similar to your competition, but it is not identical. Make it distinct and differentiate yourself from the pack. Integrating Sustainability will make your organization truly unique from end-to-end. It will you give you a better perspective, viewed through a lens that includes not only internal viewpoints, but external aspects of outside influences. As a leader of Sustainability you have a unique opportunity to lead your enterprise through a fresh Vision, based on Ethics, that is a Commitment to Sustainability. Your Core Assets will be driven by business values recognizing that Sustainability aligns to the needs of the present without sacrificing resources for future generation's needs. It challenges your ideals beyond your brick and mortar walls and it is a role that legacies are made from.

In a real example, IBM reflects this approach. Based on a recent study from IBM, today's CEOs are "learning while leading". Of those surveyed, say their organization must exhibit three key characteristics: 61% must be "customer obsessed", 60% want an "inspirational leadership", and 58 % want "leadership teaming". CEOs must differentiate their organizations.[190]
* Today's Customers are looking for Sustainability factors in your products.
* Sustainability is a catalyst to move closer to all externalities and Suppliers would be a good beginning for that innovation.
* Engage your employees to develop shared values. Allow your organization to collectively develop its core values.

Applying A New Approach
CEOs of many major corporations have relied on decades old business

principles that only focused on productivity, revenue growth and shareholder value. Today's business environment has changed. These business concepts do not recognize limited resources, external influencers and regulations that can lead executives to place emphasis on maximizing shareholder value and not enough on generating value for its consumers, communities, employees and society.

We are still wrestling with the aftermath of the Great Recession. Today's business environment is still reeling from lack of financing from the banking industry. The overall economy is showing signs of revival, but is still considered cautiously optimistic. Many put the blame on the ethics of the banking system and its leadership. The financial behavior and its impact upon millions of companies and the prevailing set of beliefs to which those bankers subscribe, have deepened a widespread public distrust of financial corporations. Borrowing and lending are essential to the U.S. economy functioning. A strong banking business allows consumers and businesses to optimize their credit use and maximize economic growth. A weak banking system does just the reverse, as is currently the case in Europe. As a result, fixing the U.S. banking system, including the ongoing problems in housing finance, should be a top national priority following the presidential election, along with efforts to deal with the so-called fiscal cliff[191].

Nowadays, fixing the banking problem is essential for economic growth, but most agree it has to come from the financial industry. Other industry executives around the world have recognized this "lessons learned" and are seeking better ways of transforming their business that incorporates ethics. Sustainability provides that entree to change their enterprises. These executives are asking the question; "If we treat our customers like we have been treated, would we be in business? What do we need to do to ensure our brand image and reputation? How does ethics impact our decisions and our new thinking about Sustainability?"

In most cases, your employees genuinely care about the company's role in the world and are strongly engaged. Survey research shows employees would rather work for sustainable firms—and some would even forego higher earnings to do so[192]. Empowered employees, are far more creative and innovate, and produce better results when given the opportunity and responsibility. An engaged culture is often a reflection of cultural values, innovation focus and technology.

Are decisions always made from a profitability point of view or do you consider all of your options and decide because "it is the right thing to do?" If you know resources will be in short supply, wouldn't you want to be prepared? If the demand for those resources will be so great, wouldn't you want conserve? If you know the supply of those resources will outstrip Natures ability to regenerate, wouldn't you want protect the environment? Would you consider other alternatives? Do you plan for those contingencies now? What would you really do?

Applying Ethical Standards: Each organization should provide employees with a clear understanding of ethical standards, how they are defined, and examples of how they can be used. In a business environment, guidance and education, along ethical lines could provide direction in a global marketplace.
- Conflict of Interests
- Corporate Opportunities
- Fair Dealing
- Insider Trading
- Confidentiality
- Protection and Proper Use of Company Assets
- Compliance with Laws. Rules and Regulations
- Timely and Truthful Public Disclosure
- Significant Accounting Deficiencies

How would you apply ethics and business cases? In reality, instances occur daily that could have impact on your core assets, people, processes, products, and innovation, which is all tied to the very values embraced by your corporate culture.

Stewardship is also an ethic that embodies responsible planning and management of resources. The concept of stewardship has been applied in diverse realms, including with respect to environment, economics, health, property, information, and religion, and is linked to the concept of Sustainability[193].

Violation of Ethical Standards: When ethical standards are violated, employee should know how to report a suspected violation, how to account for that event, and ensure that compliance to those procedures are utilized.
- Reporting Known or Suspected Violations: most of these occurrences are violations of laws and can be clearly communicated in video or computer-based programs for employees.
- Accountability for Violations: Your policies and actions should clearly provide guidance to all employees, from the executives to from line workers.
- Compliance Procedures and Policy: The document should be available for all employees and supported with training programs that stress corporate values.

Establish an Ethics Based Culture

Direction and definition of an ethics based corporation may come from the founder, board of directors or the executive suite. Those values are spread through sensitivity training to ethical issues, a practiced method for exploring the ethical aspects of a decision, weighing the considerations that should impact our choice of a course of action, and observing management's behavior that applies ethical practices.

If your company has not established ethics, legal standards or a clear business philosophy, then your enterprise is exposed to high risks that could foster law suits, environmental fines, or dramatic environmental consequences such as the Love Canal[194] crisis. Defining good ethical standards are products of well thought out values, recognizing their consequences, and penalties should behavior violate those standards

Having a method for ethical decision-making is absolutely essential. When practiced regularly, the method becomes so familiar that we work through it automatically without consulting the specific steps.

The more novel and difficult the ethical choice we face, the more we need to rely on discussion and dialogue with others about the dilemma. Only by careful exploration of the problem, aided by the insights and different perspectives of others, can we make good ethical choices in such situations.

We have found the following framework for ethical decision making a useful method for exploring ethical dilemmas and identifying ethical courses of action.

- Make sure you have all the facts. In order to reach the right solutions, we must be as informed as possible.
- Ask yourself: What specifically am I being asked to do? Does it seem unethical or improper? Use your judgment and common sense. If something seems unethical or improper, it probably is.
- Clarify your responsibility and role. In most situations, there is shared responsibility. Are your colleagues informed? It may help to get others involved and discuss the problem.
- Discuss the problem with your supervisor. This is the basic guidance for all situations. In many cases, your supervisor will be more knowledgeable about the questions, and he or she will appreciate being consulted as part of the decision-making process.
- Seek help from Company resources. In rare cases where it would be inappropriate or uncomfortable to discuss an issue with your supervisor, or where you believe your supervisor has given you an inappropriate answer, discuss it locally with your office manager or your human resources manager.
- You may report ethical violations in confidence without fear of retaliation. If your situation requires that your identity be kept secret, your anonymity will be protected to the maximum extent consis-

tent with the Company's legal obligations. The Company in all circumstances should prohibit retaliation of any kind against those who report ethical violations in good faith.

- Ask first, act later. If you are unsure of what to do in any situation, seek guidance before you act[195].

Defining Key Ethics

Simply stated, ethics refers to standards of behavior that tell us how human beings ought to act in the many situations in which they find themselves-as friends, parents, children, citizens, businesspeople, teachers, professionals, and so on. Fundamentally, cataloging ethics is as varied as direction of the winds; however, for basic discussion needs defining ethics in a straight forward framework is important. Here are five ethical standards illustrating what ethics include:

The Utilitarian Approach: Some ethicists emphasize that the ethical action is the one that provides the most good or does the least harm, or, to put it another way, produces the greatest balance of good over harm. The ethical corporate action, then, is the one that produces the greatest good and does the least harm for all who are affected-customers, employees, shareholders, the community, and the environment. Ethical warfare balances the good achieved in ending terrorism with the harm done to all parties through death, injuries, and destruction. The utilitarian approach deals with consequences; it tries both to increase the good done and to reduce the harm done[196].

The Rights Approach: Other philosophers and ethicists suggest that the ethical action is the one that best protects and respects the moral rights of those affected. This approach starts from the belief that humans have a dignity based on their human nature per se or on their ability to choose freely what they do with their lives. On the basis of such dignity, they have a right to be treated as ends and not merely as means to other ends. The list of moral rights - including the rights to make one's own choices about what kind of life to lead, to be told the truth, not to be injured, to a degree of privacy, and so on-is widely debated; some now argue that non-humans have rights, too. Also, it is often said that rights imply duties-in particular, the duty to respect others' rights[197].

The Fairness or Justice Approach: Aristotle and other Greek philosophers have contributed the idea that all equals should be treated equally. Today we use this idea to say that ethical actions treat all human beings equally-or if unequally, then fairly based on some standard that is defensible. We pay people more based on their harder work or the greater amount that they contribute to an organization, and say that is fair. But there is a debate over CEO salaries that are hundreds of times larger than the pay of others; many ask whether the huge disparity is based on a defensible standard or whether it is the result of an imbalance of power and hence is unfair[198].

The Common Good Approach: The Greek philosophers have also contributed the notion that life in community is a good in itself and our actions should contribute to that life. This approach suggests that the interlocking relationships of society are the basis of ethical reasoning and that respect and compassion for all others-especially the vulnerable-are requirements of such reasoning. This approach also calls attention to the common conditions that are important to the welfare of everyone. This may be a system of laws, effective police and fire departments, health care, a public educational system, or even public recreational areas[199].

The Virtue Approach: A very ancient approach to ethics is that ethical actions ought to be consistent with certain ideal virtues that provide for the full development of our Humanity. These virtues are dispositions and habits that enable us to act according to the highest potential of our character and on behalf of values like truth and beauty. Honesty, courage, compassion, generosity, tolerance, love, fidelity, integrity, fairness, self-control, and prudence are all examples of virtues. Virtue ethics asks of any action, "What kind of person will I become if I do this?" or "Is this action consistent with my acting at my best[200]?"

What is Not an Ethic

Corporations are seeking better ways to understand and respond to social and environmental impacts, persuade and influence governance regulations, manage business risks, identify new services, and manage external relationships. Ethics will drive those projects and clarity is often gained through comparison and contrast. In that vein, here are five examples of what Ethics are **NOT:**

Ethics are Not the same as Feelings: Feelings provide important information for our ethical choices. Some people have highly developed habits that make them feel bad when they do something wrong, but many people feel good even though they are doing something wrong. And often our feelings will tell us it is uncomfortable to do the right thing if it is hard.

Ethics are Not Religion: Many people are not religious, but ethics applies to everyone. Most religions do advocate high ethical standards but sometimes do not address all the types of problems we face.

Ethics are Not Following the Law: A good system of law does incorporate many ethical standards, but law can deviate from what is ethical. Law can become ethically corrupt, as some totalitarian regimes have made it. Law can be a function of power alone and designed to serve the interests of narrow groups. Law may have a difficult time designing or enforcing standards in some important areas, and may be slow to address new problems.

Ethics are Not Following Culturally Accepted Norms: Some cultures are quite ethical, but others become corrupt or blind to certain ethical concerns (as the United States was to slavery before the Civil War). "When in Rome, do as the Romans do" is not a satisfactory ethical standard.

Ethics are Not Science: Social and natural science can provide important data to help us make better ethical choices. But science alone does not tell us what we ought to do. Science may provide an explanation for what humans are like. But ethics provides reasons for how humans ought to act. And just because something is scientifically or technologically possible, it may not be ethical to do it[201]

Defining A Stewardship Vision

The word Stewardship was first documented usage in the 15th Century. The concept of stewardship was used in the context of managing the assets of an estate or church. It was entrusted in one's care who would manage and supervise assets in a careful and responsible manner.

Today, stewardship is now generally recognized as the acceptance or assignment of responsibility to shepherd and safeguard the valuables of others. Stewardship is an ethic that embodies the responsible planning and management of resources. The concepts of stewardship can be applied to the environment, economics, health, property, information, religion etc. Stewardship is often linked to the principles of Sustainability because *stewardship* of the environment is viewed as everyone's responsibility.

As our population and economy continue to expand, the U.S. can accelerate environmental progress while simultaneously strengthening our global competitiveness. In short, we have exciting opportunities to create a more sustainable future in this country and with our partners around the world. However, government alone cannot accomplish this bold goal; rather it requires the active engagement of all people. To this end, we have a vision of environmental stewardship – where all parts of society actively take responsibility to improve environmental quality and achieve sustainable results. Researchers have come to three important conclusions about environmental and conservation education:
* Ecological awareness and knowledge are not enough to cause long-lasting behavior changes, but they can provide a basis or readiness for learning and participation.

- Ownership (a personal connection with one or more natural areas, and knowledge of and/or investment in problems/issues) is critical to responsible environmental behaviors.

- Instruction and experiences intended to foster ownership and empowerment (a sense of being able to make changes and resolve important problems, and use critical issues investigation skills to do so) often permit individuals and groups to change their behavior[202].

As our population and economy continue to expand, the U.S. can accelerate environmental progress while simultaneously strengthening our global competitiveness. In short, we have exciting opportunities to create a more sustainable future in this country and with our partners around the world. However, this bold goal cannot be accomplished by government alone; rather it requires the active engagement of all people. To this end, we have a vision of environmental stewardship – where all parts of society actively take responsibility to improve environmental quality and achieve sustainable results.

Understanding ethical standards, consequences in violating standards, and the impact on your core assets can have a positive effect on your corporate culture was implemented and enforced prudently. This regarding those values, can have an underlying perception that those values are not genuine. Regular discussion, execution for ethical issues in applying those issues and business cases are helpful in ensuring sustainable development and Stewardship.

Stewardship's Key Role
In today's business world, executives make decisions regarding expenditures by the millions and billions of dollars. Now think of this: how is that decision process determined? Most companies have developed guidelines, business practices and behavior policies based on legal risks and compliance, but ethical considerations should also be part of that decision process. Sustainability introduces Stewardship and other ethics into those processes.

In terms of the environment, reusing resources without recognizing consequences. Why? Because that's the only way it's been done?! Well, this is 17th Century mindset where resources were collected locally, hewn or molded into buildings or products, and then sold in an open market. Little has really changed in the 21st Century.

We are still using 18th-Century accounting practices that only recognize sales, costs and assets. Before we get into an argument, it is true that business accounting principles have been updated and standardized for the last 150-200 years. However, I would argue that most of those adjustments, amendments, and standardized approaches are based on government regulations, tax policy and international trade conformity. Nonetheless, profitability was inherently calculated on the cost of resources, cost of production, and fulfilling market needs without regard to the consequences of resource depletion.

Many companies are still reliant on Frederick Taylor's principles that workers are incapable of understanding what to do and need to be enforced to ensure work completion. It is amazing that many businesses in today's world still use these philosophies that were originated in the 19th Century.

In today's world where competing globally, due to a 60-year-old 'free trade' policy that reduced or eliminated trade barriers to promote international trade among nations. This policy was suppose to open up trade opportunities for the United States with other countries, but it was a two-edge sword. For example, globalization emerged. It was no longer economical to produce goods in the US. It produced outsourcing of millions of call center, financial and technical positions to improve corporate processes and performance. In today's marketplace, in the US, we are tethered and constrained to a 20th-Century policy of 'free trade' at any cost and extending that policy without consideration of other environmental and social ramifications.

We can infer that this policy issue has been a critical element in our recent 'great recession'. That is, millions of US jobs have been lost permanently, US businesses must compete in a noncompetitive world, and outsourcing in many instances has undermined corporate strengths.

Comparing the 20th Century to the 21st Century is a contrast in scenarios and outcomes. In the last century, lines were drawn across geopolitical ideologies that almost produced a cataclysmic event that would have changed the world permanently. Fortunately, Humanity avoided mutually assured destruction, but in the 21st Century we are facing a similar event that will choke, starve, resort to worldwide thirst for water and potentially witness Humanity's decline by 2100. The next scenario is similar to the last scenario. In both cases, we always have a choice of our destiny.

Yet conservation of the environment, especially agrarian, goes back to common practices over 5,000 years ago. In American history, kindred spirits united for a common cause. Theodore Roosevelt and John Muir recognized the need to preserve our limited natural resources. During the beginning of the last Century people like these were responsible for reserving and establish the U.S. National Park Service. That Park Service, established in 1916, is now responsible for the Stewardship of 84 million acres of land and 4.5 million acres of oceans, lakes and reservoirs.

Also, we are seeing the expansion of sustainable infrastructure into new areas, destined to build and restore our environment. Successes are often cited in articles about Sustainability initiatives improving business, education, government and the military. Sustainability is embraced as a smart choice for future, but it is not quick fix, and will be a long-term commitment for all organizations. Business is seen as the catalyst for improvement and must manage people, products, processes, innovation on corporate values that create measurable value for their company and for future competitive advantage by including:

- Move beyond business and information alignment of strategies toward an integration of those needs with Sustainability strategies
- Manage Sustainability as a portfolio of capabilities and touch points, from operational costs to innovative technology
- Invest in innovative Sustainability as an organization aimed at delivering tangible business value
- Integrate metrics into evaluation and strategic decision-making for Sustainability investments
- Anticipate the next wave of environmental change, technology or issues that define a significant impact your business, marketplace or industry

A Lens To Stewardship: The word Stewardship was first used in the 15th Century, the concept of stewardship was used in the context of managing the assets of an estate or church. It was entrusted in one's care that would manage and supervise assets in a careful and responsible manner.

Today, stewardship is now generally recognized as the acceptance or assignment of responsibility to shepherd and safeguard the valuables of others. Stewardship is an ethic that embodies the responsible planning and management of resources. The concepts of stewardship can be applied to the environment, economics, health, property, information, religion etc. Stewardship is often linked to the principles of Sustainability because *stewardship* of the environment is viewed as everyone's responsibility.

Stewardship is an ethic that embodies responsible planning and management of resources. The concept of stewardship has been applied in diverse realms, including with respect to environment, economics, health, property, information, and religion, and is linked to the concept of Sustainability[203].

Researchers have come to three important conclusions about environmental and conservation education:

- Ecological awareness and knowledge are not enough to cause long-lasting behavior changes, but they can provide a basis or readiness for learning and participation.

- Ownership (a personal connection with one or more natural areas, and knowledge of and/or investment in problems/issues) is critical to responsible environmental behaviors.

- Instruction and experiences intended to foster ownership and empowerment (a sense of being able to make changes and resolve important problems, and use critical issues investigation skills to do so) often permit individuals and groups to change their behavior[204].

Stewardship is an Ethic: We define environmental stewardship as the responsibility for environmental quality shared by all those whose actions affect the environment. This sense of responsibility is a value that can be reflected through the choices of individuals, companies, communities, and government organizations, and shaped by unique environmental, social, and economic interests. It is also a behavior, one demonstrated through continuous improvement of environmental performance, and a commitment to efficient use of natural resources, protection of ecosystems, and, where applicable, ensuring a baseline of compliance with environmental requirements.

Environmental stewardship is not a new phenomenon. In fact, it has deep and diverse roots in our country. From farming to hunting, from conservation practices to spiritual beliefs, one can find an appreciation for natural resources and the valuable services they provide in many diverse settings.[205]

Stewardship is an ethic that embodies responsible planning and management of resources. The concept of stewardship has been applied in diverse realms, including with respect to environment, economics, health, property, information, and religion, and is linked to the concept of Sustainability.[206]

In the today's business world, executives make decisions regarding expenditures by the millions and billions of dollars. No think of this: how is that decision process determined?

Well, in terms of the environment, reusing resources without recognizing consequences. Why? Because that's the only way it's been done?! Well, this is 17th Century mindset where resources were collected locally, hewn or molded into buildings or products, and then sold in an open market. Little has really changed in the 21st Century.

We are still using 18th-Century accounting practices that only recognize sales, costs and assets. Before we get into an argument, it is true that please business accounting principles have been updated and standardized for the last 200 years. However, I would argue that most of those adjustments, amendments, and standardized approaches are based on government regulations, tax policy and international trade conformity. Nonetheless, profitability was inherently calculated on the cost of resources, cost of production, and fulfilling market needs without regard to the consequences of resource depletion.

Many companies are still reliant on Frederick Taylor's principles that workers are incapable of understanding what to do and need to be enforced to ensure work completion. It is amazing that many businesses in today's world still use these philosophies that were originated in the 19th Century.

However, in today's world where competing globally, due to a 60-year-old 'free trade' policy that reduced or eliminated trade barriers in order to promote international trade among nations. This shift in policy was suppose to open up trade opportunities for the United States with other countries. But it was a two-edge sword, for example, it produced outsourcing of millions of call center, financial and technical positions to improve corporate performance. In today's marketplace, in the United States, we are tethered and constrained to a 20th-Century policy of 'free trade' at any cost.

We can infer that this policy issue has been a critical element in our recent 'great recession'. That is, millions of US jobs have been lost permanently, US businesses must compete in a noncompetitive world, and outsourcing in many instances has undermined corporate strengths.

Core Assets With Ethics: Core Assets are based on People, Processes, Products and/or Services, Innovation and Values. These Core Assets provide a litmus test to decision-making and drive your corporate compass to determine the "right thing to do" based on those business values. Applying ethical decision-making will ensure that the approach that you may take affecting these key core assets will be in the best interest of the enterprise.

In many cases, these collective assets communicate the depth and breadth of an organization. They define the beliefs and values, enable their applications, identify those assets as underpinnings to abilities, reflect guidance for leadership and direction, and define business success. The integration of these assets also provides management's ability to comprehensively understand where their organization is now and where they need to move to in the future.

Instill Corporate Values: Especially in recent years, values have become more important to Customers, Investors, Employees and Suppliers primarily due to Corporate Social Responsibility and Sustainability principles. Those values, often established by the founder or owner, share beliefs, ethics, attitudes and mores that should commonly portray the company and its personnel to the outside world. If you want your company to embody the culture, empower people and ensure every department understands what's expected. Don't just list your company's values in PowerPoints; bring them to life in people, products, spaces, at events, and in communication.

Additionally, the binding connection points between the previous four components are based on the value system created by the founders and implemented by the executives in the corporation. Consistency and you ubiquitous understanding of those values is a foundation for your corporate culture.

A statement of company values can provide direction and rationale for the report. Wording is important. Clichéd catch-all phrases ("Building a Better Future") are unconvincing and difficult to measure. Saying that Sustainability is important but failing to reflect this in stated company values raises doubts about the sincerity of the commitment.[207]

Ethical Standards: Each organization should provide employees with a clear understanding of ethical standards, how they are defined, and examples of how they can be used. In a business environment, guidance and education, along ethical lines could provide direction in a global marketplace.
- Conflict of Interests
- Corporate Opportunities
- Fair Dealing
- Insider Trading
- Confidentiality
- Protection and Proper Use of Company Assets
- Compliance with Laws, Rules and Regulations
- Timely and Truthful Public Disclosure
- Significant Accounting Deficiencies

How would you apply ethics and business cases? In reality, instances occur daily that could have impact on your core assets, people, processes, products, and innovation, which is all tied to the very values embraced by your corporate culture. The following examples show how these external influences could have a direct impact on your organization. Examples of applied ethics as part of the corporate code of conduct include:

Violation of Ethical Standards: When ethical standards are violated, all employees should know how to report a suspected violation, how to account for that event and ensure that compliance procedures are utilized.
- Reporting Known or Suspected Violations
- Accountability for Violations
- Compliance Procedures

Sharing Values and Success

I recently received an email from a cousin of mine. She often sends stories and jokes that would interest me. This was an anecdotal story about ethics, honesty and integrity. The author is not known but the lesson discussed should make any CEO consider that their Core Values are one of the most valuable assets in their business.

A successful businessman was growing old and knew it was time to choose a successor to take over the business. Instead of choosing one of his Directors or his children, he decided to do something different. He called all the young executives in his company together.

He said, "It is time for me to step down and choose the next CEO. I have decided to choose one of you. "The young executives were shocked, but the boss continued. "I am going to give each one of you a seed today – one very special seed. I want you to plant the seed, water it, and come back here one year from today with what you have grown from the seed I have given you. I will then judge the plants that you bring, and the one I choose will be the next CEO."

One man, named Jim, was there that day and he, like the others, received a seed. He went home and excitedly, told his wife the story. She helped him get a pot, soil and compost and he planted the seed. Everyday, he would water it and watch to see if it had grown. After about three weeks, some of the other executives began to talk about their seeds and the plants that were beginning to grow.

Jim kept checking his seed, but nothing ever grew. Three weeks, four weeks, five weeks went by, still nothing. By now, others were talking about their plants, but Jim didn't have a plant and he felt like a failure. Six months went by — still nothing in Jim's pot. He just knew he had killed his seed. Everyone else had trees and tall plants, but he had nothing. Jim didn't say anything to his colleagues, however, he just kept watering and fertilizing the soil – he so wanted the seed to grow.

A year finally went by and all the young executives of the company brought their plants to the CEO for inspection. Jim told his wife that he wasn't going to take an empty pot. But she asked him to be honest about what happened. Jim felt sick to his stomach, it was going to be the most embarrassing moment of his life, but he knew his wife was right. He took his empty pot to the board room.

When Jim arrived, he was amazed at the variety of plants grown by the other executives. They were beautiful – in all shapes and sizes. Jim put his empty pot on the floor and many of his colleagues laughed, a few felt sorry for him!

When the CEO arrived, he surveyed the room and greeted his young executives. Jim just tried to hide in the back. "My, what great plants, trees and flowers you have grown," said the CEO. "Today one of you will be appointed the next CEO!"

All of a sudden, the CEO spotted Jim at the back of the room with his empty pot. He ordered the Financial Director to bring him to the front. Jim was terrified. He thought, "The CEO knows I'm a failure! Maybe he will have me fired!" When Jim got to the front, the CEO asked him what had happened to his seed, Jim told him the story.

The CEO asked everyone to sit down except Jim. He looked at Jim, and then announced to the young executives, "Behold your next Chief Executive Officer! His name is "Jim!" Jim couldn't believe it. Jim couldn't even grow his seed. "How could he be the new CEO?" the others said.

Then the CEO said, "One year ago today, I gave everyone in this room a seed. I told you to take the seed, plant it, water it, and bring it back to me today. But I gave you all boiled seeds; they were dead – it was not possible for them to grow.

All of you, except Jim, have brought me trees and plants and flowers. When you found that the seed would not grow, you substituted another seed for the one I gave you. Jim was the only one with the courage and honesty to bring me a pot with my seed in it. Therefore, he is the one who will be the new Chief Executive Officer!"

- If you plant honesty, you will reap trust.
- If you plant goodness, you will reap friends.
- If you plant humility, you will reap greatness.
- If you plant perseverance, you will reap contentment.
- If you plant consideration, you will reap perspective.
- If you plant hard work, you will reap success.
- If you plant forgiveness, you will reap reconciliation.

Think about this for a minute. Now, don't you agree Transparency needs to have a SEED of integrity as a foundation to your Sustainability approach? Can you see how its absence could produce poor business decisions that could dramatically impact your legacy? Have you considered the impact to the financial markets, too? If you plant integrity, you will reap an abundance from its benefits. It's an idea worth thinking about ...

So, be careful what you plant now; it will determine what you will reap later[208].

Business Benefits From Stewardship

From the ancient times until today, farmers, herders and ranchers have been intimately involved applying good stewardship principles and maintaining thriving ecosystems for raising crops and livestock. This was based on the body of knowledge, understanding of local environmental needs and what was then known best practices. The rules are quite simple, if you didn't produce enough produce and livestock, a local land lord could apply punishment or other sanctions for poor productivity. From an individual point of view, if you didn't take care of the environment, you wouldn't be able to take care your family, yourself or for the future.

When land ownership became available, Stewardship became a major tenant and often taught within religious groups. Although today's best practices were not known or used, It was based on the awareness and dependency of nature and how supportive the survivability of the family unit and helping community and those less blessed. It also brought into focus, the market and political changes that being a good steward would have an economic benefit of building wealth for their generation and future generations. These are basic guidelines and considerations for hundreds of years and continue to be part of modern-day agricultural enterprises.

As CEOs bet big on collaboration, there's a looming risk. Collaboration isn't a result. Innovation, fuzzy as that notion is, at least suggests an end result, some outcome that you claim to be better and new. ... That leads to the last data point I'll flag from IBM's CEO Survey. On that list about where CEOs focus to get the best out of employees, where ethics is #1, collaboration #2, and innovation #4, I didn't mention #3. That's "purpose and mission," cited by 58% of CEOs, five points behind collaboration. It's a pretty good top 3 topics for your CEO and the rest of the executive team. If the executive team gets the ethics and purpose right, and then turns employees loose with the tools and expectation that they collaborate around those two, the chances for innovation are going up[209].

Taking Ownership

The key to taking ownership is committing to the systems approach that is carried over decades and engaging all employees. As Bill Gates said; "…leaders will be those who empower others." General Mills has a mission focused on conserving natural resources and increasing sustainable resources across their supply chain. Honeywell took another approach, it decreased the usage of energy though efficient products and services.

- *Coca□Cola:* To achieve our mission, we have developed a set of goals, which we will work with our bottlers to deliver:
    - Profit: Maximizing return to shareholders, while being mindful of our overall responsibilities
    - People: Being a great place to work, where people are inspired to be the best they can be
    - Portfolio: Bringing to the world a portfolio of beverage brands that anticipate and satisfy people's desires and needs
    - Partners: Nurturing a winning network of partners and building mutual loyalty
    - Planet: Being a responsible global citizen that makes a difference
    - Productivity: Be a highly effective, lean and fast-moving organization[210]

- *General Mills:* "Our sustainability mission centers on conserving and protecting the natural resources on which our business depends. To achieve this mission, we focus on two key areas: reducing resource usage in our operations and increasing sustainable sourcing across our supply chain. Both are key to operating sustainably and supporting our business for the long term. "~ Ken Powell, Chairman and CEO[211]

- *Honeywell:* "Nearly 50 percent of our portfolio is dedicated to energy efficient products and services. In fact, the use of Honeywell technologies could reduce energy demand in the United States by 20 to 25 percent if they were immediately and comprehensively adopted." ~ David M. Cote, Chairman and Chief Executive Officer[212]

What Did Wangari Think?

Wangari Maathai (1 April 1940 – 25 September 2011); was a Kenyan environmental and political activist. She was educated in the United States and in Kenya. Maathai founded the Green Belt Movement in 1970s, which is an environmental non-governmental organization focused on the planting of trees, an environmental conservation, and women's rights. In 2006, she was awarded with the Nobel Peace Prize. She was quoted; "Today we are faced with a challenge that calls for a shift in our thinking, so that Humanity stops threatening its life-support system. We are called to assist the Earth to heal her wounds and in the process heal our own - indeed to embrace the whole of creation in all its diversity, beauty and wonder. Recognizing that sustainable development, democracy and peace are indivisible is an idea whose time has come."

"Recognizing that Sustainable Development is an idea whose time has come."

8. Good People And New Talent[213]
"The human mind is our fundamental resource."
~ John Fitzgerald Kennedy

Commitment, energy and abilities of all your people help achieve your Sustainability goals. It is the human mind, its mindset and commitment to achieve that purpose. It crosses generations and embraces different views. It crosses different cultures and embraces diversity. Here is one major global company's approach and public display of those Values and Vision for everyone to read:

All around the world, Unilever people are doing jobs that contribute to the environment and society. They are contributing to our business success and helping us to achieve our Sustainable Living Plan targets.

Some jobs involve working with our partners and partnership development, others promoting the Sustainability of our agricultural raw materials'

Some are involved in activities that help us manage our impacts — from setting environmental targets and monitoring our progress, to designing marketing programs for our brands to promote better health and hygiene practices[214].

Many corporations have recognized that their employees are the most important resource in the organization. Others are beginning to understand that argument and changing their corporate values to better support and guide employees. So, discussing the issues surrounding Sustainability, eliminating waste through changes to resolve those problems, are mostly resolved by educating and training your employees.

Sustainability Value
Moreover, companies and investors that integrate Sustainability into their business practices are finding that it enhances profitability over the long-term. Experience and research show that embracing sustainable capitalism yields four kinds of important benefits for companies:
- Developing sustainable products and services can increase a company's profits, enhance its brand, and improve its competitive positioning, as the market increasingly rewards this behavior.

   For example, Eastman extended this point into their strategies: "We have created a pipeline of new opportunities by collaborating with our key customers and leveraging our market insights to deliver innovative solutions that create more sustainable products and enable our customers to satisfy their own sustainability goals. Our commitment is that by 2015, two-thirds of revenues from our new product launches will come from products advantaged on assessed sustainability criteria[215]."

- Sustainable capitalism can also help companies save money by reducing waste and increasing energy efficiency in the supply chain, and by improving human-capital practices so that retention rates rise and the costs of training new employees decline.

- For example, Campbell's: "In 2011, we ... Reduced water use by more than 3 percent and energy use by more than 4.5 percent[216];"

-

- Focusing on environmental, social and governance (ESG) metrics allows companies to achieve higher compliance standards and better manage risk since they have a more holistic understanding of the material issues affecting their business.

-

- For example: "Fluor's global health and safety performance ... ended 2011 with excellent results, reinforcing our strong safety culture. On the environmental side, we improved our carbon footprint by reducing energy consumption by more than 1.3 kilowatt-hours per square foot[217]."

- Researchers have found that sustainable businesses realize financial benefits such as lower cost of debt and lower capital constraints.

Many banks are recognizing this trend, for example: "Citizenship at Barclays is about contributing to growth in the real economy, creating jobs and supporting sustainable growth. It is also about the way we do business: putting the interests of our clients and customers at the heart of what we do and managing our social and environmental impact responsibly[218]."

What Practitioners are Reporting

The majority of businesses say that the benefits resulting from their Sustainability initiatives have exceeded expectations, according to an international survey by Accenture. But a hard core minority of businesses does not see Sustainability as a critical or strategic investment.

The survey of 247 C-suite decision-makers in the United States, United Kingdom and China, reveals that 72 percent think the benefits of their

Sustainability initiatives exceeded expectations. Only four percent failed to meet expectations. Business leaders identify the main benefits as reputation and trust (cited by 49 percent of respondents), lower costs (42 percent) and an improved brand (41 percent).

Although two thirds (68 percent) of senior business decision-makers see Sustainability as an integrated part of their business, a hard core of 32 percent say it is peripheral. While 66 percent see Sustainability as an investment, 34 percent see it as more of a cost. And although 60 percent believe their company is investing the right level in Sustainability initiatives, 28 percent say their business invests too much or far too much. The same proportion states that businesses in general are doing too much to make their working practices more sustainable.

"93 percent of respondents say their company currently has Sustainability initiatives" and of those "72 percent think the benefits of their Sustainability initiatives exceeded expectations."

Some 93 percent of respondents say their company currently has Sustainability initiatives. The most common focus areas are reducing the amount of electricity used and green IT (both cited by 51 percent), followed by Sustainability talent and skills initiatives (47 percent) and the development of Sustainability-based new products and services (44 percent).

"The good news is that companies are already seeing Sustainability investments generate returns in terms of market success and cost performance," said Bruno Berthon, managing director, Accenture Sustainability Services. "The irony is that the hardcore third of businesses who don't enjoy these benefits are likely the ones who think Sustainability is peripheral to their business. Only by placing it at the heart of commercial strategy can Sustainability be a channel to growth and innovation."

People Make the Difference
Training a multigenerational workplace can be challenging, if not recognized. The difficulty in managing a heterogeneous workforce is the fact that each generation is attracted to different types of training. In large corporations, this can have significant implications in today's workplace. Managers and training professionals need to know about the generational differences and how to incorporate those groups under one Sustainability umbrella.

How do you minimize differences that can affect employee relations and productivity? Each group has different values and different events that shape their behaviors and what they believe in. Line, staff managers and training professionals need to be aware of these differences when planning for the on-boarding of new employees, ensuring social and sexual issues in the workplace, providing on-going development to current employees and planning for knowledge transfer from retiring employees.

There are some experts who argue that there are no differences between the generations, that all employees want the same thing in the workplace. Issues in management of the generations are defined by behavior and characteristics:

Traditionalist born between 1930 and 1945: Traditionalists value traditional morals, safety and security as well as conformity, commitment and consistency. They prefer brick-and-mortar educational institutions and traditional lecture formats to online, web-based education. In the legal workplace, they favor conventional business models and a top-down chain of command. They see work as a necessary means to take care of their families. These workers tend to be loyal to the organizations for which they work and it's not uncommon to find some of these individuals in the workplace with more than 30 years tenure.

Baby Boomers born between 1946 and 1964: Baby Boomers are extremely hardworking and motivated by position, perks and prestige. Baby Boomers relish long work weeks and define themselves by their professional accomplishments. They believe in working in teams and they herald good team players. They are much more social than their Traditionalists parents and tend to be much better at building and maintaining relationships. The Baby Boomer generation learned to use technology on the job and see it as a valuable tool for improved productivity and a good source of information.

Gen-Xers or Generation Xers are the group of individuals born 1965 between 1980: Generation X came of age in an era of two-income families, rising divorce rates and a faltering economy. Women were joining the workforce in large numbers, spawning an age of "latch-key" children. As a result, Generation X is independent, resourceful and self-sufficient. In the workplace, Generation X values freedom and responsibility. Many in this generation display a casual disdain for authority and structured work hours. They dislike being micro-managed and embrace a hands-off management philosophy. They are career oriented but are somewhat like their Radio Baby grandparents in that they prefer not to mix work with their personal lives.

Gen-Yers or Millennials are the youngest born between 1981 and 2000: This group of individuals are also referred to as Gen-Why?, Nexters, Echo Boomers and Tech-Savvy. Generation Y grew up with technology and rely on it to perform their jobs better. Armed with Blackberrys, laptops, cell phones and other gadgets, they are typically plugged-in 24 hours a day, 7 days a week. This generation prefers to communicate through e-mail and text messaging rather than face-to-face contact and prefers webinars and online technology to traditional lecture-based presentations.

Understand Your Culture: "Company cultures are like country cultures. Never try to change one. Try, instead, to work with what you've got." was the mantra of Peter Drucker. Organizations not prepared to address the internal culture will meet stiff resistance and 'pushed back' against the change. Understand how communication with employees can be enhanced by empathizing, creating a business case, providing a vision for the future and enlisting employee-led changes to improve procedures and processes. LSS will instill a "measured" culture; one that quantifies a problem, investigates the root cause and applies solutions that should mitigate the problem. One of LSS's goals is to attain process stability and efficiency.

A Generational Study: Based on a sample size of more than 1 million people across 200 countries and territories from executives to front-line staff, the Landscape of Diversity study exposes how the dramatic age diversity in organizations — in the U.S. and globally — could significantly stunt leadership growth as well as succession planning, employee performance and business outcomes.

SHL's study found that only 20 percent of Generation Y plan on staying with an organization for their entire career, compared to 65 percent of baby boomers. While baby boomers are motivated most by reward and recognition, Gen Y is driven by progression and personal growth.

The study also shows negligible differences between generational groups in the talents required to "develop the vision" and "share the goals" effectively. But significant and substantive differences appear in the talents required to gather support of ideas and proposals (favoring baby boomers), and in successfully turning those ideas into actions and deliverables (favoring Gen Y).

The new research was released as a call to action for corporate leadership. With work becoming more complex and collaborative, the profile of a successful leader has changed in more than 89 percent of organizations, according to the study[219].

In a very real sense, the skills, education and individual attitudes and desires of each employee will determine the best fit for available positions. It is all about getting the right people, doing the right thing, in the right role[220]. Human resources are assets that need reshaping to meet the current needs of enterprise and anticipate the needs of the future.

Human Resources and People Opportunities

Sometimes, management overlooks employees and their value may not be fully recognized. This can especially true if the company is unionized, in that case, they are considered as an adversary that needs to co-exist in the same business environment.

However, the flip side of that viewpoint is a leadership that recognizes that employees are linchpins to innovation, processes, products and values. Also, employees are your foundation to an effective and exemplar corporate culture. Changes are often an area of discomfort and transforming along lines of a greater values, such as Sustainability, can help motivate and lead your organization to a new level.

Convince Employees To "Let Go": Business transformation can be seen as a tool to invigorate the struggling company. It can introduce new strategies to boost revenue, introduced new products or services, or provide an opportunity to acquire a competitor. A reality surfaces when executives began to rally their troops to tackle this major change needed in the organization, resistance to change will appear. Many times this resistance reflects that employees are neither ready nor willing to change.

Corporate leadership should foster enthusiasm by offering a clear and concise vision of where they want the company, what should be sustained and supported by the employees and include in that vision, what tangible goals should be expected in the Future State. On a practical side, executives need to involve employees in establishing these new operating procedures, processes and guidelines. In a recent article in the Wall Street Journal, three companies were cited as examples of bridging this resistance.

Attracting And Retaining Employees: Top-caliber employees, particularly younger ones, might be reluctant to cast their fates with companies linked to an ecological disaster. Few people want to have their names linked to a company that allows its toxic waste to seep into the groundwater or whose safety procedures result in a massive oil spill. In addition, some employees may display higher morale, productivity and loyalty to a firm they believe to be socially responsible[221].

Cutting Resource Use Without Losing Productivity: Sustainability-driven innovation goes beyond designing green products and packaging solely on their inherent virtue. It entails improving business operations and processes to become more efficient, with a goal of dramatically reducing costs and waste. It's also about insulating a business from the risk of resource price shocks and shortages. Taken together these enhancements can deliver business benefits that go far beyond the bottom line—whether it's improving your overall carbon footprint, enhancing your brand image or engaging your employees in a more profound way[222].

Employee Engagement Proliferates: The idea that enlisting staff in Sustainability efforts is an effective way to achieve environmental and social goals, as well as to improve recruitment, retention, and the bottom line isn't brand new. But after field testing at leading organizations in recent years, it's starting to gain a foothold at mainstream companies.

The National Environmental Education Foundation recently released a major report on employee engagement including case studies and best practices. And Brighter Planet's survey report recently revealed that as engagement programs proliferate, the most successful take a data-driven approach, focus on emerging environmental issues, and make heavy use of social media[223].

Integrated Ecosystem Usage: The market is undergoing a shift to more integrated systems and ecosystems and away from loosely coupled heterogeneous approaches. Driving this trend is the user desire for lower cost, simplicity, and more assured security. Driving the trend for vendors the ability to have more control of the solution stack and obtain greater margin in the sale as well as offer a complete solution stack in a controlled environment, but without the need to provide any actual hardware. The trend is manifested in three levels. Appliances combine hardware, software and services are packaged to address your infrastructure or applications workload. Cloud-based marketplaces and brokerages facilitate purchase, consumption and/or use of capabilities from multiple vendors and may provide a foundation for ISV development and application runtime. In the mobile world, vendors including Apple, Google and Microsoft drive varying degrees of control across and end-to-end ecosystem extending the client through the apps[224].

Understand your Employee's Negative Concerns: Why the resistance to change? Would top executives not consider to anticipate resistance in their organization? Change must be taken in context. The last 20 years has witnessed significant changes in almost all industries in the United States and impacted trading partners worldwide. There has been downsizing, restructuring, takeovers, bankruptcies and significant economic instability. So, from an employee's point of view, the last thing that many want is more change. In many cases employees are stressed, angry and distrustful of management[225].

- The risk of change is seen as greater than the risk of standing still - Making a change requires a kind of leap of faith. Making a change is all about managing risk. But if you only sell your idea of change based on idealistic, unseen promises of reward, you won't be nearly as effective in moving people to action. The power of the human fight-or-flight response can be activated to fight for change, but that begins with the perception of risk[226].

- People feel connected to other people who are identified with the old way - We are a social species. As you craft your change message, you should make statements that honor the work and contributions of those who brought such success to the organization in the past, because on a very human but seldom articulated level, your audience will feel asked to betray their former mentors (whether those people remain in the organization or not). A little good diplomacy at the outset can stave off a lot of resistance[227].

- People have no role models for the new activity - Get some people on board with your idea, so that you or they can demonstrate how the new way can work. Operationally, this can mean setting up effective pilot programs that model a change and work out the kinks before taking your innovation "on the road." For most people, seeing is believing. Less rhetoric and more demonstration can go a long way toward overcoming resistance, changing people's objections from the "It can't be done!" variety to the "How can we get it done?" category[228].

- People fear they lack the competence to change - Change in organizations necessitates changes in skills, and some people will feel that they won't be able to make the transition very well. They don't think they, as individuals, can do it. The hard part is that some of them may be right, and that's why part of moving people toward change requires you to be an effective motivator. You can minimize the initial fear of a lack of personal competence for change by showing how people will be brought to competence throughout the change process[229].

- People feel overloaded and overwhelmed - Fatigue can really kill a change effort, for an individual or for an organization. You've got to motivate and praise accomplishments as well, and be patient enough to let people vent (without getting too caught up in attending to unproductive negativity[230]).

- People have a healthy skepticism and want to be sure new ideas are sound - It's important to remember that few worthwhile changes are conceived in their final, best form at the outset. Healthy skeptics perform an important social function: to vet the change idea or process so that it can be improved upon along the road to becoming reality. So listen to your skeptics, and pay attention, because some percentage of what they have to say will prompt genuine improvements to your change idea[231].

- People fear hidden agendas among would-be reformers - Reformers, as a group, share a blemished past . . . if your change project will imply reductions in workforce, then be open about that and create an orderly process for outplacement and in-house retraining. Get as much information out there as fast as you can and create a process to allow everyone to move on and stay focused on the change effort[232].

- People feel the proposed change threatens their notions of themselves - Sometimes change on the job gets right to a person's sense of identity. When resistance springs from these identity-related roots, it is deep and powerful, and to minimize its force, change leaders must be able to understand it and then address it, acknowledging that change does have costs, but also, (hopefully) larger benefits[233].

- People anticipate a loss of status or quality of life - Some people will, in part, be aligned against change because they will clearly, and in some cases correctly, view the change as being contrary to their interests[234].

- People genuinely believe that the proposed change is a bad idea - To win people's commitment for change, you must engage them on both a rational level and an emotional level[235].

Discouraging Failure: Peter Drucker was quoted to say: "Most of what we call management consists of making it difficult for people to get their work done." Micromanagement does more harm than good. So do lengthy meetings. Both keep people away from the work you need to have completed. If you are practicing either / both instances, then your organization is probably doing it as well. The cascading effect becomes a time sponge and sets your organization up for failure and continued inefficiency.

Where do top executives fail in the implementation and deployment of LSS or Sustainability? Often times management is not aware of potential problems, it is not incentivize to ensure the success of Transformation implementation, executives may not agree to the selection of the projects that are candidates for improvement or they may be politically isolated in their organization to actively participate in the methodology.

For numerous reasons, Sustainability and LSS programs can fail solely due to inactions and behavior of top executives. For illustration purposes, the following partial list of key senior management pitfalls illustrate how management undermines potential success of Transformation projects from inception:
- Lack of organizational alignment (horizontal or vertical)

- No visible leadership at the executive level
- Not having a metrics in place for management participation
- Project selection process does not identify projects related to business objectives
- Business executives do not show up for review of project reviews (conveys a lack of priority)
- Believing a single initiative can or will solve all your problems - this is a continuous improvement process
- Not having multiple projects queued up for each Master Black Belt, Black Belt, or Green Belt (so when they complete a project the next one has already been selected)

Taking Ownership

Business values and the value business places on its employees are two major trends in sustainability. PwC reflects the desire to have good people that they wish to keep informed and educated in the most current business principles, practices and knowledge. On the other hand, companies like Proctor and Gamble reflect the continuos commitment to ethical and sustainable standards that are reflected in the community that it serves.

- *PriceWaterhouseCooper (PwC):* "PwC's commitment to corporate responsibility is an integral part of our long-term business strategy. Given the PwC network's size, ability to scale and respected voice globally, PwC can play a transformative role in addressing today's social, business and environmental challenges. ... People are PwC's most important asset; their efforts enable PwC's corporate responsibility strategy to remain relevant and impactful in the communities where we live and work throughout the world. By investing in our people, our communities and our environment, we build stronger communities and a better workforce for tomorrow — and that is good for business." ~ Dennis M. Nally, Chairman[236]

- *Procter & Gamble (P&G):* "As we celebrate P&G 175th anniversary, we recognize one reason for our longevity is our commitment to growing ethically and sustainably. We know that to grow and thrive for another 175 years we must accelerate our sustainable innovation and resource efficiency so that we have less environmental impact and, at the same time, continue to invest in our communities to help create the conditions for future growth." ~ Robert A. McDonald, Chairman of the Board, President and Chief Executive Officer[237]

What Did Henry Think?

"Every human has four endowments - self awareness, conscience, independent will and creative imagination. These give us the ultimate human
freedom... The power to choose, to respond, to change." ~ Stephen R.
Covey (October 24, 1932 – July 16, 2012) was an American author, businessman, educator and keynote speaker.

**Empowering your employees is one of the best management tools you
have.**

9. Sustainability and Quality Crossroads[238]

"Pollution is nothing but the resources we are not harvesting. We allow them to disperse because we've been ignorant of their value."
~ Richard Buckminster Fuller

In today's increasingly competitive landscape, more and more companies are realizing that being sustainable is more than an environmental gesture. Sustainability makes long-term economic sense. Although most Executives would agree Sustainability is "the right thing to do" or at least a "nice to have", the reality is that change from internal or external influences are the "real" reasons.

As a methodology that pursued to improve an enterprise, Sustainability has been available for about two decades. Its savings come from reducing wastes, conserving energy and water; ensuring compliance while increasing efficiency and effectiveness. But more importantly, the two most important by-products discovered were increasing efficiency and effectiveness of an enterprise.

On the other hand, Quality has been applied and institutionalized in corporations around the globe for over a century. For over a century it was known to increase efficiency and effectiveness. Its savings come from removing waste of time, eliminating defects, identifying where the issues are, and fixing it one time to eliminate "fire fighting". It focuses on Customer Satisfaction to Internal processes to Supplier requirements and ensuring elimination of waste, too.

Why wouldn't any executive want to consider Sustainability with Quality as the spine for expanding that functionality? A survey from the UN Global Compact and Accenture found what contemporary CEOs are thinking:

- 96% of CEOs believe that Sustainability issues should be fully integrated into the strategy and operations of a company.
- 93% of CEOs believe that Sustainability issues will be critical to the future success of their business.
- 91% of CEOs report that their company will employ new technologies to address Sustainability issues over the next five years.
- 88% of CEOs believe that they should be integrating through their supply chain.
- 86% of CEOs believe see "accurate valuation by investors of Sustainability in long-term investments" as important to reaching the tipping point in Sustainability[239].

From a Sustainability viewpoint, your organization must recognize how it may be detrimental to the environment and society, but more importantly how those behaviors and practices are costly to your enterprise. The acknowledgement of this waste may be surprising. That means looking at a variety of Sustainability considerations (waste, carbon footprint, water, energy, etc.) that are present in your organization and aware to those living in the community.

Now, let us look at the Quality perspective (e.g., Lean and Six Sigma). These methodologies remove other wastes from your organization and compliment your efforts with eliminating Sustainability wastes. In a business context, it is removing other unwanted wastes, unwanted logistics, improving Customer relations, etc. and often times compliment certifications, whether ongoing or planned.

It also ensures that changes are not adrift, but secured and retain gains already identified. Peter Drucker is remembered by this famous quote; "You can only manage what you can measure." By measuring refinements changes, by your projects that are effectively implemented, your true gains will hit your bottom line. Remember this simple equation for each project:

↑ Sustainable Development + ↑ Quality + Continuous Improvement + Secured Gains = Optimizing Profitability

The results address current CEOs beliefs, as well as, uncovering new opportunities that had not been anticipated. Strategies will be better integrated, establish a common understanding of how Sustainability and Quality will be critical to their success in the future, leverage new technology, integrate methodologies into supply chain processes, and favorably impact the financial investment image of your corporation. As Drucker also said; "What's measured improves."

Sustainability indicators have proliferated globally. More than 3,500 organizations in more than 60 countries, for example, use the Global Reporting Initiative's (GRI) voluntary Sustainability standards report on their environmental, social, and governance (ESG) performance. Sustainability and related certification standards have met important needs. They have heightened corporations' awareness of their impact on society and triggered meaningful improvements in social and environmental performance.[240]

Strategic Process Alignment
Strategic processes, whether internal and external, directly impact your organization, information flow and timing of information and its availabil-

ity. These high visibility processes often rely on lagging indicators that affect Sales, Assets and Expenses. Fusing Sustainability and Quality information, system availability and performance metrics are critical to delivering reliable and accurate decision-making information. Other considerations for top level decision-making and governance processes need to encapsulate "triggers" for change and include forward looking metrics (e.g. back orders, cancellations). Business processes are a collection of interrelated tasks, which accomplish a particular goal. Your Core Assets include these three basic types of business processes:

- ***Management processes:*** Those processes that govern the operation of a system. Typical management processes include "Corporate Governance" and "Strategic Management".
- ***Operational processes:*** Processes constitute the core business and create the primary Sustainability Value stream. Typical operational processes are Logistics, Purchasing, Manufacturing, Marketing, Sales and End-of-Life.
- ***Supporting processes:*** Processes that support the core processes. Examples include Accounting, Human Resources and Recruitment, and IT-Support.

Adapt Your Business: Based on your assessment of how climate change could affect your company, develop and implement strategies for reducing energy consumption and carbon emissions. And consider how you might reinvent parts of your business to seize new opportunities.

Example: Caterpillar is making its already relatively low emission diesel engines even more efficient. It is also building a new business: making particulate filter systems that can be retrofitted on its own and other manufacturers' engines. In addition, it's studying engines that run on biofuels[241].

Apply SWOT Analysis: When do you use SWOT analysis? We first discussed, this tool is useful in developing a Commitment, Vision and Strategies. It is also useful at other levels such as Sustainability and Quality strategies. It can offer helpful perspectives at any stage of an effort. You might use it to:

- Explore possibilities for new efforts or solutions to problems.
- Make decisions about the best path for your initiative. Identifying your opportunities for success in context of threats to success can clarify directions and choices.
- Determine where change is possible. If you are at a juncture or turning point, an inventory of your strengths and weaknesses can reveal priorities as well as possibilities.
- Adjust and refine plans mid-course. A new opportunity might open wider avenues, while a new threat could close a path that once existed.

SWOT also offers a simple way of communicating about your initiative or program and an excellent way to organize information you've gathered from studies or surveys.

Do It Better Than Rivals: "Doing well by doing good" isn't enough: You have to beat rivals at reducing your exposure to climate-related risk and finding business opportunities within those risks.

Example: Honda and Toyota have bested competitors (including GM, DaimlerChrysler, and BMW) by making their fleets more fuel efficient than most rivals' and taking the lead in commercializing hybrid vehicles[242].

Carbon-Related Risks And Opportunities: Consider how the following risks could hurt— or present opportunities to help—your business:
- *Regulatory*: mandatory emissions- reduction legislation
- *Supply chain*: suppliers' passing their higher carbon-related costs to you
- *Product and technology*: rivals' developing climate-friendly offerings before you do
- *Litigation*: lawsuits charging you with negligence, public nuisance, or trespass
- *Reputation*: destructive consumer or shareholder backlash
- *Physical*: damage to your assets through drought, floods, and storms

Example: Forest products company Weyerhaeuser could ask itself questions such as: "Will milder winters spur wood-beetle populations, damaging trees? Could climate change affect demand for our products, if customers require more energy efficient building materials—or increasingly choose wood over other materials[243]?"

Sustainability Waste: Waste can be eliminated internally with Sustainability best practices. Addressing emissions, toxic materials, human rights, labor laws and alignment to communities are external to business brick and mortar structures, but influence the enterprise. Sustainability recognizes these "externalities" to gain market leadership, brand recognition, corporate ethics and Customer allegiance. Here are other areas:
- Customer engagement
- Employee engagement
- Change management
- Strategic planning
- Operational efficiency
- Innovation
- Leadership engagement

Sustainability and Quality Strategies: When preparing for the adoption of a Sustainability Transformation, seven key strategies can enhance create shared-benefits when implementing Sustainability when fused with Quality:

1. Actively pursue a Sustainability and Quality program throughout your enterprise and ensure accurate and timely reporting.
2. Ensure that those responsible for Sustainability matters do not operate in isolation from the rest of the enterprise — especially the finance function.
3. Ensure that those responsible for Quality matters do not operate in isolation from the rest of the enterprise — especially the marketing, service and operation functions.
4. Enhance dialogue with stakeholders and improve disclosure in key areas, particularly those related to social and environmental issues.
5. Ensure that directors' skills are relevant to the chief areas of stakeholder concern, including risk management tied to social and environmental matters.
6. Consider using nontraditional performance metrics, including those related to environmental/Sustainability and Quality/Sustainability issues.
7. Focus on end-of-life, product design and innovation processes to eliminate waste, recycle sub-assemblies and products, in order to eliminate emissions.

An External View

Changing before you have to is a matter of perspective: If you are looking through a lens that asks; "How is business affecting Sustainability? Then you are not asking the right questions. Rather, look through a lens that asks; "How could Sustainability affect the business?" They are two separate approaches that provide two very different sets of answers. If you are considering changing before you have to, use the second approach.

Where would you start? In the US, where is the most significant Sustainability (e.g., environmental) concerns in 2012? According to Gallup, those three top issues where:

- Contamination of soil and water by toxic waste
- Pollution of drinking water
- Pollution of rivers, lakes, and reservoirs

In fact, "the three water" concerns in this year's poll have ranked as the top three concerns over any other environmental problems nearly every time they have been asked since 1989. Pollution of drinking water has most often been the top concern[244]. This concern is the fundamental argument for frac'ing for natural gas and oil.

Has your company been contacted by customers, NGOs, partners, or shareholders that have addressed these issues? Then, this is a set of issue that should be on list to resolve.

Brand reputation and publicity: Historically, certain brands have given consumers confidence in a company or its products. The consumer's perception can determine whether a product or line sells. Once a brand is tarnished, however, it is difficult to recover. Branding your company as one that is committed to Sustainability is easier than removing the public perception that you are environmentally irresponsible. Being green not only saves money, it also creates new revenue by attracting Customers who care about a company's environmental footprint.

Although not every consumer cares about environmental issues, more consumers are paying attention to the Sustainability policies of the businesses from whom they make purchases. Social media and the Internet mean that consumers can spread the word about a company's environmental responsibility, or lack of it, instantly. Fostering positive consumer relations through sustainable initiatives generates brand value and improves a company's image.

One word, 'greenwashing', has been the bane on the reputation of Sustainability. Many companies with aggressive and unethical marketers have gone to the marketplace and sold their products on 'greenwashing' product characteristics at the cost of market share and brand image. This is when a company stakes a claim to its record on the environment regardless of whether it is genuinely involved in protecting the environment. Essentially, it does explain some of the motives behind companies touting environmentally responsible messages.

Sustainability: Fostering positive consumer relations through sustainable initiatives generate brand value and improves a company's image.

Quality: If your Customers have delivery, environmental or quality issues then you should recognize those "disconnects" and learn from them. The most valuable information comes from the dissatisfaction of products or services

Whether using automated processes or streamlining processes manually; the reduction of time to service a customer has been a key index for decades. Amazon for examples measures the time from Online Order to Actual Delivery. In addition, increased Customer Satisfaction involves a strong focus on customer needs and requirements and delivering high value to customers. If you have customer issues then having a project in that area will dramatically improve the situation.

Creating a Competitive Advantage: If Sustainability is not institutional-ized in your company, then you are not in the race. Early Adopters fore-saw the benefits almost 30 years ago and reaping tangible benefits today. My advice: do not procrastinate any longer or gravitate to "analysis pa-ralysis" and waste more time and potential opportunities.

> *Sustainability:* A 2011 survey of nearly 3,000 global executives by MIT Sloan Management Review found that about two-thirds of re-spondents believed Sustainability was necessary to being competitive in today's market.

> *Quality:* Quality directly increases your competitive advantage. As you improve your performance you will start to see a difference be-tween yourselves and your competitors. You can then use this in your marketing and sales pitches, as well.

Government Regulations: Chances are that federal, state and local gov-ernments will enact additional regulations to protect the environment. Companies that are not in compliance could find themselves excluded from government contracts. Furthermore, the regulations may apply to every business in the supply chain. Establishing a Sustainability strategy helps ensure your company will be able to meet changing regulations in a timely manner.

Resource Awareness: Sustainable development goals are balanced be-tween consumption and conservation. If we are to achieve those goals, then we need to understand environmental limits and thresholds. The con-cept of resource limits is therefore more useful generally. It focuses atten-tion on the possibilities of ecosystem collapse and the possibly more wide-spread, chronic or progressive loss of integrity that natural resource sys-tems may suffer with increasing environmental demands.

> *Sustainability:* Natural resources like fossil fuels and water are finite. As scarcity increases, cost also increases. At some point the resources with which we depend upon will be more expensive or we won't be able to get it. So companies need to be prepared to protect those re-sources so they will be plentiful or find alternate resources for their products and services. If you see yourself as a winning company, you will do both.

> *Quality:* Resource availability may also impact the quality of the original resource. This may impact internal requirements and force reformulation of the impact to your operations in a number of different ways. Internal specifications, based on product requirements will need

to be reviewed in anticipation of this scenario and extending to re-thinking your Continuous Improvement cycle.

An Internal View

An introspective view focuses on organizational structure, process flows and elimination of waste. Similar to looking at external influences, review your internal framework. If you are looking through a quality lens ask; "How could Quality affect the business?" They are two separate approaches that provide two very different sets of answers. Use Lean, Six Sigma or combine and use both in Lean Six Sigma.

So when faced with a dilemma of transforming your organization or surfer the consequences of doing nothing, what are your options? Sustainability is such option. The following items are major reasons to follow the Sustainability route:

Cost Savings: There are two basic ways of increasing profitability. First, top-line efforts are focused on selling more products and services (assuming your products/services are profitable) with improved Quality or if they meet Customer demands for Sustainability characteristics. Second, cost can be easily accomplished by cutting head count. This cost cutting approach often demoralizes the enterprise, injects fear in the personnel, can paralyze actions and hinder effectiveness. Cutting costs is a great way to help your company survive, but embracing Sustainability and Quality methodologies focuses on making the best with what you have.

> *Sustainability:* For Business to adopt Sustainability, it must have a bottom line impact and it does. Whether you are reducing resources (e.g., water), reducing consumption (e.g., energy), eliminating waste, it is all about improving the bottom line.

> *Quality:* Reduced Costs one of the primary desired benefits is a reduction in costs associated with improvements to processes to require less time (and employee resources) and to decrease defects or errors that can result in rework.

Even small changes can reduce your expenses. Choosing recycled toner cartridges and energy efficient lighting may lower your costs. Opting for laptops over desktops and multifunction machines over stand-alone printers, faxes and scanners will reduce your energy costs.

Customer demand: When it comes to Corporate Social Responsibility (CSR), Customers want more than aspirational mission statements and objectives. 84 percent of Americans hold companies accountable for producing and communicating the results of their commitments by going beyond the mission to robustly communicate progress against well-defined purpose. Some 40 percent go as far as to say that they will not purchase a company's products or services if CSR results are not communicated[245].

Sustainability: Sustainable development is based on the premise of being sensitive to the environment and society. But it also saves money, creates new products and revenue streams by attracting customers who care about a company's environmental footprint.

Quality: LSS addresses product quality requirements, design and defect issues. Often product uncertainty exists by assuming that commodity attributes are what Customers desire and that an uncertain commodity may possess attributes wanted by Customers. Merging Sustainability with Quality concepts will drive the product reputation, develop a Customer relationship, and increase brand aware news by addressing environmental and social concerns.

Employee retention*:* Employees want to work with companies who are 'doing the right thing'. Ensure employees are receiving the appropriate training to support their ongoing development, link employee skills with opportunities for growth in the company, help employees understand how their work contributes to the firm's success, give employees ongoing qualitative and quantitative feedback on their performance, and greatly increased employee satisfaction and retention based on Sustainability, Quality and empowerment.

Sustainability: "Working for a bigger cause excites employees," says Metzger (senior associate at the World Resources Institute). "It's one of the softer measures to wrap your head around, but if you talk to someone where Sustainability is embedded into the corporate culture, it's a selling-point to attract and retain workers."

Quality: Increased employee engagement can be accomplished through their participation on process improvement teams designed to help them improve processes and increase value for their customers. Oftentimes, employees will take great pride in tangible achievements. They obtain an amazing amount of self confidence, the training and being able to speak with data enable them to challenge the norm, suggest new ideas and solve problems.

Improving Productivity: Targeting one area might lead to benefits in another area. For example, you might decide to map your delivery routes in an effort to reduce fuel costs, but then discover that the streamlined routes also reduce labor and maintenance costs. In addition, you might find that your Customers are receiving their orders sooner.

Innovation: When you encourage your employees to find a better way to do something, it is seldom a one-time occurrence. Once you engage their creative side, it tends to remain engaged. While considering a method to reduce energy costs, for example, an employee may find the inspiration to a better manufacturing process.

Leadership Mindset: Sometimes companies have been oriented toward social and environmental responsibility since they were created. In most cases, this is often due to the values of the company's founders. Two companies that come to mind are the cosmetic company Bert's Bees and high-end furniture designer Herman-Miller.

From its garage inception, Bert's Bees was producing products only from natural products. Burt's Bees became a key leader in natural personal care products and convinced environmental stakeholders that the company's strategy was both sincere and significant. For example, they were the first company to post percentage of natural ingredients in their products. Their corporate culture became notorious for its natural products. In fact, Clorox's acquired Bert's Bees for its culture and leveraged it for a safer cleaning product line, introduced as Clorox's Greenworks.

Herman-Miller has strongly embraced Sustainability. It is now powered with 100% renewable energy. Herman Miller is a 100+ year old company that places great importance on design, the environment, community service, and the health and well-being of their customers and their employees.

Herman-Miller's roots originated as a clock company in the 1900s. Its innovative and design approach bought Herman-Miller entry the modular and versatile systems furniture. That tradition continues today and is highly respected as a high-end furniture designer. Today, they still focus on innovative ways to improve the performance of their customers' organizations that have become their hallmark.

In the 1940s, Charles and Ray Eames mold plywood chairs, molded plywood lounge chairs, molded plywood folding screens, and molded plywood coffee tables are introduced to the public. They are recognized for their unique designs and the New York's Museum of Modern Art installs a small exhibition called "New Furniture Designed by Charles Eames"--the museum's first one-man furniture show.

Walmart is a good example of leadership. Despite its big box reputation, in 2006 its focus shifted. CEO Mike Duke was leading the charge to make Walmart look at its environmental impact differently and that transformation changed to enterprise and many industries, as well.

However, there are exceptions. BP in the Gulf of Mexico, Union Carbide in Bhopal, India; and the Fukushima Dai-ichi nuclear disaster in Japan are all examples of man-made, natural-made and combined events. These are all leadership crisis and nightmares. Sometimes it takes a disaster to get leadership and their companies to embrace Sustainability. Companies observe and learn from other company's experiences and some of them are using Sustainability to envision a better future.

Sustainability: "Traditionally, companies adopted Sustainability strategies in order to comply with government regulations and avoid fines. Now leading-edge corporations are embracing the concept of Sustainability in order to be a part of the conversation on environmental policy", says Eliot Metzger, a senior associate at the World Resources Institute.

Quality: There will always be yield loss; accidents are to be expected; and not every customer can be fully satisfied. Instead, quality leaders adopted zero-based thinking as a countermeasure against these paradigms.

Financial Awareness

Financially, tangible benefits from Sustainability is not well known, nor seldom recognized. This one primary reason CFOs are becoming key players in Sustainability initiatives. External stakeholders are recognizing that those companies embracing Sustainability are often well managed, showing increase profitability while reducing risks.

Attracting Investors: Like consumers, many investors prefer to choose an environmentally responsible company in which to invest. Their motives are not altogether altruistic. Investors want to earn a profit. A company that is at risk for a large government fine or a massive cleanup effort will likely not be as profitable. Investors might also perceive an environmentally conscious company as one that is more innovative and therefore more competitive.

Increasing Sales: The trend has been for more large corporations to go public with their Sustainability strategies. Companies such as IBM, Walmart and Kaiser Permanente examine suppliers' Sustainability commitments when determining which supplier receives a contract. If your company can provide proof of your commitment, you will have an edge over suppliers who have yet to implement a Sustainability strategy.

"Companies like DuPont, Nike and IBM are looking ahead to see how natural resources, climate change, and energy can drive innovation and inspire new business models, products and services," said Metzger, senior associate at the World Resources Institute. "These are the factors that are going to determine future winners and losers in the marketplace."

New financial opportunities: Some companies and their CFOs are over-looking benefits from Sustainability transformation. A recent study from Deloitte report its key findings are:
1. Many CFOs are engaged with sustainability issues as they relates to core finance activities like financial auditing and reporting, compliance, and risk management,
2. Only one-third of CFOs describe themselves as fully involved in sustainability strategy and governance; one-fifth plan to get more involved in the next two years, and
3. Nearly half of the CFOs surveyed are planning capital investments that will support the implementation of sustainability initiatives.

Sustainability: "Companies like DuPont, Nike and IBM are looking ahead to see how natural resources, climate change, and energy can drive innovation and inspire new business models, products and services," said Metzger. "These are the factors that are going to determine future winners and losers in the marketplace."

Quality: The financial benefits associated with LSS and Six Sigma are well documented. Typically we see projects which on average save around $100,000 for a medium size business and higher savings for more complex enterprises.

Risk mitigation: Many Owners and Executives are ignoring the 800 pound gorilla in the living room. Uncertainty is hiding in the shadows. Ignoring responsibility for the environment has not been in the purview of most companies. In that respect Sustainability is recognizing that government may be changing the economic model. Whether through environmental awareness, court decisions, regulations, or legislation, companies and in-dustries can be forced into social and environmentally responsible prac-tices. Risks are being recognized and voluntary approach is applied, through Sustainability, which may mitigate those concerns.

Sustainability: Business runs on energy, available energy and that is one of the largest risks on the horizon. With energy costs rising, smart companies are considering their alternatives. Executives are starting to re-think how they obtain and use these resources and mitigating with renewable sources. Other areas of concern are focused on resources (financial, human, natural), food and water.

Quality: Every company process would benefit from standardization. If you implement LSS a major benefit would be that all projects would be run in a standardized same way following the same process -

DMAIC. This means that as managers you can be confident that the problems or risks are being solved properly with data to back up any decision.

Stakeholder benefits: By effectively managing Stakeholder relationships, which increases potential opportunities and lowering the risk for each relationship, a company can enhance the quality of its intangible assets and therefore increase the overall valuation of the business.

Sustainability: Externalities will take notice through your financial and Transparency reports, Media exposure, awards and other recognition of changes that affected the environment and society. Financial resources will also recognized that your organization is also better managed and have positive consequences to investments.

Quality: The key benefit in this area is the engagement of your workforce in transforming your business. Companies who have deployed LSS successfully see this engagement and reap the benefits – the whole workforce identifying and solving problems. They will not just put out fires but they will remove the root causes stopping the fires from starting again. Eliminate how much time and money have you spend fire fighting over the last year. LSS is about putting out major fires permanently.

Tax incentives: According to Area Development, federal, state, and local governments offer a range of financial incentives for undertaking environmentally responsible activities. These include investment-, production-, or consumption-based income tax credit, accelerated depreciation for certain capital expenses, exemptions from state or local sales taxes, and cash grants

Government plays an important role in providing incentives for Sustainability transformation. There are a number of tax incentives to promote the development of energy and sustainability projects. Some examples of current U.S. tax incentives include: Alternative energy, Alternative fuel vehicles, Green building related state incentives, Energy efficiency, Energy-efficient buildings, etc.

Sustainability: According to Area Development, federal, state, and local governments offer a range of financial incentives for undertaking environmentally responsible activities. These include investment-, production-, or consumption-based income tax credit, accelerated depreciation for certain capital expenses, exemptions from state or local sales taxes, and cash grants.

Quality: Quality is not promoted by tax incentives, but it does retain the gains of those initiatives, in a framework, that also promotes frugality and visibility.

Deming On Continuous Improvement

I believe Dr. W. Edwards Deming, often recognized as the father of modern-day Quality Management, would have quickly embraced Sustainability when it was fused with Quality Management. In 1993, he was quoted to say; "It would be better if everyone would work together as a system, with the aim for everybody to win." It is now difficult to find a large company that has not attempted some change at least once.

Clearly, managers attempting Quality improvement are in some way not fully prepared to go the distance. Any Quality Management visionary needs to fully understand that Business Transformation, based on Sustainability and Quality, is a holistic approach that affects everyone in the organization. That potentially includes all of your Suppliers that fulfill your Customers needs. Last, the journey for Business Transformation is a long-term commitment that must incorporate Quality strategies, Process transformation, Management tools and implementing a Continuous Improvement process.

Do You Want To Be Exceptional? Why would your company's philosophy and management style be important to the adaptation and adoption of quality programs? First, are you self-motivated to improve your financial opportunities through Business Transformation? Second, are you pursuing this course in order to garner future business and being perceived as a "quality" company? Third, are you in a crisis due to the constraints of the Great Recession and fear failure is near? Of these three scenarios, the first is most likely to succeed, since self-motivation and willingness to "adapt and adopt" are critical elements of the transformation, management's openness and conveying the desire to work smarter - not harder - will influence the workforce to improve, take pride in their accomplishments and channel that energy into measurable progress. The second scenario, driven by "certification" rather than qualifications, will ultimately fail due to lack of understanding and commitment to the quality program. Last, the company in dire straits with its back up against the wall may be looking for a silver bullet. Any quality program is not a quick fix. To be obliged to accept this change, under duress, could very well distract your true need, to focus on survival.

Knowledge: So, what business knowledge should be used in Business Transformation? Not all change is homogenous and the maturity of the concern will also be a qualifier. That means that every company has a unique set of variables, assets and needs that are dictated by various influencers (i.e. marketplace, product, service, strategic vision, etc.). So, those needs and required changes to incorporate solutions in your every day business process will require openness, critical thinking and adaptation based on your quality definition, commercial needs and recognition of your corporate culture. One of the most obvious qualifier is the maturity of the business. Is your business in a start-up phase? In that case, you may not be able to afford massive investments in automated solutions, elaborate dashboards or time required for training. However, you could benefit from non-structured techniques that reduce time, waste and costs. If your corporation is a proactive middle matured organization, you may need to start monitoring progress through your Balanced Scorecard and supporting dashboards to identify areas that need improvement and incorporate your quality program (i.e., production defects, implementation for a continuous improvement program, etc.).

Leadership: To manage, one must lead. To lead, one must understand the work that he and his people are responsible for. Who is the Customer (the next stage), and how can we serve better the Customer[246]? If we are to understand Deming's point, we must understand that work includes effective usage of resources (human, information and organization capital), a keen understanding of the processes, and a clear identification of the Customer(s).

First, if the Customer is satisfied and your team meets or exceeds expectations, then a manager will naturally focus on quality, cost, timeliness and effectiveness of resources to meet goals. Second, if the Customer is not satisfied, are you sacrificing quality, cost, timeliness and effectiveness of resources due to urgency, expediency or fear? Are you recognizing that a Customer issue or problem is an opportunity to improve your processes to ensure quality, cost, timeliness and effectiveness of resources are not sacrificed?

Baldrige Award Criteria
Some company are often directed by their leadership to excel in exceptional areas for recognition for the performance, corporate cultures, forward thinking and ensuring better Customer Satisfaction through implementation of special methodologies, community efforts, philanthropy or other areas. Fusing Sustainability with Quality offers those enterprises a number of areas for recognition. One key program is the Baldrige Award for quality.

The Baldrige model has identified the beliefs and behaviors of high-performing organizations. These 10 core values and concepts, embedded in the Baldrige Criteria and in Baldrige Award recipients, are essential to achieving performance excellence. You can find the complete list here and an explanation of each in the Criteria booklets here. So how do you get your organization from where it is today to world-class status? Twenty years of Baldrige reveal the steps you can take to create a high-performing organization:

1. *Lead the Transformation.* It won't happen without leaders committed to excellence, and it won't happen without recognizing that the steps you take will transform your organization. Plan the journey, communicate the plan, measure progress, and facilitate change.

2. *Develop management system experts.* You will need these experts to help focus resources and attention on what must happen along your journey. Take a few existing or rising stars and ask them to be Baldrige or state award examiners for at least three years. The training and experience they get will give you the internal expertise you need.

3. *Promote curiosity.* No organization can change if it is content with the way things are. Learning organizations challenge the status quo. They seek a better way. And they recognize and reward people at all levels of the organization who take responsibility for improving performance.

4. *Demand process thinking.* All work is process. You cannot prolong your journey to world-class by constantly putting out fires or blaming employees for systemic problems. Ask how you do what you do, identify the steps, and manage and improve the process.

5. *Compare with the best.* You need context to know if what you are doing is the best course and what you are achieving is truly world-class. Benchmark key processes and key results with those of high-performing organizations. Hold your organization to the highest standards and implement plans that will help you join them.

6. *Assess and apply.* The only way to keep attention focused on improving your management system is to assess and improve it using the Baldrige Criteria. Many Baldrige Award recipients submitted applications for state awards and/or the Baldrige Award annually for several years before winning the Award—and many continue to do assessments after they won. Start with a self-assessment or by applying for a state award. Use the feedback to prioritize and address your biggest gaps. Repeat the process annually and you will improve.

7. *Drive continuous improvement.* Use data and information to identify opportunities for improvement and have action planning and problem solving processes in place to address them. Build refinement steps into every process to make sure the process is systematically improved.

8. ***Align and integrate.*** Use your strategic planning and performance measurement systems to align what you do with what you want to achieve. Harmonize plans, processes, information, resource decisions, actions, results, and analyses to support your organization's goals.
9. ***Innovate.*** High-performing organizations are good at everything and great at a few things. To be good at everything you need a culture of innovation that touches all processes. To be great at a few things, you need formal approaches to developing breakthrough approaches in those areas critical to your success.
10. ***Sustain the gains.*** The first nine steps are a lot of work if you're going to slack off as soon as you get to the top. To sustain the journey, identify the factors that must be in place and managed to remain world-class and then develop and implement processes to address them.

High-performing organizations have integrated Baldrige by integrating these ten steps into the way they operate. Their success is available to any organization committed to being the best.

Analytics And Metrics

Metrics are key to realizing your objectives. Guard them, do not publicize your results and formulas. Your competitors will be looking for industry success stories and often times, in trade show and industry conventions, your employees and competitor's employees often exchange information without thinking.

Be clear as to what words mean to your Core Assets in your company. Define how you fuse Sustainability with Quality clearly. Quality is based on your definitions of activities, processes and methods of applying your workforce to accomplish tasks that create and produce goods or services. Metrics and data are not a true measure, nor a means to an end.

Short-term profits are not a reliable indicator of performance of management. Anybody can pay dividends by deferring maintenance, cutting out research, or acquiring another company[247]. Understand that MBO (management-by-objectives) and BSC are usually abused and do not empower their employees. As Deming said; "…management by numerical goal is an attempt to manage without knowledge of what to do, and in fact is usually management by fear."

Over seven decades ago, W. Edwards Deming thoughtfully discussed Quality as an interdependent system. A system based on knowledge, not information, to improve processes that would ensure products and services that Customers would rave about (e.g., Apple).

- "It is important that an aim never be defined in terms of activity or methods. It must always relate directly to how life is better for everyone... The aim of the system must be clear to everyone in the system. The aim must include plans for the future. The aim is a value judgment."
- "Profit in business comes from repeat customers, customers that boast about your project or service, and that bring friends with them."
- "It is not enough to do your best; you must know what to do, and then do your best."
- "What we need to do is learn to work in the system, by which I mean that everybody, every team, every platform, every division, every component is there not for individual competitive profit or recognition, but for contribution to the system as a whole on a win-win basis."
- "A system is a network of interdependent components that work together to try to accomplish the aim of the system. A system must have an aim. Without the aim, there is no system."
- "Let us ask our suppliers to come and help us to solve our problems."

Although tailored to fit different perspectives of an enterprise, measuring the success of Sustainability and Quality is a systematic approach that addresses two different levels. Your decision-making should be based on the knowledge why things work or fail. It is not the metric or information to create the metric - for it simply should be used as only an indicator for that success or failure.

Deming's 14 Points on Quality Management, a core concept on implementing Quality management, is a set of management practices to help companies increase their Quality and productivity. Interesting to note that many of Deming's 14 points fit well in context of Sustainability, too.

1. Create constancy of purpose for improving products and services.
2. Adopt the new philosophy.
3. Cease dependence on inspection to achieve quality.
4. End the practice of awarding business on price alone; instead, minimize total cost by working with a single supplier.
5. Improve constantly and forever every process for planning, production and service.
6. Institute training on the job.
7. Adopt and institute leadership (leadership of the system).
8. Drive out fear (don't use metrics to punish, but to learn from the information).
9. Break down barriers between staff areas.
10. Eliminate slogans, exhortations and targets for the workforce.

11. Eliminate numerical quotas for the workforce and numerical goals for management.
12. Remove barriers that rob people of pride of workmanship, and eliminate the annual rating or merit system.
13. Institute a vigorous program of education and self-improvement for everyone.
14. Put everybody in the company to work accomplishing the transformation[248].

With the improvement of performance and costs, IT leaders can now afford to perform analytics and simulation for every transaction taken in the business. In most IT environments today, mobile client linked to cloud-based analytic engines and big data repositories potentially enables use of optimization virtually everywhere and every time. These new steps provide prediction, optimization and other analytics, to empower even more flexibility at the time and place of every process transaction.

The real measure of success is not meeting the metrics or planning objectives, rather it is the real benefits to your Core Assets with respect to social capital, your cultural inclination and enhancements to your internal innovation. As expressed by Charlie Eitel, formerly of Interface, "We'll give our competitors our whole playbook – but they can't execute it! I'll tell you every play I'm going to run against you but you can't beat me! Do you know why? You don't have my people; you don't have my process; you don't have my discipline; and you don't have my culture[249]!"

Eliminating Waste To Realize Benefits

Developing and enacting a broad strategy to manage energy and resources and drive process innovation involves several steps. Briefly, these include:

- Rigorously evaluate energy and resources use—look beyond current pricing and consider volatility and availability. It also shifts the focus from individual Sustainability projects to broader programs that treat energy and other resources such as water as strategic assets[250].
- Identify key areas for improvement—not all Sustainability initiatives are created equal in terms of potential to create business value. Sustainability initiatives are the right ones to invest in—some initiatives can create both top-line value and bottom-line savings while others may only reduce operating costs[251].
- Prioritize projects—don't follow the leader, but instead prioritize projects based upon your individual company strategy. Also, consider benefits beyond the bottom line, such as increasing your brand value[252].
- Sustainability technologies are key to performance indicators and results against target: establish meaningful targets for improvement

with verifiable data. Aggressively scale the most effective improvements across the enterprise in order to increase return on investment[253].

- Consider the impact of the components in your product - recognize their types of waste - identify Zero Waste objectives, identify hazardous waste, compare current process for mitigation, build a business case for the project.

- Connect Lean, Six Sigma, and Environmental Efforts at Facilities. Environmental health and safety personnel can support operations-driven Lean and Six Sigma efforts, expanding their traditional scope, revealing hidden wastes, and improving environmental and operational results[254].

- Deliver Lean and Environment Technical Assistance. Environmental technical assistance providers can partner with Lean and Six Sigma service providers to jointly deliver Lean and environment services[255].

- Use Lean to Enhance Environmental Programs and Processes. Visual controls and other Lean concepts can improve the effectiveness of compliance-assistance efforts, and environmental agencies can use Lean to reduce waste in administrative processes such as permitting processes[256].

Taking Ownership

We are at a crossroad to decide what direction we want to go. Should we continue with the current direction with a potential dismal future or do we decide to take another route that eliminates waste, understand how the environment nurtures us, transforms our businesses, industries and countries into sustainable societies for future generations of Humanity? We do have a choice and those results will hinge on Commitment to Sustainability and Excellence.

- *CardinalHealth:* We aim to minimize the impact of our operations, products and services on the environment focusing on four key areas:

    - Pollution prevention;

    - Energy efficiency, use and sourcing;

    - Designing products, packaging and services in environmentally friendly ways; and o ▸ Promoting environmental engagement among our employees.

    - We've been included in the Dow Jones Sustainability Index since 2006, we're a founding member of the Healthcare Plastics Recycling Council, and we're a partner in the U.S. Environmental Protection Agency's SmartWay Program.

"I thank our 32,000 employees for their dedication and service to our customers, our environment, our communities and one another. And I look forward to continuing to see what we can accomplish together." ~ George S. Barrett, Chairman and CEO[257]

- ***Convergys:*** Convergys is also committed to helping sustain our environment. Our working environments are designed to optimize performance and efficiency while reducing energy consumption, waste and pollution. This is done by using ENERGY STAR® products for workstations, LCD computers and high efficiency lighting; maintaining an active corporate recycling program; reusing water; providing group transportation; and developing energy-efficient client solutions where we conserve precious resources and strive to minimize negative environmental impact.

  "We have more than 3,500 full-time equivalent employees working from home, which enables Convergys to minimize our impact on the environment by:
  - Reducing exhaust emissions
  - Lowering energy, fuel and other natural resource consumption
  - Decreasing our contribution to landfills" ~ Andrea Ayers, President and CEO[258]

What Did Irene Think?
Elimination of waste from our resources, through Sustainability, helps preserve our environment. Elimination of waste in the Value Chain, through Lean Six Sigma, helps improve efficiency in the enterprise. So how would a good business person perceive this trend? "To build and sustain brands people love and trust, one must focus—not only on today but also on tomorrow. It's not easy...but balancing the short and long term is key to delivering sustainable, profitable growth—growth that is good for our shareholders but also good for our consumers, our employees, our business partners, the communities where we live and work, and the planet we inhabit." ~ Irene B. Rosenfeld (3 May 1953), CEO of Mondelēz International.

"Quality means doing it right when no one is looking."
~ Henry Ford

10. Identifying Inefficiencies and Waste[259]

"Usually, if you're greening an industrial process, it means you're turning waste into profit." ~ Amory Lovins

William McDonough, one of the co-authors of Cradle-to-Cradle that is widely acknowledged as one of the most important environmental manifestos of our time, once said; "You don't filter smokestacks or water. Instead, you put the filter in your head and design the problem out of existence." Whether you are designing a new LEED® certified building, designing an end-of-life process or simply integrating CSR into your Strategic Planning framework, the idea is the same - "you put the filter in your head and design the problem out of existence."

The percentage of companies reporting a profit from their Sustainability efforts rose 23 percent in 2012, to 37 percent in 2013, according to the most recent global study[260]. The extent to which a company incorporates Sustainability concerns into its business model often correlates with its increase in profit, the survey found. For example, 50 percent of respondents said they profited by changing three or four business model elements to reflect more sustainable practices, while 60 percent said they profited by including Sustainability as a permanent fixture in their management agenda[261].

Your organization has opportunities in various forms of waste waiting to be harvested to reduce your cost of doing business. The following sections demonstrate areas for governance, planning, methodologies and reduction or elimination of your wastes for your success:
- CSR Strategies Targeting Waste
- Building a Business Case
- Waste Elimination Tools
- Identifying and Baseline Current Wastes
- New Construction and Major Renovation
- IT Opportunities in Data Centers
- Creating Onsite Energy Alternatives
- Supply Chain Efficiencies
- Reduce, Reuse, Recycle
- Waste Management
- Water Conservation
- Think It Through

CSR Strategies Targeting Waste
Look for effectiveness of each strategy and determine its success through

tangible benefits. These are areas of improvement linked to strategies with key processes. This is the only true way of measuring the success of your strategies. Remember, Executive Commitment to Sustainability begins with the completion and integration of these key points:

- Sustainability should be woven into your current business strategies.
- Sustainability gains through compliance and regulations.
- Sustainability and Quality gains through elimination of wastes and retains gains.
- Costs seen through the lens of Sustainability and Quality.
- Branding products and services as a "differentiation" wanted by Customers.
- Mitigate risks with Externalities (external Stakeholders) and influence Internalities (internal Stakeholders).
- Sustainability investments generate returns in terms of market success and cost performance.

Strategies addressing customers, culture, emissions, energy, products, wastes and a vast array of other considerations for sustainable development will demonstrate tangible benefits and improvements. Successful Corporate Social Responsibility is now becoming more apparent in corporations across the globe. In many cases, their experience has been meeting or exceeding objectives before their original timelines.

> *Cooper Industries:* Sustainability has become embedded into our culture — whether through our products and solutions targeted at making the electric grid more efficient, reducing energy consumption via our energy-efficient lighting and controls products, or our relentless focus on reducing our carbon footprint from our manufacturing and distribution facilities.

> *Ernst & Young:* In addition, our sustainability efforts have reduced our per head carbon footprint by 14 percent. Our Americas CFO champions efforts to modify business processes so that, as the economy improves and our business travel increases, we mitigate the impact on our carbon footprint.

> *KPMG:* KPMG is committed to reducing our overall carbon footprint by an additional 10 percent per employee by 2015.

> *Qualcomm:* Qualcomm's energy efficiency efforts to date have saved 26.6 million kilowatt hours of electricity annually and prevented approximately 8,740 metric tons of GHG emissions per year — the equivalent of eliminating the annual emissions of 1,589 cars.

Building a Business Case

Building a business case for each transformation project will quantify and qualify its value to the enterprise. For it can be the bridge from your corporate values to the actual "go-no go" decision-making processes for a variety of Sustainability projects and initiatives. It can help steer efforts into avenues that could otherwise be overlooked. Addressing Ethics, Legalities and Stewardship in context of approving funding would help ensure your strategic directions are met and align with other business constraints (i.e., ROI, cost reduction, new product development, etc.).

Current State - Megaforces Impact: Over the next twenty years, these groups of megaforces, will drive market and industry changes. Companies that recognize this fact and position themselves at the forefront stand to reap sizable competitive advantages. Consider the following emerging realities in considering their impact in a business case:

- *Resource Constraints:* Prices for food, water, energy, and other resources are growing increasingly volatile. Companies that have optimized their Sustainability profile and practices will be less exposed to these swings and be more resilient.

- *Energy Usage:* As the population grows, consumption increases and so does the demand for energy. While the developed countries have decreased energy consumption in the last decade, developing countries are increasing their usage.

- *Demographic Global Concerns:* Human population on Earth has surpassed 7 billion people. Mega-urbanization and the rise of megacities, increased growth in human populations in Africa and Asia, increased population migration to coastal geographies, increased middle-class wealth and demands for consumer products will dramatically impact the biosphere (deforestation, ecosystem decline, etc.).

- *Stakeholder Intervention:* Customers, other Stakeholders and the Government are paying more attention to Sustainability and putting pressure on companies to change. Stakeholders concerns are becoming more apparent relating to economic, environmental and social issues.

- *Future Government Laws And Obligations:* Governments' agendas increasingly advocate for Sustainability. Companies that are proactively pursuing this goal will be less vulnerable to sudden regulatory changes. They will also be better positioned to have a voice in shaping policy—rather than simply reacting to it.

- ***Growing Financial Resources:*** Capital markets are paying more attention to Sustainability and using it as a gauge to evaluate companies and make investment decisions. Sustainable Developed enterprises are considered better managed and are more sensitive to their customers, quicker to their needs and listen to their externalities.

- ***Supply Chain Impact:*** Businesses are often defined as a constant for change, and that unique characteristic provides multinational corporations (MNCs) the ability to impose demands on suppliers faster than governments can craft legislation.

Key Ethic and Legal Drivers: The business case provides the corporate guidance, direction and boundaries for acceptable behavior and limits decisions that are consider unethical, irresponsible or illegal in the communities which you operate.

- ***Core Assets:*** Core Assets are based on People, Processes, Products and/or Services, Innovation and Values.

- ***Corporate Values:*** Especially in recent years, values have become more important to Customers, Investors, Employees and Suppliers primarily due to Corporate Social Responsibility and Sustainability principles.

- ***Ethical Standards:*** Each organization should provide employees with a clear understanding of ethical standards, how they are defined, and examples of how they can be used.

- ***Legal Requirements:*** Most companies have developed guidelines, business practices and behavior policies based on legal risks and compliance, your business case should include those considerations, too.

- ***Stewardship:*** We define environmental stewardship as the responsibility for environmental quality shared by all those whose actions affect the environment.

Business Case: Your business case reframes a company's purpose and should take into account the social, ethical, and environmental effects of its activities on its staff and the residing community. Your business case should compare costs and offsetting benefits. Here are ten areas for consideration:
1. Reduce costs
2. Gain competitive advantage
3. Manage/reduce risk

4.   Comply with regulations
5.   Reach new markets, add new products / services
6.   Increase productivity
7.   Attract new talent and keep staff
8.   Gain Trust and loyalty of Customers / Stakeholders
9.   Improve reputation, "license to operate"
10.   Innovate, learn, grow

Analysis and Governance: Each project needs careful review and under-standing to its scope and resources required for its success. Involvement of proper stakeholders are also required for "buy-in" and understanding its impact on their organizations. The review process should include these steps:

1.   Understand Sustainability issues and impacts to your business
2.   Understand Quality issues and impacts to your business
3.   Investigate opportunities to be more sustainable; set goals / benchmarks
4.   Implement initiatives, communicate, promote, engage stakeholders
5.   Each Sustainability and Quality project needs review and approval.
6.   For approved projects, embed into Mega Planning, Business Planning and governance processes
7.   Evaluate, report, adapt, reinvent

Objectives: Quantifying areas of waste often under value that impact on the organization. For example: a single project, a cost savings objective could be $300,000 in savings, but in actuality exceed that objective by an additional $350,000. The key is setting your visibility on tangible and measurable results, such as:

- Cost savings
- Risk mitigation
- Innovation driver
- Market opportunity
- Asset value improvement
- Brand enhancement
- Employee attraction and retention

Tools and Methodologies: Lean, Six Sigma, Lean Six Sigma (LSS) and Sustainability goals will provide a pragmatic strategy and structured methodology for transformation, on-going change, refinement and innovation. Each project will need to choose one or more methodologies in order to fulfill its objectives:

- Sustainability
- Lean
- Six Sigma
- Lean Six Sigma

Future State - Tangible Benefits: In house experts from your team will identify "take-aways" or tangible benefits from projects and the enterprise initiative at large. They are looking for revenue, cost reductions, improved services, qualities in products and other more complex areas of benefit. Audits will reconfirm those gains and verify the project's rewards. Most areas of improvement and transformation will originate from these areas:

- Cost savings
- Risk mitigation
- Innovation driver
- Market opportunity
- Asset value improvement
- Brand enhancement
- Employee attraction and retention

Waste Elimination Tools

Develop a Zero Waste strategy that sets levels and expectations. Zero Waste, like Zero Defects of the 1980s, is unattainable and costly if pursued 100 percent of the time. Qualify your strategy with costs and benefits at various levels (i.e., start at 90 percent levels until your goals are reached, then reset your objectives to 95 percent, etc.). This strategy should align your other strategies on Stewardship based on Customers, Community and the Environment.

Corporations and Governments commit to minimizing waste through small changes in individual behavior. Sustainability technologies reduces water waste by the use of more efficient fixtures, better water management, and distribution of effluent water for use by mechanical and irrigation systems. Solid waste is diverted from the landfill through recycling, repurposing, reusing, and composting. Waste is averted through reduced consumption. However, "The 5 big things", those technologies of the future: solar energy, close loop recycling, zero waste [strategies], harmless emissions, and resource efficient transportation[262].

Companies and Governments commit to minimizing waste through aversion, too. Companies and Governments reduce water waste by the use of more efficient fixtures, better water management, and distribution of effluent water for use by mechanical and irrigation systems. Solid waste is diverted from the landfill through recycling, repurposing, reusing, and composting. Waste is averted through reduced consumption.

Using Structured Methodology: Peter Drucker once said; "Do not simply cling to your past successes, be willing to change, adopt new ideas and continually review all the different segments of business." Lean Six Sigma (LSS) provides a pragmatic strategy and structured methodology for transformation, on-going change, refinement and innovation. So, when beginning the journey of change, recognize that pitfalls can start with false assumptions or exaggerated expectations. However, balance understanding that LSS includes these inherent traits:

*   A LSS deployment is no different from any other business initiative. You make plans and develop metrics to evaluate the progress. When the deployment is not going as expected, you make adjustments.

    What is your Current State? In today's business environment, every LSS deployment has had some form of failure. Recognize that failure is a part of the learning experience and can be viewed as a benefit to your Corporation, if managed, controlled and reviewed as a learning exercise.

    If management doesn't allocate enough resources or personal attention to a LSS program from the beginning, it will never get off the ground. Inadequate training, or even too much training and not enough application of the tools and techniques, is a sure ticket to failure. Eventually, through training and application of knowledge, and steady progress, a successful culture of continuous improvement becomes organic, which then must be carried forward by succeeding generations of management.

*   If managers decide to hire outside consultants, then everyone should be trained in LSS, including the top executives. First, they should start by training the executive team in core ideas and concepts. A company's leaders have to be fully on board for LSS to have a lasting impact. Consultants can bring the managers together to talk about the issues and help make sure a program stays on track.

    Most LSS consultants typically define successful deployments in the following way: A successful Six Sigma deployment is one that provides an acceptable return to the business and leaves a stand-alone program, not requiring further consulting resources.

    Most successful programs may have required some level of assistance once the consulting resources are gone. However, you should be left with a cadre of subject matter experts. Most on-site Master Black Belts, Black Belts and Green Belts will do what it takes to support the business.

*   Beware of high expectations! For example, a project result that does not meet expected Return On Investment (ROI). Understand that any company that has invested a significant sum of money and resources to do a LSS deployment, is highly unlikely they will

publicly admit failure, regardless of the ROI outcome. Recognize that like all business initiatives, ROI estimated at the outset rarely align to the final ROI.

- Most programs that have failed to deliver the exaggerated promises of savings (usually $250,000 per project per black belt trained (4 per year)), which are the result of the consultants' salesmanship and the companies' acceptance. Anecdotally, senior Master Black Belts have shared their highest savings averaged $230,000 per project, whereas, most deployments produce a range of savings, from $100,000 to $200,000 per project.

Lean Alone: Lean methodology is the simplest approach to improved Quality that is tool driven and combines "experience and common sense" in evaluating waste. Lean or sometimes called lean transformation. It is a common sense approach, observations, analysis and using tools to support the effectiveness and eliminating of waste.

Lean is based on a three step approach. Managers and executives embarked on Lean transformations think about three fundamental business issues that should guide the transformation of the entire organization:
1. *Purpose:* What customer problems will the enterprise solve to achieve its own purpose of prospering? How can Customer Satisfaction be improved? How can services be improved?
2. *People:* Are Owners assigned to processes? How can the organization insure that every important process has someone responsible for continually evaluating that value stream in terms of business purpose and lean process?
3. *Process*: How will the organization assess each major value stream to make sure each step is valuable, capable, available, adequate, flexible, and that all the steps are linked by flow, pull, and leveling?

Historically referred to as Lean Manufacturing — refers to the principles and methods of the Toyota Production System. Lean methods focus on the systematic identification and elimination of non-value added activity (called "waste") or sometimes called Lean's "Deadly Wastes".

How can everyone touching the value stream be actively engaged in operating it correctly and continually improving it[263]? Lean waste is identified with Lean methodology on eight separate areas of investigation:
- *Transport*: Unnecessary movement of people, equipment, products and information (excess transport of work-in-process or products[264])
- *Inventory*: Excess storage of parts, documentation and materials – ahead of requirements (excess material and information[265])

- *Motion*: Unnecessary movement by the people working on the job (human movements that are unnecessary or straining[266])
- *Waiting*: Waiting for instructions, information, equipment and parts in a production line (idle time and delays[267])
- *Over-production:* Making more than what is needed at a point in time (manufacturing items ahead of demand[268])
- *Over-processing:* More work than is required for the job (process steps that are not required[269])
- *Defects:* Waste due to rework, scraps and incorrect documentation (production of off-specification products[270])
- *Skills/talent:* Underutilized skills, knowledge and talent of people, inadequate training for delegated tasks

Lean methodology is a Quality improvement concept designed to reduce waste and process cycle time. Lean tools and rules include focusing on the customer goals, avoiding batching if customers will be delayed, waste elimination, and continuous flow. Understand that waste of time is often not recognized outside Quality practices and can significantly increase productivity, performance and profitability.

Lean is generally an effective stand-alone approach. But when incorporated into Six Sigma, becomes an effective compliment, due to Six Sigma's more robust execution method. Both methodologies recognize the input-process-output model to determine disconnects and issues. Examples how Lean could prevail include:
- Just-In-Time inventory
- Agile manufacturing
- Higher value-added percentage
- Overall equipment effectiveness
- Work flow standardization

Six Sigma Alone: Six Sigma is the most sophisticated methodology and is a set of strategies, techniques, and tools for process improvement. It originated from terminology associated with the maturity of a manufacturing process can be described by a *sigma* rating indicating its yield or the percentage of defect-free products it creates (e.g., six sigma represent 3.4 defects per million).

While Lean tackles the "eight wastes", Six Sigma takes another approach of eliminating variation and wastes in processes. It was originally designed to suite high volume, complex transaction or manufacturing companies, but is flexible and can be applied in medium and large corporations.

The Six Sigma goal is to refine all processes that do not provide value-added features or qualities with the intent to perfect processes and eliminate inspection of products or services for the Customer. The goals of Six Sigma include:

- **Specialized training:** Methods include specific training used to create special infrastructures of certified individuals in the organization who are experts in these methods. These individuals are referred to as 'belts'; yellow, green, black, or master black depending on their levels of expertise.
- **Quality Strategy:** The enterprise reviews quality of all factors involved in production. It places emphasis on elements like job management, controls, performance and integrity criteria.
- **Measurable improvements:** Six Sigma delivers real improvements in terms of quality and revenue. The aim is to identify, analyze and remove causes of errors and defects in the organization.
- **Continuous Improvement:** This management philosophy aims at improving quality of processes and products continuously. It capitalizes on the involvement of customers, suppliers, workforce and management in order to exceed or meet the expectations of customers.
- **Reducing variability:** Reducing variability in business and manufacturing processes. This shrinks the process variations dramatically. It also sets financial targets that are quantified such as profit increase or cost reduction.
- **Six Sigma Level:** The ultimate goal of Six Sigma lies in zero defects within the products or services offered by an organization. A sigma rating can be used to describe the maturity of manufacturing processes. Six Sigma is less than 3.4 defects per million opportunities.
- **Data-driven decision-making:** The data-driven approach of analyzing the root causes of defects helps to deliver real improvements to the bottom line of the enterprise. Six Sigma focuses on root cause and analysis and fixes the problem "right, the first time". It is clear that the techniques and tools the Six Sigma system provides are effective methodology to boost sales and savings.

Developed by Motorola and popularized by General Electric—refers to a method and set of tools that utilize statistical analysis to measure and improve an organization's performance, practices, and systems with a prime goal of identifying and eliminating variation to improve quality.

- **Fast and Dramatic Results:** Lean produces compelling results quickly. Lean events typically last 2–5 days, during which teams dramatically reduce production lead times and costs, while improving product quality and customer responsiveness. Leveraging Lean efforts to include environmental issues can yield impressive environmental results as well.
- **Continual Improvement Culture:** Lean and Six Sigma tools engage employees throughout an organization in identifying and

eliminating production wastes. When environmental wastes are included, Lean and Six Sigma become powerful vehicles for engaging employees in identifying and implementing environmental improvement opportunities.

- *Avoided Pitfalls:* Integrated "Lean and environment" efforts can minimize environmental impacts and navigate regulatory and permitting issues that may arise in operational changes from Lean and Six Sigma.
- *New Market for Environmental Improvement Ideas:* By connecting with Lean and Six Sigma practitioners, environmental professionals can connect the wealth of environmental resources with those who are driving strategic and fundamental operational changes[271].
- *Six Sigma discovery points that produce tangible benefits are:*
  - Customer Satisfaction of Product & Service improvements
  - Defect prevention and elimination
  - Six sigma is a statistical term defined as 3.4 defects per million
  - Reducing variation in your processes
  - Predictable processes
  - Solve complex problems
  - Improve value stream

Lean and Six Sigma (LSS): LSS provides a powerful combination of the Lean Manufacturing approach and Six Sigma. LSS works on the philosophy of increasing speed by focusing on waste reduction or elimination. The result of Lean applications is shown in the improvement of quality and on reduced processing times and costs. Combining Six Sigma with Lean Manufacturing augments short-term results with the power of comprehensive changes. The result is LSS.

Corporations increasingly prefer implementing LSS over any other methodology. Here are the six top reasons that organizations prefer LSS.

1. *LSS is applicable across industry sectors:* Although Lean manufacturing was originally developed as a quality management tool with a manufacture-centric approach, of late, industries across the board have accepted and successfully implemented the seamless LSS tool. The notion that LSS can't be applied to non-manufacturing sectors doesn't hold true any more.
2. *LSS results in immediate functional improvements:* Implementation of LSS results in faster-than-expected reduction of production time and costs. This is because of the application of its tools such as kaizen (method of constantly analyzing process flow and its ap-

plication), kanban (helps pull up production) and poka yoke (mistake-proofing).

3. ***Helps create value for consumers:*** The combined application of Lean manufacturing and Six Sigma results in tangible and real value creation for consumers. Consumers of products and services can enjoy better experiences in terms of increased utility and reduced prices. More and more organizations are showing an inclination to implement LSS for obvious reasons - it improves their bottom lines.

4. ***Practicality of execution:*** LSS facilitates transformation of organizations by creating a powerful linkage between strategic priorities and improvements in operations. Strategic priorities are the goals set by the top management team for higher returns on investment and improved customer experiences.

5. ***Focus on sustainable management capability:*** LSS's highly sustainable approach, being woven into every aspect of business, leads to the creation of sustainability from top down. Sustainability results from the quick realization of tangible benefits of implementing the program.

6. ***Timeliness:*** By implementing the LSS approach, organizations have realized time and again that it is possible to streamline their operations and to create value for both management and customers alike. The bottom lines of companies have soared with the successful implementation of LSS. As a result, many companies have created enormous value for their shareholders. Organizations are drawn to the LSS approach due to its fast implementation and results, in addition to creating additional value for the consumer at no extra cost.

Sponsors and champions must continue to ask the right questions, use the DMAIC process, and be genuinely involved in selecting the best projects. The days of "shooting from the hip" must be over and decisions should now be made with the analysis of data[272].

Identifying and Baseline Current Wastes
To begin your Sustainability journey, Leadership can implement these straightforward areas of waste elimination. Add their sections to monthly or weekly reports to show the progress in the organization. Recognize all participating Human Resources, not only the leaders for their effort, but all employees. For this important exercise will help motivate your organization to adopt more Sustainability efforts and learn from experience.

Additionally, it is not uncommon to find that different departments manage the costs associated with different waste streams and no ***one*** department has ever taken the time or responsibility to add up the various waste streams cross-department to get a clear under-standing of how much total waste is generated and how much is spent on waste removal.

The amount and costs for each waste stream is dependent on current environmental programs, regional regulations and hauling fees. This early assessment is an opportunity to identify these gaps. Only through capturing details on the types, amounts and associated costs for material removal, can one set goals and track performance.

Your transformation teams can uncover various levels and areas of opportunities where energy could be utilized better and managed more efficiently. Let us take a minute and look at where a little planning and investigation could pay out large benefits:

- Where are your energy wastes? What are your energy needs? What are your energy costs? Could your energy needs be scheduled for off-peak use to lower costs?
- What your HVAC costs? What are your HVAC needs? How can your HVAC costs be reduced?
- Where are your lighting wastes? What are your lighting needs? What are your lighting costs? Could lighting be improved, if so, how much would that cost? What are the benefits? Look at lighting use / practices. Are safety issues created by lack of lighting?
- Have you made a cost / benefit analysis on alternative energy - solar, wind, water - that competes with current energy utilities?
- If you have an auto or truck fleet, have you compared vehicle total cost of ownership (electric, gasoline, diesel, propane, etc.)?
- Energy usage and carbon footprints are higher in IT centers. So are issues concerning computer efficiency and use of current technology. Has their been a total cost of ownership of the center and possible outsourcing to reduce costs? What are the risks and costs for having your data centers in the US vs. Outsourcing in another country? Are there technology vendors that can reduce you operating costs and increase your Sustainability efforts?

Air Emissions Examples: The following examples demonstrate how other companies have gained Sustainability improvements through reduction of emissions. Although verification could not be accomplished regarding methodology at Walmart , their approach, used in this example, would be similar to Lean analysis. Again, waste was identified and provided a business and environmental opportunity to eliminate waste. Results from "lean and environment" efforts:

- 3M reduced volatile air emissions by 61% and toxic inventory releases by 64% from 2000 to 2005 using Lean and Six Sigma techniques in coordination with pollution prevention.

- Woodfold Manufacturing reduced volatile organic compound (VOC) emissions by nearly 1,000 lbs. per year and diverted 6 tons per year of solid PVC waste from the landfill through opportunities identified in a value stream mapping event.
- Canyon Creek Cabinet Company: Through a combination of value stream mapping and weeklong kaizen events, Canyon Creek saved almost $1.2 million per year, reduced volatile organic compound (VOC) emissions by 55,100 lbs per year, and decreased hazardous wastes by 84,400 lbs per year.
- General Electric: GE conducted over 200 energy "treasure hunts"—a Lean strategy of identifying wastes—at facilities worldwide in 2005–07. This effort cut greenhouse gas emissions by 250,000 metric tons and saved $70 million in energy costs[273].

New Construction and Major Renovation

In most cases, buildings represent one of the largest energy and cost savings for the enterprise. In the United States, buildings account for:
- 36 percent of total energy use and 65 percent of electricity consumption
- 30 percent of greenhouse gas emissions
- 30 percent of raw materials use
- 30 percent of waste output (136 million tons annually)
- 12 percent of potable water consumption[274]

LEED® is a certification process that ensures specific categories are reviewed and planned for from the inception of building project. LEED® assesses, evaluates and investigates building proposals in a five-part review process. As an executive, this is what LEED® will do for you:
- Lower operating costs and increase asset value
- Conserve energy, water and other resources
- Be healthier and safer for occupants
- Qualify for money-saving incentives, like tax rebates and zoning allowances[275]

A new version (v4) of the Project Checklist will be phased in to include updates of the LEED's methodology used by Architects, Contractors and the certification body - USGBC (U.S. Green Building Council). As in the past, LEED® is helping to deliver energy and water efficient, healthy, environmentally-friendly cost saving buildings, homes and communities. Its objectives are:
- Identify the intent, requirements, and strategies for success with LEED® v4 credits in the Building Design and Construction rating system
- Identify strategies between credits both within and between credit categories

- Plan for key considerations and requirements for LEED® documentation
- Recognize how credit requirements lead to higher performing buildings and market transformation[276]

The building industry now uses the LEED® rating system on a wider variety of project types than ever before. From stadiums to convention centers, commercial offices to hospitals, each space type has unique needs. LEED® v4 provides new solutions for:
- Existing schools
- Existing retail
- Data centers (new and existing)
- Warehouses and distribution centers (new and existing)
- Hospitality
- Mid-rise residential[277]

LEED® provides an opportunity to move costs from 36 percent of total energy usage and 65 percent of electrical consumption to a much lower level of consumption with efficient equipment, as well as, new processes within a new or renovated building. Energy consumption is also intertwined with GHGs, therefore, reducing energy also reduces your GHG emissions, as well.

In the United States, LEED® standards are best practices that provide consistent and predictable results. When retrofitting or rebuilding, engage your subject matter professionals (i.e., architects, builders, realtors, developers, etc.) and consider these LEED® items:

Location and Transportation: Explore the LEED® Location & Transportation credits, which encourage project teams to take advantage of the infrastructure elements in existing communities that provide environmental and human health benefits.

Sustainable Sites: This is a main credit category. Sustainable sites credits encourage strategies that minimize the impact on ecosystems and water resources[278].

Many Corporations and Governments are insisting on Sustainability technologies requirements, to the fullest extent practicable, with LEED® certification for all new construction[279].

Recycling of Construction & Demolition (C&D) debris and waste is a common consideration in new construction and renovation projects, as it redirects materials targeted for the landfill and thus meets the intent of building sustainably. This waste stream is compromised of bulky material generated during deconstruction, construction and renovation projects including ceiling tiles, plumb-ing fixtures, carpeting, concrete, bricks, fill dirt, etc.

Energy and Atmosphere and Water Efficiency: This is another main credit category. Energy & atmosphere credits promote better building energy performance through innovative strategies and the use of high energy efficient HVAC equipment. Water efficiency credits promote reduced use of water, inside and out, to reduce potable water consumption[280].

Review a portfolio of LEED® buildings, both current and pending, along with all other recently completed buildings. Results can be used to illustrate the effectiveness of managing energy and water consumption, waste disposal and inefficient building infrastructure.
- Identify the intent, requirements, and strategies for success with Water Efficiency and Energy and Atmosphere sustainable features.
- Recognize ways to reduce water use inside and outside the building and implement water metering to support improved water management.
- Recognize how the holistic approach of addressing the reduction of energy use, energy efficient design strategies, and renewable energy sources are reflected in the specific sustainable pathway for each project.
- Recognize synergies between multiple sustainable categories in the LEED® program.

Materials and Resources: This is a main credit category. Materials & resources credits encourage using sustainable building materials and reducing waste[281].

Originally, the LEED® 2009 program were based on single attributes of materials, such as recycled content. The Materials & Resources section of LEED® v4 is different in that it applies lifecycle thinking at the whole-building and product level. The LEED® v4 approach presents a more complete picture of materials and products, enabling project teams to make more informed decisions that will have greater overall benefit for the environmental, human health, and communities[282].
- Identify the intent, requirements, and strategies for success with Materials and Resources features
- Recognize how LEED® goals for product transparency and optimization are reflected in program requirements
- Recognize how the program requirements support a life-cycle approach to building material selection
- Recognize synergies between multiple program categories

Indoor Environmental Quality: Also a main credit category, Indoor environmental quality features promote better indoor air quality and access to daylight and views.

Explore the LEED® Indoor Environmental Quality credits, which address key factors such as indoor air quality, lighting, acoustics, and the occupant experience to promote happier and healthier building occupants.
- Identify the intent, requirements, and strategies for success with Indoor Environmental Quality features
- Recognize how credits address issues related to improving indoor air quality by reducing sources of contaminants
- Recognize how features in this category focus on the quality of spaces and human behavior and experiences
- Recognize synergies between multiple sustainable features in this category

Innovation: This is one of two additional bonus categories. Innovation in design or innovation in operational features that address sustainable building expertise as well as design measures not covered under the five LEED® program. Six bonus points are available in this category.

Innovation and having a LEED® accredited professional on the team to address or purpose new ideas potentially be credited for use or involvement in the new building. Various application of efficient energy, lighting, facilities and optimization of power.

Regional Priority: This is the second of two additional bonus categories. Regional priority credits address regional environmental priorities for buildings in different geographic regions. Four bonus points are available in this category[283].

(NOTE: For updated information or further research, please go to LEED http://www.usgbc.org/LEED/.)

IT Opportunities in Data Centers
IT Operation strategies need to cross functional areas and collaborate with multi-level organizations to ensure elimination of energy waste.
- Turn off the lights when the center is unoccupied. This can be accomplished by having a contractor install vacancy sensor light switches and by encouraging good occupant behavior. This strategy reduces lighting and cooling loads.
- Develop relationships between IT and facilities staff by conducting regular meetings for employees to review the data center's energy performance and adjust operations to maximize energy savings.

- Building owners, data center managers, and IT staff should make energy consumption a part of total cost of ownership analysis to justify changing data center operations or procuring new IT equipment[284].
-
- There are specific opportunities, for every data center, that is based on the use, configuration or otherwise management of servers to support your end-user community. These are areas of performance and efficiency. Let us take the discussion to data storage, consolidation, decommissioning old or unused servers and virtualization. The benefits of Energy Star for Data Centers are many, including:
- Data Center Specific: Unlike LEED®, this is focused on data centers.
- Free! There is no out-of-pocket hard cost to certify or renew your Energy Star for Data Centers designation.
- Energy Efficiency Focused: Focuses on energy efficiency related items that have a high return on investment for owners, operators and end-users.
- Lower Operational Costs: Energy Star buildings typically use 35% less energy and cost $0.50 per square foot less to operate than their comparison buildings according to the EPA.
- Validation of Building Performance: A top tier PUE will result in operational savings through reduced energy use.
- Higher Revenue: Evidence suggests that higher lease rates can be charged and higher occupancy rates are common – as is similar to LEED®.
- Marketing/Branding: The Energy Star program is widely recognized. Perhaps not to the same extend in the building community as LEED®, but it still carries great value[285].

Server Virtualization: Until fairly recently, data center operators typically installed at least one physical server per application. Server virtualization offers a way to consolidate servers by allowing you to run multiple different workloads on one physical host server. Virtualization improves scalability, reduces downtime, and enables faster deployments. In addition, it speeds up disaster recovery efforts because virtual servers can restart applications much more rapidly than physical servers.

Decommissioning of Unused Servers: Surveys of data centers often identify aged servers with no use still running–so–called "comatose" servers. Estimates of the prevalence of comatose servers vary:
- Surveys have found that 8 to 10% of servers with no use are still running -- 150 of 1800 in one study; 354 of 3500 in another[286].
- According to Kenneth Brill, executive director of the Uptime Institute, "unless you have a rigorous program of removing obsolete

servers at the end of their lifecycle...is very likely that between 15% and 30% of the equipment running in your data center is co-matose. It consumes electricity without doing any computing[287]."

Consolidation of Lightly Utilized Servers: For most data centers, an assessment of all servers and their utilization rates will uncover servers that are performing single, infrequent, or limited tasks. Consolidating these servers will eliminate systems and reduce energy, hardware, and support costs. According to the Uptime Institute, decommissioning a single 1U rack server can annually save $500 in energy, $500 in operating system licenses, and $1,500 in hardware maintenance costs[288].

Better Management of Data Storage: The concept of energy efficient data storage is simple — use less storage to use less energy — and can result from the better data storage best practices available today through storage resource management tools. Examples for best practices include:
- Automated Storage Provisioning
- Data Compression
- Duplication
- Snapshots
- Thin Provisioning
- RAID (Redundant Array of Independent Disks) Level - a way of storing the identical data in different places
- Tiering Storage

Purchasing More Energy-Efficient Servers, UPSs, and PDUs: The ENERGY STAR Server specification, effective May 15, 2009, requires servers that display the ENERGY STAR label to have:
- More efficient power supplies,
- Improved power quality, which provides building-wide efficiency benefits,
- Capabilities to measure real-time power use, processor utilization, and air temperature,
- Advanced power management features, and
- Data sheet for purchasers that standardizes key information on energy performance, features and other capabilities[289].

Airflow Management Strategies: Conventional IT equipment and data center spaces can consume more than 100 times the energy of standard office spaces. So energy conservation and elimination of that waste has huge potential for energy savings. Some IT strategies do not have measurable savings, such as Airflow Management. But the proof is in implemented procedures as "best practices" in many IT equipment and data center spaces.

- Conventional Airflow Management - Hot air from server racks freely mixes with cold supply air.
- Best Practices Airflow Management - An airtight envelope prevents supply and exhaust air from mixing and allows for waste heat recovery.

Hot Aisle/Cold Aisle Layout: Hot aisle/cold aisle arrangements lower cooling costs by better managing airflow, thereby accommodating lower fan speeds and increasing the use of air-side or water-side economizers. When used in combination with containment, DOE estimates reduction in fan energy use of 20% to 25[290]%.

Containment/Enclosures: Containment structures lead to higher allowable temperatures in data centers. Higher temperatures save energy because fan speeds can be lowered, chilled water temperatures can be raised, and free cooling can be utilized more often[291].

Variable Speed Fan Drives: CRAC (computer room air conditioning) unit fans consume a lot of power and tend to account for 5% to 10% of a data center's total energy use[292]. A reduction of 10% in fan speed reduces that fan's use of electricity by approximately 25%. A 20% speed reduction yields electrical savings of roughly 45%[293].

Properly Deployed Airflow Management Devices: All airflow management strategies strive to either maximize cooling by supplying cooling ("supply") air directly to equipment, or by eliminating the mixing and recirculation of hot equipment exhaust air.
A long–term monitoring study of 19 data centers by the Uptime Institute concluded that only 60% of the cool air being pumped into the data center was cooling equipment. It also found that 10% of the data centers had hot spots[294].

HVAC Equipment: Before purchasing HVAC equipment you should determine whether your climate zone is appropriate for free or evaporative cooling. To see how much energy savings can be achieved in your location through airside economizing, direct evaporative cooling, and indirect evaporative cooling, refer to Metzger et al. (2011[295]).

Server Inlet Temperature and Humidity Adjustments: A typical data center uses a great deal of energy maintaining humidity through multiple CRAC units. Each CRAC unit has the ability to humidify, de-humidify, heat and cool. When humidity gets too low, a typical CRAC unit will raise the humidity by using inefficient infrared or steam canister humidifiers[296].

Air-Side Economizer: An air-side economizer brings outside air into a building and distributes it to the servers. Instead of being re-circulated and cooled, the exhaust air from the servers is simply directed outside[297].

Water-Side Economizer: For data centers with water or air-cooled chilled water plants, a water-side economizer uses the evaporative cooling capacity of a cooling tower to produce chilled water and can be used instead of the chiller during the winter months.[298]

(NOTE: For updated information or further research, please go to Department of Energy
- http://www.doe.gov/ or for Energy Star - http://www.energystar.gov/.)

Creating Onsite Energy Alternatives

A key link in the Sustainability value chain is the use of energy in transportation. Inbound logistics, outbound logistics, inter company transportation, import/export services, air freight and ocean freight are a few examples of tremendous use of energy. Disregarding the criticisms of carbon fuels, demand for energy will outstrip all energy sources in the next 40 years. The reality is that alternative energy supplies must be created and consideration for all types of energy sources must be analyzed on a cost-benefit basis.

Maria van der Hoeven, executive director of the International Energy Agency, said; "Energy efficiency is what we have termed the hidden fuel, and it is a key component in our efforts to achieve energy security, energy affordability, and environmental sustainability." ... Policies that boost the energy efficiency of urban transport systems could help save as much as US$70 trillion in spending on vehicles, fuel and transportation infrastructure between now and 2050[299].

Look at Apple's plans: Using fuel cells at this scale potentially changes how data center operators use grid power and traditional back up diesel generators. With Apple's combination of its solar power and fuel cells, it appears the facility will be able to produce more than the 20 megawatts it needs at full steam. That means Apple could sell power back to the utility or even operate independently and use the grid as back up power—a completely new configuration[300].

Apple hasn't disclose how much it's paying for all this, but the utility commission filing indicates it plans to monetize its choice of biogas, rather than natural gas. The documents show that Apple is contracting with a separate company to procure biogas, or methane that is given off from landfills. Because it's a renewable source, Apple can receive compensation for renewable energy credits[301].

Data center efficiency is a strategic issue: Building and operating these centers consumes growing portions of corporate IT budgets, leaving less available for high-priority technology projects. Data center build programs are board-level decisions. At the same time, regulators and external stakeholders are taking keen interest in how companies manage their carbon footprints[302].

For data centers that use on-site renewable energy to offset their energy use, reducing data center loads can reduce capital costs. For example, operators in the National Renewable Energy Laboratory's (NREL) new data center were tasked with meeting computing needs as efficiently as possible to reduce the costs for the photovoltaics (PV) required to offset energy use. NREL saved about $2.2 million in PV costs by reducing data center loads and more than $1.5 million in PV costs by reducing workstation loads[303].

The demand for energy will continue to grow and to meet that need will require expansion of energy options. Commercial needs, urban transportation, product distribution and other infrastructure needs will place a tremendous pressure on stressed energy framework. Businesses and governments alike regardless of size, will build decentralized energy facilities to augment future utility networks. Energy generation could very well originate from the following sources in the near future:

Biomass energy: Many different kinds of biomass, such as wood chips, corn, and some types of garbage, are used to produce electricity. Some types of biomass can be converted into liquid fuels called biofuels that can power cars, trucks, and tractors. Leftover food products like vegetable oils and animal fats can create biodiesel, while corn, sugarcane, and other plants can be fermented to produce ethanol[304].

Fuel cell: Fuel cells and solid oxide fuel cells (SOFCs) are devices that convert fuel into electricity through a clean electro-chemical process rather than dirty combustion. They are like batteries except that they always run. For example: Each Bloom Energy Server provides 200kW of power, enough to meet the baseload needs of 160 average homes or an office building ... day and night, in roughly the footprint of a standard parking space. For more power simply add more energy servers[305].

Geo-thermal energy: Tapping into underground temperatures to heat and cool a building is another source of energy commonly available around the world. The United States has more geothermal capacity than any other country, producing more than 3,000 megawatts in eight states. Eighty percent of this capacity is in California, where more than 40 geothermal plants provide nearly 5 percent of the state's electricity[306].

Ocean and tidal energy: Tremendous amounts of energy can be extracted from the tides and ocean currents around the world. Like wind generation, it is limited to the type of energy source, which would primarily be coastal applications. This technology is considered to be in its infancy and no specific technology has yet emerged as the best means to produce the energy. However, the European Marine Energy Centre recognizes six principal types of tidal energy converters. They are horizontal axis turbines, vertical axis turbines, oscillating hydrofoils, venturi (devices that measure flow rates) devices, Archimedes screw and tidal kite[307].

Photovoltaic energy: Solar photovoltaics is a sustainable energy source. By end of 2012, the 100 GW installed capacity milestone was achieved[308]. Solar photovoltaics is now the third most important renewable energy source in terms of globally installed capacity. Crystalline silicon solar cell prices have fallen from $76.67/Watt in 1977 to an estimated $0.74/Watt in 2013. … This is seen as evidence supporting Swanson's law stating that solar cell prices fall 20% for every doubling of industry capacity[309]. This is an industry that thrives on competition.

Wind energy: The Great Plains states, in the center of the U.S., and key areas of the Atlantic and Pacific coasts are "sweet spots" for generating electricity from wind generation turbines. Wind power is the second largest produced sustainable energy source. In addition to current wind farms, new construction trends incorporate wind turbines on top of high rise buildings, water towers and other roof top placements that can access wind movement.

Supply Chain Efficiencies
To realize opportunities for improvement in the Supply Chain, energy must be managed across organizations, industry sectors, supply chains and regions, which will require significant new and increasingly more transparent data, common metrics and analytics.
- Engage leading companies to identify high-quality suppliers for pilot supply chain energy efficiency improvements.
- Create one or more sector-based collaborations for improving supply chain energy efficiency by assembling groups of peer manufacturers within a supply chain and using benchmarking, process capability analysis and best practice sharing to identify and improve energy efficiency and industry competitiveness.
- Increase transparency and standardization of energy use, audits and supply chain information.

- Create finance and credit risk approaches and models for portfolio-level energy efficiency and energy management projects[310].

Fleet Efficiency: Many corporations have automobile, truck or a combination of fleets in service for their company needs. Costs associated with the vehicles are often a point of analysis and discussion, especially in context to the total cost of ownership and the impact of those assets in a Sustainability setting.

In a study produced by UPS, they recognized the importance of reducing inefficiencies and wastes in their supply chain. The linkage between energy usage and carbon footprint are common sense relationships. This is their story of success:
- Fuel represents about 5 to 6 percent of their costs.
- Anytime they reduce fuel usage, they reduce costs.
- Anytime they make our global supply chain more efficient, we reduce costs.
- In the process, they reduce carbon emissions.
- This is relevant to anyone whose company ships goods.
- An efficient supply chain is a more sustainable supply chain, especially in these days when goods are as likely to come from across the world as across the street[311].

Yet grandiose plans (e.g. Pickens Plan) for applied methods of improving fuel efficiency exists, which in turn, reduces carbon emissions. Here are a few of statements from the Pickens Plan web site that proposes the use of natural gas to replace diesel for major transportation fuel. There are several pillars to the Pickens Plan:
- Use America's abundant natural gas to replace imported oil as a transportation fuel;
- Build a 21st century backbone electrical transmission grid;
- Develop renewable energy sources, such as wind and solar power; and,
- Provide incentives to homeowners and the owners of commercial buildings to upgrade their insulation and increase efficiency[312].

Fuel Alternatives: Many corporations are becoming more aware that energy consumption in their fleets have increased over the years. Transportation costs have increased due to cost of resources, inefficiencies, obsolescence and acknowledging the total cost of ownership. In today's environment there are many energy alternatives to consider:
- Automobile and trucks conversions in natural gas applied technology providing vehicle conversion, compression, adjustment and natural gas transport equipment.
- Bi-fuel operates with just a flip of a switch, for example use either gasoline or natural gas.

- CNG (compressed natural gas) fleets leverage the Pickens Plan to replace the existing need for diesel fuel and in turn reduce emissions.
- Dual-Fuel vehicles are designed to run on two different types of fuel, usually gasoline and a type of fuel that does not cause pollution (e.g. electric hybrid).
- New gas and diesel vehicle efficiencies have increased miles per gallon and emissions ratings.

System Supported Optimization: GPS tracking system gives your company management and logistic tools that will dramatically reduce your costs in fuel, manpower and equipment maintenance. For example, American Air Liquide provides industrial gases and related services to a variety of customers including those in large industry, industrial manufacturing, electronics and healthcare marketplaces. Using biomimicry, scientist discovered that ants use an efficient algorithm to find the most direct route to forage food that uses the least amount of energy. Air Liquide applied that knowledge and discovered that trillions of mathematical outcomes of distribution routes exist across the U.S. However, further analysis determined they could simplify and optimized a route that would not duplicate or intersect previous paths and efficiently service their entire customer community.

Reduce, Reuse, Recycle

Where do you find these areas of waste? Again, look in your supply chain. Read what Walmart accomplished. Examining records can provide insight into your organization's waste generation and removal patterns. Look for areas of CO_2 by-products, as well. Manufacturing products produces an average 4-8 pounds of CO_2 for every pound of manufactured product. The types of records you might find useful include:
- Purchasing, inventory, maintenance, and operating logs.
- Supply, equipment, and raw material invoices.
- Waste hauling and disposal records and contracts.
- Contracts with recycling facilities and earned revenues from recycling[313].

Here are suggested areas for gathering information, investigation and elimination of waste:
- Some of following examples were taken from the Walmart website to illustrate how a targeting areas of waste, then extracting that waste from your system is a methodical process, often support by Lean and Six Sigma, but always by Sustainability objectives established to reduce their corporate footprint[314].
- Remember that Walmart had an aspirational objective "to create zero waste". That was the lofty desire of the corporation and what

translated were the results from three specific areas: reduce, reuse and recycle. Walmart focus on the three "R's" when thinking about your waste – reduce, reuse and recycle.
- In other cases, examples or issue areas are inserted in the reduce, reuse, recycle model.

Reduce: Where do you find by-product waste? Reduce, reuse, recycle are fundamental saving blocks, usually found on the first rung of change, for protecting the environment. Most key managers, especially IT managers, must master the understanding applying sustainability improvement and efficiency (LSS).

Plastic Bag Initiative: In 2008, we committed to reduce the plastic shopping bag waste at our stores around the world by an average of 33 percent per store by 2013 using a 2007 baseline. If we achieve this goal, we:
- could reduce our plastic bag waste by the equivalent of 9 billion bags,
- avoid producing 290,000 metric tons of greenhouse gases,
- prevent consuming the equivalent of 678,000 barrels of oil every year, and
- expect to eliminate more than 135 million pounds of plastic shopping bag waste globally[315].

Junk Mail: To help reduce each department's junk mail services like 41pounds.org can stop annoying catalogues and mail. They provide a non-profit service that contacts dozens of direct mailers to remove employees who are no longer in a company. This decreases the volume of catalogs, magazines or other advertising mail.

Reuse: Reuse also has much potential to limit environmental impact and cut costs. For example, data centers are regularly upgraded to keep pace with the latest technology and by extending this idea to surplus office equipment and items like these that may no longer be needed in current departments, but can be transferred and utilized and reused elsewhere. This concept could be extended to the community, transferred to another subsidiary, facility or local clinic (donations could be deductible, but check first with you CPA or internal accountants for compliance of tax regulations).

> *Reusable Bags:* In October 2007, we started selling reusable bags at Sam's Club and Walmart stores in the U.S. In 2008, we expanded our reusable bag selection at Walmart stores to include two bags, a black bag and blue bag, which are both made out of recycled materials and can be recycled when they wear out. We estimate over their lifetime, the bags can eliminate the use of 75 to 100 plastic shopping bags[316].

Paint Reuse Program. Reuse of different paint can be filtered and stirred together with odd lots of old paint for reuse on small projects around the office and the community, in the process, eliminating a hazardous waste that would not go to the landfill, thus eliminating a hazardous waste.

Recycle: Recyclables are items and materials bound for the waste stream that can be converted into a reusable material. Most organizations can recycle common waste such as aluminum, paper, cardboard, plastic (beverage and food containers), metal and glass. But when recycling electronic equipment, be careful to work with highly ethical, environmentally responsible recyclers – or your discarded gear might end up in a toxic dump overseas.

Walmart stores around the world are recycling millions of pounds of materials generated from the back of our stores. We're reducing the amount of waste sent to landfills and our need to use virgin materials.

Closed Loop: We are developing a closed-loop program to send some of our materials to suppliers who then use the material to make new products that return to Walmart's shelves or operations. For example:

- In 2008, 2.5 million of the tires we recycled from our Tire and Lube Express went into Majestic™ Rubber Mulch, a product sold in our stores. The product prevents tires from going to landfills and reduces the number of trees needed to make traditional mulch. This closed-loop system saves money for us, our Suppliers and our Customers.

- In 2009, we announced that fifteen Class 8 trucks would be retrofitted to run on reclaimed grease fuel made of waste brown cooking grease from Walmart stores. This partnership provides us opportunity to develop a closed loop solution for the waste cooking grease it generates in its stores and Sam's Club locations.

Super Sandwich Bale: Many recyclable trash items – such as loose plastic, plastic hangers, office paper, aluminum cans – are unruly and hard to collect for recycling, so we implemented a super sandwich bale at all of our stores and clubs in the U.S. Like a sandwich, the recyclable items are pressed between two stacks of cardboard then bundled for transportation. This process helps us recycle more than 30 commodities, including:
- loose plastic and bags,
- cardboard,
- aluminum cans,
- plastic hangers,
- plastic water and soda bottles,
- office paper, and

- paperback books amongst other items[317].

Since integrating this process into our facilities, we have redirected: 182 million pounds of plastic, 18.9 million pounds of plastic hangers, 12.4 million pounds of office paper, and 1.3 million pounds of aluminum from going to landfills[318].

Community Garden: Contribution to local community gardens can bolster brand image and help promote the benefits of recycling. Governments have created community gardens to supported neighborhood needs. The garden encourages residents to learn about permaculture and sustainable food practices, creates a sense of community, and transforms an underutilized area to one that is more vital and engaging. It also engages the community in planting and harvesting food to provide fresh, local produce for food kitchens, for charity and for sale.

Recycle Electronic Devices: Recycle your electronic devices, as much as possible. Selling or recycling surplus items, to third parties, provide another industry that harvests and sells metal from retired property. Recycle or sell your old blackberrys, PDAs, laptops, tablets or smartphones to YouRenew.com (or similar sites) and help support your clean air projects.

Waste Management
Hazardous waste is defined and regulated by the US Environmental Protection Agency (EPA) and is either a "listed" waste or meets the characteristics of a hazardous waste. Individual states may have stricter regulations than the EPA, so management requirements can vary state-to-state. The costs vary, depending on the material but common Resource Conservation and Recovery Act (RCRA) hazardous wastes include hazardous pharmaceuticals, bulk chemotherapeutic agents, mercury, xylene and other solvents, some paints, aerosol cans etc. The EPA has categorized these hazardous waste into four groups. In addition, solid wastes are common in most business:
- Listed Wastes
- Characteristic Wastes
- Universal Wastes
- Mixed Wastes
- Solid Wastes

Listed Wastes: Wastes that EPA has determined are hazardous. By definition, EPA has determined that some specific wastes are hazardous and these wastes are incorporated into lists published online. The lists include:
- F-list (wastes from common manufacturing and industrial processes) this list identifies wastes from common manufacturing and

industrial processes, such as solvents that have been used in cleaning or degreasing operations.

- K-list (wastes from specific industries) this list includes certain wastes from specific industries, such as petroleum refining or pesticide manufacturing.
- P-list and U-list (wastes from commercial chemical products) these lists include specific commercial chemical products in an unused form. Some pesticides and some pharmaceutical products become hazardous waste when discarded.

Characteristic Wastes: Wastes that do not meet any of the listings above but that exhibit ignitability, corrosivity, reactivity, or toxicity. Products exhibiting one of the four characteristics are considered a hazardous waste.

- Ignitability: Ignitable wastes can create fires under certain conditions, are spontaneously combustible, or have a flash point less than 60 °C (140 °F).
- Corrosivity: Corrosive wastes are acids or bases (pH less than or equal to 2, or greater than or equal to 12.5) that are capable of corroding metal containers, such as storage tanks, drums, and barrels.
- Reactivity: Reactive wastes are unstable under "normal" conditions. They can cause explosions, toxic fumes, gases, or vapors when heated, compressed, or mixed with water.
- Toxicity: Toxic wastes are harmful or fatal when ingested or absorbed (e.g., containing mercury, lead, etc.). When toxic wastes are land disposed, contaminated liquid may leach from the waste and pollute ground water.

Universal Waste: EPA has designated via its Universal Waste Rule that certain hazardous wastes—when sent for recycling, may be managed under a less stringent set of regulations and do not have to be counted toward total hazardous waste volumes that determine generator status. Universal waste rules were devel-oped to encourage recycling materi-al. Materials eligible to be handled as Universal Waste include:

- Batteries,
- Pesticides,
- Mercury containing equipment (e.g., thermostats),
- Bulbs (e.g., fluorescent and mercury bulbs), and in some states
- Electronic equipment such as computers also qualify for the Universal Waste designation[319].

Mixed Wastes: Waste that contains both radioactive and hazardous waste components. As a result, both treatment and regulation are complex. The RCRA and the Atomic Energy Act (AEA) regulate mixed wastes. In cases where requirements of the two acts are found to be inconsistent, the AEA takes precedence.

Solid Wastes: This waste stream is also called municipal waste, black bag, clear bag, or non-regulated medical waste. This is general trash, similar to what you would find in a hotel but with more plastics and packaging.

Water Conservation
Water security is a 21st century megaforce that pits the needs of Humanity to other needs in the environment. This includes industrial needs and usage. Although this planet has over 70 percent water surface, only less than one percent of that water can be used for human and animal consumption. Here are five examples how water can be better manage in your business:

- *By-product Contamination:* Look for instances where water and by-product contamination occurs. Columbia Paint & Coatings recovered 49,200 lbs per year of paint solids from wash water and reduced wastewater by 36,900 gallons per year based on a few Lean and environment events[320].

- *Composting:* An enterprise's Facilities Management department can institute several practices for composting. This waste stream is primarily compromised of food and landscaping waste (e.g. grass clipping, mulch, wood chips, etc). Organic material will naturally breakdown within a short time period under proper temperature and pressure conditions. Consider your community and similar partners, investigate possible composting with a local farmers, who may already convert waste into compost. Your maintenance crew can use the compost as fertilizer and weed barriers on your office grounds. These efforts remove tons of material from landfill. each year.

- *Landscaping Water Conservation Practices:* The Facilities Management department can institute several practices designed to reduce the amount of water used in landscaping. Time irrigation at night or early morning is one way. This will prevent evaporation of about two-thirds of the water. To take a step closer to environmental conditions, automate irrigation systems so that different plants will receive water based on both current weather conditions and a given plant's evapotranspiration rate.

  Where possible, use with a gray water system for plant irrigation. Domestic wastewater composed of wash water from kitchen sinks and tubs, clothes washers, and laundry tubs is called gray water (USEPA, 1989). Gray water can be used by homeowners for home gardening, lawn maintenance, landscaping, and other innovative uses[321].

- *Low-flow Fixtures:* Continuous improvement in Sustainability technologies have reduced water usage through the installation of low-flow water fixtures such as sinks, showers, toilets, and in special circumstances, waterless urinals. In many cases, these efficient appliances use approximately 30 percent less water than their conventional counterparts.

  The average American uses about 9,000 gallons of water to flush 230 gallons of waste down the toilet per year (Jensen, 1991). In new construction and building rehabilitation or remodeling there is a great potential to reduce water consumption by installing low-flush toilets[322].

- *Review Your Value Stream:* Often times, just looking into current practices to discover water misuse. A Baxter Healthcare facility in the U.S. Southeast conducted a three-day value stream mapping event focused on water use, and developed an action plan to save 170,000 gallons of water per day and $17,000 within 3 months, with little or no capital investment. With this project, the facility no longer needed to expand its wastewater treatment plant[323].

- **Water Reuse**: Some potential applications for the reuse of wastewater or reclaimed water include other industrial uses, landscape irrigation, agricultural irrigation, aesthetic uses such as fountains, and fire protection (USEPA, 1992). Factors that should be considered in an industrial water reuse program include (Brown and Caldwell, 1990):
- Identification of water reuse opportunities
- Determination of the minimum water quality needed for the given use
- Identification of wastewater sources that satisfy the water quality requirements
- Determination of how the water can be transported to the new use[324]

Think It Through
Before engaging projects and committing resources, think through what each project should be addressing. While being pragmatic, provide some flexibility until each team understand the commitment and serious nature of this transformation. Communication at milestone review gates are important, overall communication of progress through the organization, measuring results correctly and validating those assumptions; while bring-

ing in financial and internal auditors to ensure results are calculated appropriately and that accounting systems reflect those improvements. Ask yourself these ten points:

- Are you saving energy, reducing energy costs and / or moving to renewable energy sources?
- Are you reducing emissions (e.g., land, water, etc.)?
- Are you using the three R's (reduce, recycle, repurpose)?
- Are you redesigning your products to use the three R's and / or eliminating use of resources?
- Are you increasing your productivity?
- Are you increasing your Quality?
- Are your Customers more engaged and do you know what they want?
- Are your processes more efficient, especially for Customer Services?
- Are you improving your brand image?
- What are your measurable goals for Sustainability and Quality projects (e.g., increased revenue, reduced costs, increased inventory turnover, etc)?

Taking Ownership

Identifying inefficiencies in your organization, or in the case your enterprise is a supplier to outside consultant, can provide solutions that reap benefits in eliminating waste or increasing efficiency. Take Abbott who has identified areas of waste that had a global impact in waste reduction in their packaging. Accenture was another example of aligning their business practices with social needs. They provided sage advice to a client utility that reduced peak consumptions, they controlled their carbon footprint and implemented volunteer teams to apply eco-friendly business practices.

- *Abbott:* Abbott is committed to sustainability and is honored to have received recognition for our leadership in countries around the world. Our continued focus on patient needs, our changing times and the environment will guide our sustained success. ... Through recent efforts, we have reduced the amount of packaging we use and distribute to customers by 12.3 million pounds annually — the equivalent of eliminating trash generated by approximately 4,500 U.S. families each year. ~ Miles D. White, Chairman of the Board and Chief Executive Officer[325]

- *Accenture:* We believe that a company's business purpose is most powerful when it aligns with the potential for greater social impact. As we help clients achieve high performance, we strive to make a measurable, sustainable difference in our communities. ... At the same time, our efforts to ensure sustainable growth span our entire operations, from internal operations to the services we provide our clients to how we engage with our employees and suppliers. In the last year:

- Our disclosure score on the Carbon Disclosure Project's Global 500 remained at 93 out of a possible 100.

- We helped Baltimore Gas and Electric implement a smart meter network for its 1.2 million customers, aimed at reducing peak electricity demand, increasing customer service and enhancing operational performance.

- Our employee volunteers on Eco Teams across our U.S. offices implemented eco-efficient office practices. ~ Jorge Benitez, Chief Executive, United States and Senior Managing Director, North America[326]

What Did W. Edwards Think?

W. Edwards Deming (October 14, 1900 – December 20, 1993) was an eminent scholar and teacher in American academia for more than half a century. He was a key thought leader and consulted with almost all of Japan's industries after World War II to resurrect their industries. He was also often referred to as the Father of Quality Management. The impact of his revolutionary ideas has been compared to those of Copernicus, Darwin and Freud[327]. Deming was quoted to say; "The result of long-term relationships is better and better quality, and lower and lower costs."

"A man who carries a cat by the tail learns something he can learn in no other way" ~Mark Twain

11. Transformation's Four Phases[328]

"Process change has become embedded in individual functions and business units, and they have seen the benefits to their bottom lines. So they come to IT because they want to know what other parts of the company have done. We've gone from being the engineers of new processes to being the movers of innovation across the company."
~ Lee Scott, former CEO of Walmart

"Much more remains to be done to help companies turn Sustainability goals into action," said Georg Kell, Executive Director of the UN Global Compact. "CEOs clearly see the need to instill Sustainability at all levels and roles within organizations, and this unprecedented level of data and analysis will enable us to help them on their journey to truly embedded long-term Sustainability."

Business Transformation, when designed as an Opportunity, is the alignment of Business Strategies, Objectives and Requirements that orchestrate your enterprise resources (i.e., Customers, Operations, Financial, IT, Suppliers, etc.). The desired change is directed by unique Roadmaps and is measured by metrics for Growth, Performance and Savings.

Business Transformation can be defined as the "combination of strategic, process, organizational change, and technology development focused around one clear vision, resulting in a significant change in the organization and substantial financial benefits[329]." This has been the theme in previous chapters and now we need to link the value of transformation into actions and milestones.

A 2013 survey asked executives; "What factors have led to changes in your business model? (Please choose all that apply.)"
* Customers prefer sustainable products/services - 52%
* Resource scarcity - 39%
* Competitors increasing commitment to sustainability - 38%
* Legislative/political pressure - 37%
* Owners' demand for broader value creation - 36%
* Customers are willing to pay a premium for a sustainable offering - 30[330]%

Leadership Driven
From the beginning, all of your employees should be engaged in the Transformation. This should not be presented to internal Stakeholders as a choice, for that will send a negative message that the Transformation is not important. Early in the transition, set CSR objectives, aligned them

with your existing strategic objectives and train your team to execute from a system viewpoint. Have your Executive Team work together to integrate metrics. Let these key managers take ownership for their efforts and revisit those intermediate measures every one or two years later.

- A clear Sustainability Vision is formulated and communicated to all levels of your organization. The CEO should lead this journey and be willing to share expectations, failures and celebrate achievements. Ensure Employees are informed, motivated, and actively engaged in the company's Sustainability program.

- Ensure that Ethical and legal boundaries are clearly established with all employees. In the event of a transgression a line of reporting will be channeled through the management line or appropriate special offices (e.g., Legal, Human Resources, etc.).

- Company has a genuine commitment to Sustainability by management at the highest level, with Sustainability principles present in core values and business strategies.

- Sustainability strategies are cascaded down through management and are incorporated into organizational and individual performance goals.

- Establish clear Key Performance Indicators (KPIs) for Sustainability that are fully integrated into the business processes, corporate performance, and employee recognition.

- Company has active dialog with key stakeholders on Sustainability issues, including customer to understand how Sustainability issues relate to different market segments.

- Product stewardship is integrated into the development process, with production and procurement decision-making supporting more sustainable choices.

- A Supply Chain Management strategy that aligns company and supplier performance targets to deliver a sustainable supply and stimulate product innovation.

- Business risks and opportunities associated with sustainable development are well understood and communicated to key stakeholders, especially investors.

- Defined strategies to ensure business Sustainability initiatives add value both to the company and community and to the business.

- Transparent reporting on Sustainability concepts and sensitive issues, with both positive and negative results.

- Verify results through internal SMEs (finance / auditing) or through external services or professionals (CPAs, Auditors).

CEO: The industry analysis shows that some sectors may be ahead of the pack when it comes to integrating Sustainability into core business. For example, 80% of utilities CEOs report their company has embedded metrics to track Sustainability performance, ahead of the cross-industry average of 64 percent. Similarly, 83 % of CEOs in the energy sector, and 81 % of those in infrastructure say their company measures both positive and negative impacts of their activities on Sustainability outcomes, a finding which suggests Sustainability performance management capabilities are beginning to take root in leading industries[331].

"Insights from the study have helped us to understand the executive business lens for Sustainability across industries," said Peter Lacy, Managing Director, Accenture Sustainability Services for Europe, Middle East, Africa and Latin America and the overall study lead. "Most importantly, we heard from a growing number of CEOs that Sustainability is becoming part of their innovation and growth agenda. That may not be new for certain well-known companies, but it marks a significant departure to see this more widespread across industries. There are many challenges ahead--and legitimate questions about scale and real impact--but we're starting to see signs of high performing businesses aligning Sustainability with the top line[332]."

Nevertheless, performance gaps remain between CEOs' ambition and execution: 95% of automotive executives, for example, believe that companies should invest in enhanced training of managers to integrate Sustainability into strategy and operations, but just 52 % report that their company already does so[333].

CFO: "Costs, gains, opportunities, retention and risks." That's how to speak the language of the CFO when you're talking about Sustainability. In fact, I would like to lay out five reasons that CFOs should care about Sustainability. They are:
- You can cut costs and enhance efficiency.
- You can mitigate risks.
- You can open up new competitive and revenue opportunities.
- You can drive innovation.
- And you can improve employee development and retention[334].

Sustainable Development is rooted in doing more with fewer resources. This implies Sustainability will be wasting less and making responsible decisions about how to operate a company. As Peter Drucker used to say; "What's measured improves." A quarterly update of tangible benefits should include, at least, report the impact to your Value Chain and reflect your Sustainability efforts:

Value Chain	Sustainability
Customer satisfaction	Carbon emissions
Customer cycle time	Energy usage
Employee retention	Safety data
Innovation (Product, Processes, Services)	Wastes generated
Material costs	Wastes eliminated
Material cycle time	Water usage

*

Champion: In addition to executive management playing a critical role in the success of a company, business Sustainability requires leadership across the entire organization. This is a catalyst position that interfaces with the teams, is a leadership position in your Executive Team, and provides facilitation between enterprise organizations to dislodge existing and potential roadblocks. While Executive management may ultimately carry the responsibility of Sustainable business results, employees have a major part to play in the definition and implementation of the company's business Sustainability programs. The key role for the employees is based on their ownership and engagement. Whether led by a member of the Executive Team, a Champion, or led by a Steering Committee and Project Management Office, your Sustainability initiative has many teams and key roles for individuals seeking to become leaders:

*   Supply Chain Professionals: a key in-bound interface which can reduce your carbon footprint, implement new sources of supplies or work with current suppliers to incorporate Sustainability concepts that improve operations.

*   Sales and Marketing Professionals: a key out-bound interface which represents the brand image and quality of the company's sustainable developed products, services and corporate action.

*   Health and Safety Professionals: a key internal interface, often based on compliance and insurance requirements, which functions as one the internal business Sustainability voices of the company.

- Human Resource Professionals: a key employee and community interface that plays a key role in employing, training and acclimating new Human Resources into the organization.

- Environmental Legal Professional: a key external interface, often based on environmental compliance regulations for federal and state EPA and other regulatory agencies.

- Facilities Professional: a key internal interface, often responsible for implementing various systems (e.g., heating, cooling, energy conservation, waste disposal, etc.) throughout the enterprise.

- Operation Professional: a key internal interface, often responsible for day-to-day operation of goods and warehousing which plays a key role in energy consumption (production energy consumption, logistics, fleet operations, warehousing transfers, etc.)

- IT Professional: a key internal interface, responsible for enterprise-wide system support and is a key energy consumption area (servers, PCs, internets and internet capabilities, networks and backup systems, etc).

Incorporate Trends from the Beginning: Sustainability and understanding its impact is still evolving. Currently, growing trends are addressing those new ideas to Corporate Sustainability.

- What is measured and reported will change. That is why Sustainability reporting is growing, but the tools are still developing. From the beginning, actively pursue a Sustainability and reporting system that exemplifies the same Transparency and rigor as used in the system for financial reporting[335].

- The CFO's role in Sustainability is key to the initiative. Remember, they are responsible for signing fiduciary reports along with the CEO. Gain their respect and engage CFOs in Sustainability efforts, such as choosing appropriate tools to measure, monitor and report on environmental and Sustainability issues in a way that can measure progress, create value and enhance investor confidence. Additionally, encourage them to embed the Sustainability strategy into the core strategy of the business[336].

- Recognize that employees are key stakeholders and a vital source of Sustainability engagement and ideas to enhance the company's Sustainability journey. Employees emerge as a key stakeholder group for Sustainability programs. Employee involvement is needed to embed Sustainability into the corporate culture[337].

- Despite regulatory uncertainty, greenhouse gas reporting remains strong, along with growing interest in water. Understand that greenhouse gas disclosure has value outside of the regulatory arena due to its utility for stakeholders, investors, customers and suppliers. Independent verification of GHG emissions is important, not only for accuracy but also for its usefulness by both internal and external stakeholders[338].

- Awareness is on the rise regarding the scarcity of business resources. Assess the availability and reliability of strategic business materials and resources from a Sustainability perspective. Develop a risk management plan addressing contingencies for disruptions in access to key resources, and integrate risk assessments and plans in Sustainability reporting[339].

- Rankings and ratings matter to company executives. Understand the value of Sustainability reporting to ranking and ratings organizations, particularly those of interest to investors. Consider third-party assurance in order to enhance the value of such reporting by shareholders and others[340].

Some of the trends are based on Executives roles and participation, training and employees, your culture, other stakeholders, Transparency and reporting, but most significantly; that your competitors are becoming more aggressive assured by their implementation of Sustainability. Industries vary in embracing new concepts and Sustainability is no exception. Some companies may be far behind; while others may not.

Transformation Paradigm

Corporate Social Responsibility, CSR, is a company's obligation to be accountable to all of its stakeholders in all its operations and activities (including financial stakeholders as well as suppliers, customers, and employees) with the aim of achieving sustainable development not only in the economic dimension but also in the social and environmental dimensions. Developing and enacting a broad strategy to manage energy and resources and drive process innovation involves several steps. Control and visibility of your Transformation is important for both Sustainability and Quality initiatives. The Transformation Paradigm is designed to address four key areas:

- ***Decision 1: Executive Commitment*** is a driver of the process. What is your Vision and how did you define it?
- ***Decision 2: Meta Planning*** is the portfolio of projects, their priority, assessed potential for savings, actual benefits and status.

- *Decision 3: Transformation* is the intervention of trained LSS teams to resolve identified problems and improve the performance of processes, both internally and externally.
- *Decision 4: Realization* is the verification of assessed and remediated projects. These are completed by financial or audit professionals in your organizations and can be reevaluate by eternal auditors and third party companies. Their purpose is to validate that reported gains in each project actually produce verifiable tangible benefits.

Executive Commitment

Executive commitment is focused long-term strategies addressing Customers' needs and Satisfaction of those needs through Sustainability and Quality. This commitment is based on a vision for products, processes and services and how that vision can be effectively implemented in a competitive landscape.

Evaluate energy and resources use—look at current pricing, but consider volatility and availability: Collect and consolidate data from the different silos across your enterprise (direct and supply chain use, across the business units). Your teams to establish a reference point, a baseline, for measuring and monitoring the impact of your energy and resource strategy, supports external benchmarking and makes it easier to define goals that support your overall business strategy. It also shifts the focus from individual Sustainability projects to broader programs that treat energy and other resources such as water as strategic assets[341].

Management Mindset: Make it clear that change is not an option and must be a team effort, no exceptions. They will need to participate, be trained, collaborate with employees and find solutions to problems, collectively. "Change programs" fail in that they are seen as just that: "programs". Clearly understand that a rigid management style, a poorly thought out transformation process and implementation will always result in resistance, poor quality and increased costs. Management must recognize that all organizational levels will need to accept and embrace change for clear success. Transparency, honest communication, incentives and visible commitment to Quality will be your initiative linchpins[342].

Emphasize Team Leadership: Use of LSS does involve some technical skills – the ability to process and analyze data, for example. But good leadership skills are even more important. This emphasis on leadership also relates to how a company chooses people to fill Black Belt roles. Placing the most promising people in the Black Belt role is painful at first, yet it yields fast results and a rapid transformation of the organization.

Sustainability issues can be used to harvest "low hanging fruit", especially in immature organizations. Recycling, reusing and repurposing wastes are easy Lean tactics to implement and physically show the entire organization which direction your corporate Vision is taking.

Managers will never fully support Six Sigma if they view it as taking away from their resources rather than adding capability and helping them become more successful in achieving their goals; nor will they actively support it if they think it is eating up vital budgetary allotments rather than setting the stage for significant financial payback. To avoid such pitfalls, a company must involve all key business leaders in helping to design its Six Sigma deployment. By giving them a voice in project selection, priorities and ongoing monitoring, an organization can be assured of their commitment to the effort[343].

Empower and Support Transformation: Senior leadership should provide access to tools to guide your organization with Sustainability Transformation. The Toolbox approach is intended to be an interactive, dynamic resource that enables departments to understand, as well as, to utilize the "tools" in the Toolbox. How leadership can help is to provide goals and expectations, but includes provision and report standards to all departments. This includes easy access to a comprehensive set of resources and tools. A conscious workplace and clear application of zero-waste goals will be the drivers for change, eliminating waste and discovering opportunities.

Sustainability Center: Serve as a catalyst for empowering people and mobilizing ideas. Use your Sustainability Centre for resources, tools and organizations to help encourage sustainable practices, locally and globally. For individuals who wish to take the lead in helping to build Sustainability into their organizations. Your Sustainability Centre should provide in-depth professional development courses for Sustainability, Quality, construction and courses on green building and the   LEED® certification system.

Sustainability Goals: All employees should have a clear understanding of their role in applying Sustainability and Quality. They should also understand that if they are actively involved, day to day, in making these practices work; then consequences that impact those goals will be create. Clearly communicate the strategies and objectives of the corporation and link the policies and goals that filter through the organization to improve the enterprise.
* Leadership needs to communicate the Vision, Mission, Strategies, Objectives and Goals for Sustainability and Quality to everyone
* Specific policies and goals to protect biodiversity, water quality, benign greenhouse-gas emissions and energy use

- Specific policies and goals concerning improvement of corporate values, people, processes, products and innovation
- Specific policies and goals to encourage employee use of tele-commuting / teleconferencing to reduce GHGs

Sustainability Provisioning: This should include provision elements in your organization that can ensure that certified and approved channels for business and government needs are expedited for day-to-day use. This would include: Sustainable Business Practices group, Procurement / Purchasing, Facilities Management, Surplus Property, and many other departments to create an even more comprehensive and cohesive database of sustainability practices.

Sustainability Reports: Today, interactive web tools are available to enable users to examine real-time energy and water use; by individual building, building type, or the entire office complex. There are now third party companies interested in obtaining this information for research. Web sites also perform another duty; extended string of new information and practices that increases Sustainability, save costs and leverage "lessons learned" from other departments or projects. Web tools provide interactive visibility enabling users to examine real-time energy and water use by individual building, building type, or your entire facilities.

Sustainability Training: Knowledge is important and your business transformation is no different. New policies, new methods, new vocabulary, new ways to do work and better serve your Customers are all critical. Training addresses the much needed education and knowledge transfer. This fills the gaps in each individual and helps expand understanding in your growing culture. Those corporate values that leadership wants to be embraced will affect organization behavior and link goals clearly. Training should include:
- Training programs to shift employees from manual labor into skilled positions
- Training programs that educate why Sustainability is important to them and their organization
- Training programs that educate why Quality is important to them and their organization

Sustainability DIY Toolbox: Create your own Sustainability Toolbox as an online collection of strategies, policies, procedures, tools (spreadsheets, databases, etc.) and other resources for Companies and Governments departments interested in sponsoring "green" teams and hosting sustainable events. Standardize the "look and feel" of your themes that be used in demonstrations, presentations or displays so they will reflect your brand image properly. Engage your employees and ask for their help in building the tools, especially if those tools can analyze cost savings, productivity and analysis on emissions.

Beginning of tools are available through the US EPA web site:
- EPA Lean Manufacturing and Environment Website (www.epa.gov/lean) provides Lean and environment case studies resources
- The Lean and Environment Toolkit (www.epa.gov/lean/toolkit) describes practical strategies and tools for integrating environmental aspects into common Lean methods
- The Lean and Energy Toolkit (www.epa.gov/lean/energytoolkit) outlines how to use Lean methods to reduce energy use, energy costs, and associated greenhouse gas emissions
- Lean Manufacturing and the Environment Report (www.epa.gov/lean/leanreport.pdf) describes the relationship of Lean manufacturing to environmental performance and the environmental regulatory framework

Meta Planning

Is focused on the enterprise landscape and the Sustainability and Quality vision. It is the control center for the Transformation initiative. It addresses business alignment, business concepts, and addresses the need for innovation of Products, Services, and Processes.

Preliminary Assessment: Identify key improvement areas and estimate the benefits and length of time for the project. Some business operations require more resources than others. Weight your projects on criteria: Sustainability and Lean Six Sigma savings. Track and analyze data across the facilities and processes to compare apples to apples. Then you can identify and prioritize areas with the most potential for improvement and return on investment. Not all Sustainability initiatives are the right ones to invest in—some initiatives can create both top-line value and bottom-line savings while others may only reduce operating costs[344].

Prioritize projects based upon your company strategies: With many Sustainability projects competing for limited dollars, you need to prioritize and pay close attention to sequence and timing. For example, instead of assuming that the cost of a particular resource will rise uniformly across the entire enterprise, look at current and anticipated costs for individual locations. Also, consider benefits beyond the bottom line, such as increasing your brand value[345].

Develop a collaborative project selection based on potential value: The most effective Lean Six Sigma companies have a rigorous project selection process driven by an evaluation of how much shareholder value a project can generate. It can be characterized as a trade-off decision comparing value delivered to effort expended. The most effective Six Sigma companies have a rigorous project selection process driven by an evaluation of how much shareholder value a project can generate. It can be characterized as a trade-off decision comparing value delivered to effort expended[346].

Critical mass of projects and resources: Some companies start their deployments by training a handful of people and launching a few "pilot" projects. Some companies engage one locality after another, in a satellite approach to transformation. Meanwhile, others often ramp-up for immediate corporate-wide deployment, training hundreds of Black Belts and launching dozens of projects within the first six months. In any case, your decision in approach is workable, but for every company there is a critical choice of LSS and interleaving Sustainability principles and efforts: Above that level, excitement and momentum build into a sustainable advantage and tangible benefits.

Projects-in-Process: The pursuit of cost savings can hamper results. Most companies want to generate measurable, significant results within six months or a year, the tendency is to push as many projects into Sustainability and LSS deployment as possible. But one of the most important lessons that Lean principles teach is that pushing excess work into a process slows down the process and dramatically increases lead times (avoid wasting time and "bottle necks"). Combining other projects that are only Sustainability and other that are combination of Sustainability and LSS, this "traffic jam needs to be monitor and understanding projects-in progress.

Be aware of your resources. With the right resources working on the right projects, learning and results are maximized by short cycle times (typically 6-8 weeks for Lean projects). Avoid poor decisions under time constraints (this is not a "beat the clock" approach) and instill in your team members, "do it right the first time". An example cited when a business 'rammed' certain functions with little regard to the overall business (i.e. they had changed one part of the process and not considered the impact up or downstream). In short, do not panic and do not make your LSS team make quick wins or to declare victory too soon. This decision led to process disconnects and poor quality that also required additional rework.

Transformation
Is accomplished through integrated solutions based on LSS methodology. Those components include Quality Strategies, Process Transformation, Quality Evaluation, and Learning Transformation throughout the Business Transformation initiative. Management must recognize that Business

Transformation will affect the corporate culture, begin accumulating information on corporate effectiveness, and provide a mind-set that sets expectations for management and employees alike.

Measure key performance indicators, results vs. target. Use baseline data and your investment plan as reference points to verify that you are getting the results you expect. Make sure employees understand how their behavior affects their use of a particular resource and what they can do to help implement and sustain improvements. Aggressively scale the most effective improvements across the enterprise in order to increase return on investment[347].

Avoid Complexity: When implementing a business transformation initiative, avoid complexity and choose an approach that is suited for your business. Ensure that your method methodology is a "cookie-cutter" approach that encourages replication and ease of transition. Do not layer the complexity of your transformation by piling methodology upon methodology, program upon program. One example of an organization that included Six Sigma, Balanced Scorecard and IIP methodology all at the same time. The results were dismal[348].

Emphasize team leadership skills: Use of Sustainability and LSS does involve some technical skills – the ability to process and analyze data, for example. But good leadership skills are even more important. This emphasis on leadership also relates to how a company chooses people to fill Black Belt roles. Placing the most promising people in the Black Belt role is painful at first, yet it yields fast results and a rapid transformation of the organization[349].

Transformation Supports your Business Strategy: Sustainability and LSS techniques are powerful in reducing process variation. So what does reduced variation in your process imply? First, measuring for variation will provide control over what your process is designed for. Second, in a manufacturing environment, production processes that can reduce variation, will produce a higher quality product at reduced cost levels. Another example, in a service process, variation could impact the delivery of a product or service to a Customer, therefore impacting Customer satisfaction. Today, an increasing number of companies are also implementing LSS approaches to business excellence as part of the business strategy[350].

Transformation supports and facilitates Business Objectives: Senior management must be clear about the reasons for change in the overall objectives. Successful deployments are based on a sense of urgency were the company's business leaders have a clear understanding as to how to adopt strategies based on Sustainability and LSS principles. In many cases, management recognizes major business challenges or risks that the company can overcome only through LSS. Those challenges could be a need to regain market competitiveness, introduce new products or services, attract new Customers, retain existing Customers or simply improve profitability[351].

Realization
Is the phase that recognizes the tracking of efforts and translating those efforts into tangible benefits for the Corporation that are verified by your internal Auditing group. This is done through the institutionalization of best practices; the periodic review of Products, Services and Processes; the integration and application of any systematic approach to two fundamental strategies, Continuous Improvement; and the cultural integration of LSS principles and developing an environment for learning.

Track Tangible Results: Too many companies discount the necessity of having a reliable means to judge project results and impact, or they underestimate the difficulty in creating such a system. Sustainability and LSS results must be quantified so a company can appropriately evaluate their impact and make good decisions about whether resources are being used wisely. Post audits are strongly encouraged to verify the results and implementation of the principles.

Retrospective
Sustainability is not an expendable marketing campaign; rather it's a reflection of benefits established with honest strategic effort, results, and best practices. It must be a long-term commitment and transparent to all stakeholders. It must be interwoven with business strategies. It must engage with external organizations. Sustainability is about measurable transformation, internally and externally. Sustainability is more than platitudes and recycling efforts. It should be able to show financial benefits directly relating to waste reduction, conservation, improvement of internal processes and engagement with external publics (i.e., NGOs, Governments, Customers, Suppliers, etc.).

A recent survey from MIT Sloan Management Review and The Boston Consulting Group validated those assumptions. It asked; "Has sustainability caused your company to increase its collaboration with any of the following? (Please choose all that apply.)
- Customers - 40%
- Suppliers - 40%
- Governments/policy makers - 34%
- Industry associations - 32%
- Internal business units across functions - 29[352]%"

Taking Ownership

Ownership responsibility is not limited to anyone industry, but it is an opportunity for any enterprise whose leadership has chosen that route. BNSF is in the freight transportation industry and they provide transportation services for capital goods, as well as, consumer goods. They have discovered fuel efficient methods of moving these products more effectively that benefits their Customers in reducing GHGs and other emissions.

- *BNSF:* BNSF is one of North America's leading freight railroads operating on 32,500 route miles of track in 28 states and two Canadian provinces. BNSF is a top transporter of consumer goods, agricultural products, low-sulfur coal and industrial goods. BNSF works to continuously improve the safety, service, energy and environmental benefits we provide to our customers and communities. … BNSF's chief contribution to growth and sustainability is our ability to provide our customers with innovative options to ship their products more efficiently by rail. Rail is four times more fuel efficient than trucking, and in 2012, BNSF's intermodal, automotive, industrial products and agricultural products customers reduced carbon dioxide emissions by about 30 million metric tons by moving freight via rail instead of over the road. This is equivalent to reducing the annual fuel consumption and resultant greenhouse gas emissions of more than 6 million passenger vehicles. ~ Matthew K. Rose, Chairman and Chief Executive Officer[353]

What Did Ben Think?

Sustainability is a new paradigm, yet it has been in existence for over 25 years. Those Executives who embrace the concept will reap significant tangible benefits. It will take open minds to recognize that this approach views the business impact not only internally, but externally as well, within a context of shared value. Each enterprise is a change agent. Each enterprise will be more competitive using a Sustainability model, whether small, medium or large. Benjamin Franklin said; "We are all born ignorant, but one must work hard to remain stupid." In the 21st century, we cannot afford to be either ignorant nor stupid in a global economy.

Is your enterprise mired in distrust?
What are you doing to change that image?
What is your industry doing to change that situation?
If nothing is being done, then start it.

12. Realization - Audit and Validation[354]

"A corporation is a living organism; it has to continue to shed its skin. Methods have to change. Focus has to change. The sum total of those changes is transformation." ~ Andy Grove, former CEO of Intel

---

Corporations, whether small, medium or larger, are always faced with refinement and improvement of complex business systems and strategic processes. Often these key structures are intertwined, so Transformation must be controlled and managed. Transformation is controlling business change in order to reposition your organization by exploiting potential increases in Growth, Performance or Savings. In today's environment, success can be derived from applied best-in-class solutions.

Successful transformation can be implemented incrementally, based on a project's focus such as efficiency, productivity, profitability or a selected combination. In the beginning, select the "low lying fruit" that is easy to complete, build team confidence and can quickly apply the new tools and training for your entire organization.

Management of risk and its mitigation are key to any successful project. In a low reward scenario, a single project that is positioned to take advantage of technology could also be applied in order to streamline processes and provide efficiencies with little downside risks. At the operating or department level, productivity gains and financial rewards can be gained through streamlined processes and/or technology. In another scenario, co-transformations between departments can produce a synergistic effect, and again the efficiency increases rewards. Last and most significant is the strategic scenario of transformation that would encompass the whole organization providing systematic rewards and results.

One of the by-products of any audit is reusing the validated information as source for transparency to external stakeholders and shareholders. The word commonly used now is "transparency" and it is a tool for the Principles of Sustainability. The following areas should be considered as useful description of Sustainability acceptance and practices:
- Awareness: Learning how to adopt Sustainability principles to produce a corporation's awareness of resource consumption like carbon, water, and electricity in order to run their businesses in compliance with existing regulations is very important to build knowledge and understanding. Awareness promotes forward thinking that will also anticipate future issues and regulations.

- Brand Differentiation: Companies often leverage Sustainability principles to differentiate their products and services to the market. Companies often acknowledge sustainable features or components in their products and services. Build brand value through setting, keeping, and communicating Sustainability promises to all stakeholders, including customers and suppliers.

- Core Values: Corporate values, based on demonstrable ethics, forms your leadership's fundamental assessment and decision-making model. Integrity based communication, incentives, and visible commitment to Sustainability and Quality will be your linchpins to address stakeholder and shareholder requests, and a push for cost reductions through greater efficiency. Be thoughtful that your corporate culture will change and core values will be the hub for your transformation.

- Integrated Strategies: Creating an isolated, siloed Sustainability strategy will create a fiasco and potentially bring failure to your initiative. Sustainability strategies must be woven into overall corporate strategies, like quality management strategies, to reap true tangible benefits.

- New Talent: Brand image promotes adoption of Sustainability principles, which in turn, often attracts higher-quality talent that aligns to prospective personnel values, as well.

- Risk Mitigation: Open mindedness and eliminating practices of "sweeping problems under the rug" will acknowledge business risks to brand, revenue, operations and utilization of resources. Openly recognizing issues and creating mitigation plans reducing risk exposure, avoiding unnecessary costs, loss of time and potential threats to your company.

- Structured Optimization: Organizations often use this increased awareness to optimize their processes, compelled by financial benefits through cost savings, increased productivity and elimination of waste.

Sustainability Adoption

Corporate commitments to sustainability-driven management are strengthening. Enterprises overall are strengthening their commitments and a gap has emerging between Sustainability strategy leaders ("embracers") and laggards ("cautious adopters"). Embracers are implementing Sustainability driven strategies widely in their organizations and have made the business case for Sustainability. Cautious adopters, by contrast, have become engaged in Sustainability initiatives for reasons of efficiency, risk mitigation and regulatory compliance. Who are the embracers and what do they do differently to reap tangible benefits? Here are the seven most significant steps:

1. Move early – even if information is incomplete. Embracers are willing to charge ahead even in the case of ambiguity.
2. Balance broad, long-term vision with projects offering concrete, near-term "wins." Embracers have both big vision and specific positive bottom-line projects.
3. Drive sustainability top-down and bottom-up. Enlisting employees at all levels in sustainability yields many benefits.
4. Aggressively de-silo sustainability – integrating it throughout company operations. Rather than solely a position or a team, sustainability is an embedded process or a mindset.
5. Measure everything (and if ways of measuring something don't exist, start inventing them). Companies are measuring everything from the obvious – waste, energy efficiency, and water conservation – to the more nuanced – impact on brand, innovation and productivity.
6. Value intangible benefits seriously. Embracers make investment decisions based on a combination of tangible benefits, intangibles and risk scenarios.
7. Try to be authentic and transparent – internally and externally. Embracers do not overstate motives or set unrealistic expectations, and they communicate their challenges as well as their successes[355].

Realization Phase of Transformation Paradigm

Corporate Social Responsibility, CSR, is a company's obligation to be accountable to all of its stakeholders in all its operations and activities (including financial stakeholders as well as suppliers, customers, and employees) with the aim of achieving sustainable development not only in the economic dimension but also in the social and environmental dimensions. Developing and enacting a broad strategy to manage energy and resources and drive process innovation involves several steps. Control and visibility of your Transformation is important for both Sustainability and Quality initiatives.

The Transformation Paradigm is designed to address four key areas and the last validates the results of the effort each transformation team has produced. **Realization**, *the last phase*, is the verification of assessed and remediated projects. It is the phase that follows **Transformation** and is a check and balance stage that verify tangible results. These are completed by financial or audit professionals in your organizations and can be re-evaluate by eternal auditors and third party companies. Their purpose is validate that reported gains in each project actually produce verifiable tangible benefits.

Prioritize projects based upon your company strategies: With many Sustainability projects competing for limited dollars, you need to prioritize and pay close attention to sequence and timing. For example, instead of assuming that the cost of a particular resource will rise uniformly across the entire enterprise, look at current and anticipated costs for individual locations. Also, consider benefits beyond the bottom line, such as increasing your brand value[356].

Develop a collaborative project selection based on potential value: The most effective Lean Six Sigma companies have a rigorous project selection process driven by an evaluation of how much shareholder value a project can generate. It can be characterized as a trade-off decision comparing value delivered to effort expended. The most effective Six Sigma companies have a rigorous project selection process driven by an evaluation of how much shareholder value a project can generate. It can be characterized as a trade-off decision comparing value delivered to effort expended[357].

Projects-in-Process: The pursuit of cost savings can hamper results. Most companies want to generate measurable, significant results within six months or a year, the tendency is to push as many projects into Sustainability and LSS deployment as possible. But one of the most important lessons that Lean principles teach is that pushing excess work into a process slows down the process and dramatically increases lead times (avoid wasting time and "bottle necks"). Combining other projects that are only Sustainability and others that are a combination of Sustainability and LSS, creates a potential "traffic jam" that needs to be monitored and considerate of projects-in progress.

Be aware of your resources. With the right resources working on the right projects, learning and results are maximized by short cycle times (typically 6-8 weeks for Lean projects). Avoid poor decisions under time constraints (this is not a "beat the clock" approach) and instill in your team members, "do it right the first time". An example cited when a business 'rammed' certain functions with little regard to the overall business (i.e. they had changed one part of the process and not considered the impact up or downstream). In short, do not panic and do not make your LSS team make quick wins or to declare victory too soon. This type of decision will lead to process disconnects and poor quality that also require additional rework; thus loosing time, increasing manpower and costs.

Transformation Confirmation

The Realization, the last of four phases, is the validation of what was purported to have been accomplished in the Transformation phase. Sustainability strategies integrated with Quality Strategies follow the four levels of Kaplan and Norton perspectives (Financial, Customer, Internal and and Learning Transformation) create value throughout the Business Transformation initiative. Management should recognize that Business Transformation will affect the corporate culture, begin accumulating information on corporate effectiveness, and provide a mind-set that sets expectations for management and employees alike. Take results into account and assess these points:

- Definitions of Sustainability and Quality and how it affects business
- Assessment of the drivers of Sustainability and understanding opportunities
- Assessment of the drivers of Quality and understanding opportunities
- Translated analysis into action items by defining Sustainability as a business issue or risk
- Translated analysis into action items by defining Quality as a business issue or risk
- Develop a business case for your short term Sustainability and Quality efforts
- Modeled a long term business case for Sustainability investments
- Established targets for your Sustainability and Quality efforts along with metrics for visibility
- Sustainability and Quality strategy receives sufficient focus from senior management
- Sustainability and Quality strategy is integrated with your products, processes, and culture (changes to Core Assets)
- Sustainability agenda is aligned with the relevant external stakeholders
- Your company has the required capabilities and tools to execute your Sustainability and Quality strategies

Measure key performance indicators, results vs. target. Use baseline data and your investment plan as reference points to verify that you are getting the results you expect. Make sure employees understand how their behavior affects their use of a particular resource and what they can do to help implement and sustain improvements. Aggressively scale the most effective improvements across the enterprise in order to increase return on investment[358].

Audits support and facilitate Business Objectives. Communication and clarity furnished by Senior Management to all employees explain reasons for change and how it will promote business transformation to meet or exceed overall objectives. Successful deployment is not about finding and remediating "low hanging fruit" for it does not stop there. Metrics measured through your processes give a perspective, comparing successes and issues for all stakeholders. Leveraging audits provide verified information to take clear actions to problems or risks.

Resource Audit: The resource audit identifies the resources available to a business. Some of these can be owned (e.g. plant and machinery, trademarks, retail outlets) whereas other resources can be obtained through partnerships, joint ventures or simply supplier arrangements with other businesses[359].

Value Chain Analysis: Value Chain Analysis describes the activities that take place in a business and relates them to an analysis of the competitive strength of the business. Influential work by Michael Porter suggested that the activities of a business could be grouped under two headings:
- Primary Activities - those that are directly concerned with creating and delivering a product (e.g. component assembly);
- Support Activities, which whilst they are not directly involved in production, may increase effectiveness or efficiency (e.g. human resource management). It is rare for a business to undertake all primary and support activities[360].

Core Competence Analysis: Core competencies are those capabilities that are critical to a business achieving competitive advantage. So the goal is for management to focus attention on competencies that really affect competitive advantage[361].

Performance Analysis: The resource audit, value chain analysis and core competence analysis help to define the strategic capabilities of a business. After completing such analysis, questions that can be asked that evaluate the overall performance of the business include:
- How have the resources deployed in the business changed over time; this is "historical analysis"
- How do the resources and capabilities of the business compare with others in the industry - "industry norm analysis"
- How do the resources and capabilities of the business compare with "best-in-class" - wherever that is to be found / "benchmarked"
- How has the financial performance of the business changed over time and how does it compare with key competitors and the industry as a whole? - "ratio analysis[362]"

Portfolio Analysis: Portfolio Analysis analyses the overall balance of the strategic business units of a business. Most large businesses have operations in more than one market segment, and often in different geographical markets. This is important - a business should always consider which markets are most attractive and which business units have the potential to achieve advantage in the most attractive markets[363].

SWOT Analysis: SWOT is an abbreviation for Strengths, Weaknesses, Opportunities and Threats. This is an important tool to identify strategic opportunities and risks. SWOT analysis is also important tool for auditing the overall strategic position of a business and its environment[364]. Feedback during auditing provides insight and refinement of of your business planning system, Sustainability and Quality efforts.

Realization: Validating Tangibles

Realization is the phase that identifies and recognizes those efforts that produced tangible benefits for the Corporation. Your internal financial experts and internal Auditing group will verify benefits and recommend improvements. This is done through institutionalization of best practices; periodic review of new Products, Services and Processes; integration and application of any systematic approach, cultural integration of LSS principles and developing an environment for learning (e.g., lessons learned to improve Sustainability, LSS and best practices).

Track Tangible Results: A senior level finance person, Champion or Steering Committee should participate in the development of results visible through dashboards, reflecting key performance indicators of tangible financial results. At a minimum, project cycle times and project values must be measured on a regular basis and to gain an understanding of the level of variation in these numbers.

Prepare for success. A consulting report, produced by the Aberdeen group, identified a new breed of manufacturing company where management of energy and greenhouse gas (GHG) emissions is central to corporate strategy. Aberdeen's report cited a number of key business capabilities that characterize the leading companies in energy and carbon management:

- Establishment of a "formal energy and carbon program" with executive sponsorship and cross-functional support and execution
- Development of an "enterprise-wide framework" providing "a clear understanding of the organization's energy management programs"
- Establishment of "maintenance schedules and alerts" based on the real-time condition and energy efficiency of particular assets
- Adjustment of production schedules based on energy costs.

Consider using these or similar questions in the reviews your Auditors will conduct.

- Did a process owner(s) assist the project team?
- Did a resource manager(s) assist the project team?

- Did the team properly apply the definitions of savings, cost avoidance, and revenue generation?
- Did the team properly apply the definitions of emission decrease, water conservation, energy conservation or other resource reduction or waste elimination?
- Did the team properly use the MetaPlanning screen for ROM (rough order of magnitude), projected, forecasted, and final cost estimates?
- Did the team develop and maintain supporting documentation and attach it to the project in the MetaPlanning system?
- Does the supporting documentation adequately explain how the team developed the cost data?
- Did the team comply with guidance on personnel costing and inflation?
- Are the financial benefits shown in MetaPlanning reasonable and reliable? If not, what is a reasonable, reliable estimate for savings?
- Did all key stakeholders sign off on the project documentation and recommendations (e.g., deliverables illustrating details and cost savings, cost avoidance, and revenue generation)?

This level of visibility and control can only be achieved with integrated information technology that gives decision-makers the "the ability to drill down the performance of their energy and carbon programs across product line, geography and facility," Aberdeen said. Such information systems also need to provide a level of analysis that shows management the financial effects of the decisions they make and benchmark the company's performance against peers and competitors[365].

Audits validate tangible benefits. Your Auditors and other financial experts identify and verify "take-aways" or tangible benefits from projects and the enterprise initiative at large. They are looking for revenue, cost reductions, improved services, qualities in products and other more complex areas of benefit as the organization scales the rungs of the maturity ladder. The following table provides beginning points of projects for verification that can have a bottom line impact:

Sustainability	Lean	Six Sigma
Reduce, Reuse, Recycling	Over-production	Defects
Emissions (Air, Land, Water)	Inventory	Variation
Energy Conservation or Energy Aversion	Defects	Predictability
Water Conservation or Water Aversion	Transport	Complexity

Sustainability	Lean	Six Sigma
LEEDs construction	Motion	Value stream
Auto and Truck fleet efficiency	Over-processing	Inventory
IT Data Centers	Lead times	Customer service
Hazardous Wastes	Waiting	Innovation
Solid and Landfill Wastes	Rework	

Verify Results and Audit. All the big four accounting firms are expanding their practices to audit all of these disclosures and are also sponsoring the expanded fourth edition of the Global Reporting Initiative Guidelines, which outline standard CSR disclosures. In 2012 a promising new initiative, the Global Initiative for Sustainability Ratings, will endeavor to standardize the ratings framework, but beyond that there is little relief in sight for the survey-fatigued CSR manager[366].

Henry Ford was an astute industrialist who encapsulated "business truths" into succinct and often pragmatic phrases, such as; "One of the greatest discoveries a man makes, one of his great surprises, is to find he can do what he was afraid he couldn't do." Mr. Ford was ahead of his time, and would probably agree that resistance to change is one of the first hurdles to climb when introducing change to an organization. The key point is to make this change work for you and become a benefit for the company, and more importantly, provide your organization with an experience that fosters a "can do" attitude.

There are a number of benefits that can be identified and verified by your auditors. For example, the following table compares examples of Operations indices and Financial indices. Pre-planning and standardization of those metrics are important to share across your enterprise. Remember that behavior of your employees will be rewarded by those indices that are incentivized for areas of improvement.

Operational Benefits	Financial Benefits
Process Cycle Time	Savings
Percentage of end items that meet quality specifications	Cost avoidance
Customer satisfaction	Revenue generation

EATON Is A Good Example

At Eaton, we reinforce our accountability by making sustainability information and results widely available to the public. By improving our performance, and posting our data, we can serve as an example for positive change in global environmental and social conditions, while managing our own sustainable growth. Eaton partners with many organizations that collect data and provide a rating or "grade" for our annual performance.

Disclosures & Rankings
    Carbon Disclosure Project (CDP)
    The CDP is an independent, not-for-profit organization holding the largest public database of primary corporate climate change information in the world. In 2010, CDP featured Eaton as one of only 50 companies in its prestigious Leadership Index.

    CRO Magazine
    In 2012 "Corporate Responsibility Officer Magazine" named Eaton one of the nation's top 100 companies in Corporate Social Responsibility for the fifth consecutive year.

    Dow Jones Sustainability Index
    Eaton participates in the Dow Jones Sustainability Index (DJSI), one of the worlds' leading indicator's for corporate responsibility. In 2010, Eaton was one of six companies on the DJSI list of sustainable leaders in the "Diversified Industrial" sector.

    Global Reporting Initiative (GRI)
    The Global Reporting Initiative is one of the world's most widely used reporting frameworks for performance on human rights, labor, environment, anti-corruption, and corporate citizenship. More than 1,500 organizations from 60 countries use these guidelines to produce annual sustainability reports.

Annual Report & Sustainability Report - illustrate Sustainability progress, reported quarterly for:
    •   carbon emissions
    •   water and energy use
    •   wastes generated
    •   safety data

"More than a responsibility, sustainability is pivotal to the company's future success, helping us to drive the energy efficient power management solutions that customers and consumers need and the world demands." – Sandy Cutler, Eaton Chairman and CEO[367]

Taking Ownership:

Tangible results are what every CXO wants from Sustainability. Conoco-Phillips, Avery Dennison and Principal Financial Group have at least on thing in common: ownership. All of these companies, working independently and in separate industries, demonstrate where a company can change when committed to Sustainability.

- *ConocoPhillips:* ConocoPhillips was honored to be recognized in 2012 for sustainable development success. We were named one of the 100 Best Corporate Citizens by Corporate Responsibility Magazine. We also made the Dow Jones Sustainability North America Index for the sixth consecutive year. And we earned a much better environmental disclosure and performance score from the Carbon Disclosure Project. ~ Ryan M. Lance, Chairman and Chief Executive Officer[368]

- *Avery Dennison:* Whether it is a new adhesive or label material, a smarter inventory system, a leaner manufacturing process, or a philanthropic grant, sustainability is integral to our vision of making brands more inspiring and the world more intelligent. We invite you to visit www.averydennison.com to learn more. ... We are also making our own operations more sustainable. We are on track to reduce our global carbon index 15 percent from 2005 levels and to keep 85 percent of our facilities' waste out of landfills by 2015. Through reduction, recovery and recycling programs, we are targeting to divert 100 percent over the long term. Our employee safety results are among the world's best, and we are making excellent progress in ensuring worldwide compliance with our workplace and supplier standards. ~ Dean A. Scarborough, Chairman, President and Chief Executive Officer[369]

- *Principal Financial Group:* The Principal Financial Group® (The Principal®) is a global investment management leader. As part of our company's core value of integrity, we're committed to create, grow and maintain positive sustainability solutions. ... During 2012, we made significant progress in several areas, including:
  - We established formal goals to reduce our carbon footprint: 2 percent for 2012, 3 percent for 2013 and a 10 percent reduction by 2016. Our initial results show we're already well on our way — achieving a 9 percent reduction in the first year alone.
  - We saw a big improvement in our Carbon Disclosure Project score — jumping from 56 to 84.
  - We implemented a single-stream recycling program and a mandatory white paper shredding program late in 2011.

During 2012, our first full year of measurement, we reduced the amount of waste going to the landfill by about 40
percent or 600 tons.

- We made several energy management improvements that
  improved the efficiencies of our owned and occupied properties.

- We extended an agreement with our local transit authority
  that provides local bus service to all our employees at no
  cost to them.

- We completed The Principal Riverwalk — a 10-year project that allows people to enjoy the natural habitat of the
  riverfront. ~ Larry Zimpleman, Chairman, President and
  CEO[370]

What Did Ray Think?

Mr. Ray Anderson incorporated his philosophy and concern for Sustainability into the day-to-day operations of Interface. In his Forward to <u>Busi-
ness Lessons from a Radical Industrialist</u>, he wrote; "I'll end on a positive
note, with an update on Interface's climb up Mount Sustainability—the
latest metrics on our eco-odyssey (as of year-end 2009), and a restatement
of my central thesis. This is the "carrot":

- 80 percent reduction in the landfill waste per unit of production
  since 1996
- Water intake, down 80 percent per unit of production since 1996
- Total energy, down by 43 percent per unit of production since
  1996
- With changing energy mix to include renewables, fossil fuel intensity reduced by 60 percent
- With verified offsets, net GHG reduced 94 percent (absolute)
- 30 percent of global energy is from renewable sources
- 36 percent of total raw materials (by weight) is recycled or bio-
  based materials
- 100 percent renewable electricity in Europe (89 percent worldwide) in our factories
- 111 million square yards of climate-neutral carpet produced since
  2003: "Cool Carpet"
- 100,000 tons (200 million pounds) of reclaimed product via Re-
  Entry, our reverse logistics carpet reclamation program
- 200 million airline passenger miles offset by some 106,000 trees
- Overall footprint reduction, more than 60 percent
- Cumulative avoided waste costs totaling $433 million since
  1994—costs down, not up—waste elimination paying for the entire
  mountain climb

If we can do it, anybody can. If anybody can, everybody can. That includes you[371]."

"It ain't what you don't know that gets you into trouble. It's what you know for sure that just ain't so." ~ Mark Twain

Lexicon[372]

Definitions for these terms are derived from a variety of sources: the Biomimicry Institute, Dictionary of Sustainable Management, Dictionary.com, BusinessDictionary,com, International Union of Pure and Applied Chemistry (IUPAC) and other designated definitions by Jarvis Business Solutions, LLC.

A
Accountability
Accountability is being answerable, or responsible, to stakeholders. In Sustainable Management this goes beyond financial stakeholders to include any natural or social systems affected by a business, including customers, employees, and communities.

Automated Storage Provisioning[373]
Automated storage provisioning: 1) improves storage efficiency through right-sizing; 2) identifies and re-allocates unused storage, and; 3) increases capacity of by improving utilization of existing storage.

B
Best Practices
A set of learned practices and procedures an organization finds successful in accomplishing its goals. Best practices are most successful when clearly described or codified, part of employee training, and shared throughout an organization. These are sometimes shared with partners and competitors in order to set standards for an industry.

Biomass
Biomass is organic, non-fossil material that is available on a renewable basis. Biomass includes all biological organisms, dead or alive, and their metabolic by products, that have not been transformed by geological processes into substances such as coal or petroleum. Examples of biomass are forest and mill residues, agricultural crops and wastes, wood and wood wastes, animal wastes, livestock operation residues, aquatic plants, and municipal and industrial wastes.

Biomimicry[374]
Applying lessons learned from the study of natural methods and systems to the design of technology. Science writer Janine Benyus articulates nine principles in her 1997 book Biomimicry:

1. Nature runs on sunlight
2. Nature uses only the energy it needs
3. Nature fits form to function
4. Nature recycles everything
5. Nature rewards cooperation
6. Nature banks on diversity
7. Nature demands local expertise
8. Nature curbs excesses from within
9. Nature taps the power of limits

Biosphere
Coined in 1875 by Eduard Suess, the biosphere is that part of a planet's outer shell—including air, land, and water—within which life occurs, and which biotic processes alter or transform. From the broadest geophysiological point of view, the biosphere is the global ecological system integrating all living beings and their relationships, including their interaction with the elements of the lithosphere (rocks), hydrosphere (water), and atmosphere (air).

Branding[375]
The process of developing a brand or brand strategy for a product, service, or organization.

C
Carbon Footprint
The total amount of greenhouse gases emitted directly and indirectly to support human activities, usually expressed in equivalent tons of either carbon or carbon dioxide. Carbon footprints are calculated by countries as part of their reporting requirements under the Kyoto Protocol, as well as by companies, regions, or individuals.

Ceres Principles[376]
A ten-point code of environmental conduct that is publicly and voluntarily endorsed by companies as an environmental mission statement or ethic. Formed in 1989, Ceres is a partnership among environmental groups, labor unions, and institutional investors devoted to using shareholder power to move companies to more sustainable practices.

Climate Change
The global climate has changed as human activity has released more and new substances and gases into the atmosphere. This has many results, including global warming, the effect of consistently increased average global temperature, particularly in the oceans. One of the most common term associated with climate change is global warming, which can be con-

fusing since climate change can take many forms, including higher temperatures in some areas, lower ones in other areas, and more powerful natural disasters (such as hurricanes). The term global weirding, coined by Paul Hawken, describes this inconsistent (but elevated) weather change around the world.

Competitors[377]
Any person or entity which is a rival against another. In business, a company in the same industry or a similar industry which offers a similar product or service. The presence of one or more competitors can reduce the prices of goods and services as the companies attempt to gain a larger market share. Competition also requires companies to become more efficient in order to reduce costs.

Compliance
Compliance can be the first step to sustainability. Compliance can be achieved through a commitment to social expectations and the law or simply by observing the letter of a law. For businesses striving to achieve restorative, sustainable practices, compliance becomes not a motivation, but simply a minimum baseline against which to measure achievable cost savings increases in profitability, market share, share price, and stockholders' equity.

Core Assets
Your Core Assets are driven by business Core Values recognizing that Sustainability aligned to the needs of the present without sacrificing resources for future generation's needs. It challenges your ideals beyond your brick and mortar walls and it is a role that legacies are made from. They are composed of five internal segments that include:
* Corporate Values
* Innovation
* Products And Services
* People
* Processes

Corporate Values
Core beliefs and values should be based on legal considerations, as well as, bedrock beliefs in ethics and Sustainability. For these Sustainability Values, if adhered to, will guide your decision-making process from resource management to brand image in a Sustainability context.

Cradle-to-Cradle
A phrase invented by Walter R. Stahel in the 1970s and popularized by William McDonough and Michael Braungart in their 2002 book of the same name. This framework seeks to create production techniques that are not just efficient but are essentially waste free. In cradle to cradle produc-

tion all material inputs and outputs are seen either as technical or biological nutrients. Technical nutrients can be recycled or reused with no loss of quality and biological nutrients composted or consumed. By contrast cradle to grave refers to a company taking responsibility for the disposal of goods it has produced, but not necessarily putting products' constituent components back into service.

CSR (Corporate Social Responsibility)
A business outlook that acknowledges responsibilities to stakeholders not traditionally accepted, including suppliers, customers, and employees as well as local and international communities in which it operates and the natural environment. There are few accepted standards and practices so far, but a growing concern that the actions organizations take have no unintended consequences outside the business, whether driven by concern, philanthropy, or a desire for an authentic brand and public relations.

CXOs (Corporate Executives - CEO, CFO, COO, etc.)
Executives, C-suite executives, who are responsible and accountable for sections of the enterprise. This is a general term that encapsulates all executives (i.e., CEO, CFO, COO, etc.).

D

Data Compression[378]
For a long time, data compression has been used to minimize transmission traffic and reduce the amount of data stored. In fact, a recent survey revealed that over half of IT administrators use**d data compression.**

E

Ethics
From a professional viewpoint, ethics typically pertains to a code of professional standards that contain aspects of fairness and duty to the profession and to the general public. A useful distinction between ethics and morals is that morals are influenced by established social customs (which may over time present ethical dilemmas). As applied to sustainability, the consideration of ethics lies at the core of our business, governmental, and collective decision making. In many ways, choices revolving along sustainable concerns are simultaneously ethical as well.

Externalities
Externalities arc effects of services, products, or production on third parties who were not involved in the buyer/seller relationship (organizations outside the brick and mortar boundaries). Externalities occur when a third party incurs unintended consequences from the market behaviors of oth-

ers. Externalities can be either negative (pollution, waste clean-up fees that a community must bear, rather than the generator of the waste), or they can be positive (The Clean Water Act generates positive effects for many who were not involved in enacting the bill).

G

GHG (Greenhouse gases)[379]
Greenhouse gases are any of the gases whose absorption of solar radiation is responsible for the greenhouse effect, including carbon dioxide, methane, ozone, and the fluorocarbons.

Governance
The systems and processes of management that govern an organization's behavior and conduct. Governance covers accountability, auditing, transparency (openness), reporting and disclosure, responsibilities and representation of various stakeholders (including shareholders, board of directors, advisory boards, employees, etc.) as well as charters, by-laws, and policies document the rights and responsibilities of all parties. Governance often includes strategy, risk management, and compensation, benefits, and evaluation of senior management. There is growing inclusion of governance issues within international certification systems, such as the GRI.

GRI (Global Reporting Initiative)[380]
The GRI is a leading organization in the sustainability field. GRI promotes the use of sustainability reporting as a way for organizations to become more sustainable and contribute to sustainable development.
A sustainable global economy should combine long term profitability with ethical behavior, social justice, and environmental care.

Greenwashing
A term merging the concepts of "green" (environmentally sound) and "whitewashing" (to conceal or gloss over wrongdoing). Greenwashing is any form of marketing or public relations that links a corporate, political, religious or nonprofit organization to a positive association with environmental issues for an unsustainable product, service, or practice. In some cases, an organization may truly offer a "green" product, service or practice. However, through marketing and public relations, one is wrongly led to believe this "green" value system is ubiquitous throughout the entire organization.

I

Innovation

The goal of many organizations who seek to differentiate their offerings by finding new and more valuable solutions that others have not. Most organizations who seek to innovate, do so as a separate, occasional function by a designated subset of employees or consultants. However, true innovation requires cultural change throughout the organization to sustain as well as participation by as many stakeholders as possible. Ultimately, innovation can be a source of transformation for a company that can increase effectiveness of all operations and processes but requires understanding and value placed on its products as well as a tolerance for change.

Internalities
Internalities are internal stakeholders and components intended to facilitate and fulfill Sustainability strategies and action plans to create an awareness that your enterprise does not exist in an isolated setting internalities (your Core Assets: people, processes, products, innovation, values). Business activities are in contrast to its impact on Economic Environmental and Social perspectives. These actions are measurable and intertwined with your Sustainability Value Chain.

L
LSS (Lean Six Sigma)[381]
A management approach for problem solving and process improvement based on a combination of the different tools of Six Sigma and Lean Manufacturing.

M
MNC (Multinational Corporation)[382]
An enterprise operating in several countries but managed from one (home) country. Generally, any company or group that derives a quarter of its revenue from operations outside of its home country is considered a multinational corporation.

N
NGO (Non-Governmental Organization)
A non-profit group or organization that is run neither by business or government created to realize particular social or economic pursuits, through research, activism, training, promotion, advocacy, lobbying, or community service.

P

PDUs
A device used in data centers to distribute AC power to multiple servers and other equipment. Power distribution units (PDUs) range from simple 120v power strips to units that break out 120 volts from 240v and three-phase power.

People
People are the most important resource of a corporation. Communicate the values of the company and share information to acknowledge progress and issues. Leaders are responsible to ensure incentives and direction of their human resources. This persuades employees, who share a common direction, get to where they are going more quickly by leveraging each others experiences, knowledge, skills and trust.

Processes
A business process is a collection of related , structured activities or tasks that produce specific services or products for a particular Customer or set of Customers. Business Processes are designed to add value for the Customer and should not include unnecessary activities. The outcome of a well designed business process is increased effectiveness adding value for the Customer. and increased efficiency, while minimizing costs for the company.

Products and Services
Customers are the most important stakeholder of a corporation. Without Customers, there is no revenue. Nurture your corporate culture and recognize that the products and services reflect your brand image. Your products and services reflect the level of Sustainability. Push for Continuous Improvement in Sustainability, Quality and Excellence.

R

RAID Level[383]
RAID (redundant array of independent disks) is a storage technology that combines multiple disk drive components into a single logical unit.

Rare Earths or Rare Earth Elements (REEs)[384]
As defined by IUPAC, rare earth elements or rare earth metals are a set of seventeen chemical elements in the periodic table, specifically the fifteen lanthanides plus scandium and yttrium. Because of their geochemical properties, rare earth elements are typically dispersed and not often found concentrated as rare earth minerals in economically exploitable ore deposits.

S

SIG (Special Interest Group)
Special Interests Groups [SIG, example: AFL-CIO] are groups of persons working on behalf of or strongly supporting a particular cause, such as an item of legislation, an industry, or a special segment of society.

Stakeholders
Individuals or organizations with an interest in the success or failure of a project or entity. Potential stakeholders in a company may include customers, clients, employees, distributors, wholesalers, retailers, suppliers, partners, creditors, stockholders (shareholders), communities, government courts and departments (city, state, federal, and international), banks, media, institutional investors and fund managers, Labor Unions, Insurers and re-insurers, NGOs, media, business groups, trade associations, competitors, the general public, and the environment (local, regional, and global). Different stakeholders can exercise different types of power, including: voting, legal, economic, and political, and can form coalitions with others. Sustainable organizations should identify stakeholders and maintain dialog with them in order to better understand how to help address stakeholder concerns, operate more effectively, and make better strategic and tactical decisions.

Snapshots[385]
A form of duplication and formally known as "delta snapshots" and sometimes referred to as "cloning", snapshots are particularly important when running simulations or modeling on large data sets.

T

Thin Provisioning[386]
In the past, servers were allocated storage based on anticipated requirements. Over provisioning (i.e., "fat" provisioning) of storage would result because applications would suffer performance issues if these limits were then exceeded.

Tiering Storage[387]
Stored data typically becomes less used/accessed more infrequently as it ages and therefore does not have to be stored on high-performance drives.

Transparency
A self-regulatory tool to expose ethics and real time results of a business entity's performance through accessible publication of the entity's practices and behavior. Transparency often leads to greater accountability and fewer opportunities for corruption or abuse. There is a strong movement to

increase the transparency of business processes in service of corporate responsibility reporting.

U

UN Global Compact[388]
The UN Global Compact works toward the vision of a sustainable and inclusive global economy which delivers lasting benefits to people, communities, and markets. To help realize this vision, the initiative seeks to:
- Mainstream the Global Compact's Ten Principles in business strategy and operations around the world; and
- Catalyze business action in support of UN goals and issues, with emphasis on collaboration and collective action.

UPSs
A device that provides battery backup when the electrical power fails or drops to an unacceptable voltage level. Small UPS systems provide power for a few minutes; enough to power down the computer in an orderly manner, while larger systems have enough battery for several hours.

V

Vision (Corporate)
The state or world in which an organization seeks to create or participate within. Whereas a mission defines an organization's direction and priorities, its vision is the description of the destination this direction is heading. A vision is often a description of an organization, market, or world that is different than current state and embodies its values and objectives.

Value Chain
Described and popularized by Michael Porter in his 1985 best-seller, Competitive Advantage: Creating and Sustaining Superior Performance, the value chain identifies the various value-adding activities of an organization or network. Often used as a tool for strategic planning because of its emphasis on maximizing value while minimizing costs.

Z

Zero Waste
The goal of developing products and services, managing their use and deployment, and creating recycling systems and markets in order to eliminate the volume and toxicity of waste and materials and conserve and recover all resources. Implementing zero waste eliminates all discharges to

land, water, or air that may be a threat to planetary, human, animal or plant health. Many cities and states already have set zero-waste goals. For example, San Francisco and other cities have set a goal to create zero waste by 2020.

Source Origination:

Dictionary of Sustainable Management; Presidio Graduate School Copyright © 2013 - All Rights Reserved, Published under the Creative Commons license; www.sustainabilitydictionary.com.

This Dictionary of Sustainable Management is an open dictionary for business leaders and students of sustainability and business-related terms. It is a project of the alumni and students of the Presidio Graduate School. The purpose of this endeavor is to inspire people to better understand how sustainability concepts are creating new understandings (or reinvigorating old ones) in the spheres of business, government, and society. All of this in the pursuit of a more sustainable world.

Dictionary of Sustainable Management by the alumni and students of the Presidio Graduate School is licensed under a Creative Commons Attribution - Non Commercial - ShareAlike 3.0 Unported License.

Unless otherwise noted, designated definitions by Jarvis Business Solutions, LLC Copyright © 2013 - All Rights Reserved

Bibliography

A

A New Era of Sustainability, UN Global Compact – Accenture CEO Study 2010

ABB; Create, Grow, Sustain; How Companies Are Doing Well by Doing Good; 2013 Report; Business Roundtable; April 2013

Abbott; Create, Grow, Sustain; How Companies Are Doing Well by Doing Good; 2013 Report; Business Roundtable; April 2013

Accenture; Create, Grow, Sustain; How Companies Are Doing Well by Doing Good; 2013 Report; Business Roundtable; April 2013

Air-Side Economizer; Energy Star; http://www.energystar.gov

AKSteel; Create, Grow, Sustain; How Companies Are Doing Well by Doing Good; 2013 Report; Business Roundtable; April 2013

Alcoa; Create, Grow, Sustain; How Companies Are Doing Well by Doing Good; 2013 Report; Business Roundtable; April 2013

Anadarko; Create, Grow, Sustain; How Companies Are Doing Well by Doing Good; 2013 Report; Business Roundtable; April 2013

Anderson, Ray C., with White, Robin; Forward, Business Lessons from a Radical Industrialist; St. Martin's Griffin, March 2011; ISBN: 978-0-312-54455-3, ISBN10: 0-312-54455-3,

Anderson, Ray C.; Mid-Course Correction, Chelsea Green Publishing Company, copyright 1998, pgs. 78

Anderson, Ray C.; Mid-Course Correction, Chelsea Green Publishing Company, copyright 1998, pgs. 78

Anderson, Ray C.; Mid-Course Correction, Chelsea Green publishing Company, White River Junction, Vermont, 3rd printing September 2005

Anderson, Ray C.; Mid-Course Correction, Chelsea Green publishing Company, White River Junction, Vermont, 3rd printing September 2005, Page 12

Avery Dennison; Create, Grow, Sustain; How Companies Are Doing Well by Doing Good; 2013 Report; Business Roundtable; April 2013

Avery Dennison; Create, Grow, Sustain; How Companies Are Doing Well by Doing Good; 2013 Report; Business Roundtable; April 2013

B

Barclays, Business Roundtable 2012, www.barclays.com/citizenship

Barwise, Patrick and Meehan, Sean; Is Your Company As Customer-Focused As You Think? MIT Sloan Management Review; 10 Apr 2010. Prod. #: SMR348-PDF-ENG; pgs 1-8

Bausch + Lomb; Create, Grow, Sustain; How Companies Are Doing Well by Doing Good; 2013 Report; Business Roundtable; April 2013

Bayer; Create, Grow, Sustain; How Companies Are Doing Well by Doing Good; 2013 Report; Business Roundtable; April 2013

Berkshire Hathaway Inc. Code Of Business Conduct And Ethics, http://english6.net/c/code-of-ethics---berkshire-hathaway-inc.-w11208.html, Berkshire Hathaway Inc.. Retrieved: 29 Nov 2012

Biomass Energy; EPA; www.epa.gov; Retrieved: 15 Oct 2013

Biro, Meghan M.; 5 Leadership Behaviors Loyal Employees Trust; Forbes; 4 Jun 2012

Bloomenergy; www.bloomenergy.com/; Retrieved: 15 Oct 2013

BNSF; Create, Grow, Sustain; How Companies Are Doing Well by Doing Good; 2013 Report; Business Roundtable; April 2013

Bockstette, Valerie and Stamp, Mike; Creating Shared Value: A How-to Guide for the New Corporate (R)evolution; FSG at www.fsg.org; Sponsored by Hewlett-Packard Company

Boeing; Create, Grow, Sustain; How Companies Are Doing Well by Doing Good; 2013 Report; Business Roundtable; April 2013

Bottom-line benefits of sustainable business practices, Six growing trends in corporate sustainability:an Ernst & Young survey in cooperation with GreenBiz Group; based on over 1,600 online participants; 2012

Bouton, Shannon; Creyts, Jon; Kiely, Tom; Livingston, John ; Nauclér; Tomas; McKinsey Sustainability & Resource Productivity

BP Goals; http://www.bp.com/en/global/corporate/sustainability/bp-and-sustainability.html;Retrieved: 10 July 2013

Bredenberg, Al; Energy and Carbon Management Are Increasingly on Manufacturers' Radar; ThomasNet http://news.thomasnet.com/green_clean/2012/08/27/energy-and-carbon-management-are-increasingly-on-manufacturers-radar/; August 27th, 2012

Brewer, Stuart; COO beat sustainability drum; DNV (Det Norske Veritas); http://www.dnv.com; 29 Oct 2010; Retrieved: 6 Aug 2013

Brito, Michael; 8 Cultural Indicators of Social Business Transformation; Social Business News; http://www.socialbusinessnews.com; 14 May 2012

BusinessDictionary; http://www.businessdictionary.com/definition/competitor.html#ixzz2h4Vf Vjnn

C

Campbell's, Business Roundtable 2012, wwcampbellsoupcompany.com

Campbell's, Grow, Sustain; How Companies Are Doing Well by Doing Good; 2013 Report; Business Roundtable; April 2013

Capozucca. Peter and Sarni, William; Sustainability 2.0 - Using sustainability to drive business innovation and growth., Deloitte Review, Retrieved: 23 Nov 2012

Capozucca. Peter and Sarni, William; Sustainability 2.0 - Using sustainability to drive business innovation and growth., Deloitte Review, Retrieved: 23 Nov 2012

Capozucca. Peter and Sarni, William; Sustainability 2.0 - Using sustainability to drive business innovation and growth., Deloitte Review, Retrieved: 23 Nov 2012

Capozucca. Peter and Sarni, William; Sustainability 2.0 - Using sustainability to drive business innovation and growth., Deloitte Review, Retrieved: 23 Nov 2012

Capozucca. Peter and Sarni, William; Sustainability 2.0 - Using sustainability to drive business innovation and growth., Deloitte Review, Retrieved: 23 Nov 2012

CardinalHealth; Create, Grow, Sustain; How Companies Are Doing Well by Doing Good; 2013 Report; Business Roundtable; April 2013

Cawein, Jenni; Et.al.; The Environmental Professional's Guide to Lean and Six Sigma; U.S. Environmental Protection Agency (EPA); Aug 2009

Ceres Principles, a ten-point code of corporate environmental conduct to be publicly endorsed by companies as an environmental mission statement or ethic. UN Global Compact includes ten widely recognized humanitarian rights. GRI's 11 principles, covering the economic, environmental and ethical indicators of a company's performance.

Ceres; http://www.ceres.org/about-us/our-history/ceres-principles; Retreived: 10 August 2013

Ceres; http://www.ceres.org/roadmap-assessment/company-performance/disclosure

Ceres; http://www.ceres.org/roadmap-assessment/company-performance/governance-for-sustainability

Ceres; http://www.ceres.org/roadmap-assessment/company-performance/performance-employees

Ceres; http://www.ceres.org/roadmap-assessment/company-performance/performance-operations

Ceres; http://www.ceres.org/roadmap-assessment/company-performance/products-and-services

Ceres; http://www.ceres.org/roadmap-assessment/company-performance/stakeholder-engagement

Ceres; http://www.ceres.org/roadmap-assessment/company-performance/supply-chain

Ceres; http://www.ceres.org/roadmap-assessment/company-performance/transportation-and-logistics

Chevron Way; http://www.chevron.com/about/chevronway/

Christensen, Clayton; The Innovator's Dilemma

Coca-Cola Vision; http://www.coca-cola.co.uk/about-us/coca-cola-mission-vision-statement.html

Collins, Jim; Great by Choice, HarperCollinsPublisher, 2011, p. 136

Collins, Jim; Great by Choice, HarperCollinsPublisher, 2011, p. 45

Conceptual Issues, The Sustainability Report, Affiliated with the Institute for Research and Innovation in Sustainability; http://www.sustreport.org/; Retrieved: 27 July 2011

ConocoPhillips; Create, Grow, Sustain; How Companies Are Doing Well by Doing Good; 2013 Report; Business Roundtable; April 2013

Consumers Demand Sustainability Results, Survey Says; Environmental Leader; 24 Oct 2012; Retrieved: 7 Aug 2013

Containment/Enclosures; Energy Star; http://www.energystar.gov

Convergys; Create, Grow, Sustain; How Companies Are Doing Well by Doing Good; 2013 Report; Business Roundtable; April 2013

Corporate Social Responsibility, Reference for Business; Encyclopedia of Small Business; Retrieved: 12 Sep 2011

Corporate Social Responsibility, Reference for Business; Encyclopedia of Small Business; Retrieved: 12 Sep 2011

Corporate Social Responsibility: a new definition, a new agenda for action; European Commission, MEMO/11/730, Brussels, 25 October 2011

Creating a Workable Company Code of Conduct 2003, Ethics Resource Center

Customer; BusinessDictionary.Com; www.businessdictionary.com/definition/customer.html

D

De Morsella, Tracey; CEOs See Sustainability As Engine For Growth But Industry Sectors Split On Priorities, FastCompany, 25 May 2011

De Morsella, Tracey; CEOs See Sustainability As Engine For Growth But Industry Sectors Split On Priorities, FastCompany, 25 May 2011

Deming, W. Edwards; Ch.2 Principles for Transformation; Out of the Crisis; 1982; p. 20

Deming's 14 Points; American Society of Quality; https://asq.org/; Retrieved: 31 Oct 2013

Disclosures & Rankings; Annual Report & Sustainability Report; Eaton. http://www.eaton.com/Eaton/OurCompany/Sustainability/AccountabilityTransparency/index.htm

DNV's Chief Operating Officer Bjørn K. Haugland underlines growing interest in sustainability as business case.

Douglass, Keith and DeCosse, David; The Ethical Dimension of Sustainability, Markkula Center for Applied Ethics at Santa Clara University, May 2009

Dow Jones Sustainability Indexes, http://www.sustainability-index.com/dow-jones-sustainability-indexes/; Retrieved: 11 September 2011

Dow; Create, Grow, Sustain; How Companies Are Doing Well by Doing Good; 2013 Report; Business Roundtable; April 2013

Drucker, Peter; The Five Most Important Questions You Will Ever Ask About Your Organization; Leader to Leader Institute, 2008.

E

Eastman, Business Roundtable 2012, www.eastman.com/sustainability

EMEC. "Tidal Energy Devices". 5 October 2008, Retrieved: 15 Oct 2013

EPA source: http://water.epa.gov/polwaste/nps/chap3.cfm

EPA source: http://water.epa.gov/polwaste/nps/chap3.cfm

EPA source: Source: http://water.epa.gov/polwaste/nps/chap3.cfm

EPA, Everyday Choices: Opportunities For Environmental Stewardship, United States Environmental Protection Agency , Washington, D.C. 20460 , November 9, 2005, p. 1

EPA, Everyday Choices: Opportunities For Environmental Stewardship, United States Environmental Protection Agency , Washington, D.C. 20460 , November 9, 2005, p. 1

Epstein-Reeves, James; The Six Reasons Why Companies Actually Wind Up Embracing CSR, Forbes, The CSR Blog - Corporate Social Responsibility 10/17/2012

Ernst & Young; Create, Grow, Sustain; How Companies Are Doing Well by Doing Good; 2013 Report; Business Roundtable; April 2013

European Commission, Final EU CSR Forum Report; http://ec.europa.eu; June 2004

European Multi-stakeholder Forum On CSR; Final Report; 29 June 2004; p. 8

Evans, Tony; Humidification Strategies for Data

Externalities; BusinessDictionary.com; http://www.businessdictionary.com

F

Fiksel, Joseph; Eason, Tarsha; Frederickson, Herbert; A Framework for Sustainability

Finding the Green in Green Computing, by Mark A. Monroe, Director, Sustainable Computing, Sun Microsystems, Inc. Sep, 2009. Slide 34.

First Solar; Create, Grow, Sustain; How Companies Are Doing Well by Doing Good; 2013 Report; Business Roundtable; April 2013

Fluor, Business Roundtable 2012, www.flour.com

FMC; Create, Grow, Sustain; How Companies Are Doing Well by Doing Good; 2013 Report; Business Roundtable; April 2013

Fun Facts - Energy and Water; UCLA Sustainability; http://www.sustain.ucla.edu; Retrieved 12 July 2013

G

General Mills; Create, Grow, Sustain; How Companies Are Doing Well by Doing Good; 2013 Report; Business Roundtable; April 2013

Geothermal Energy Association (GEA) 2009. U.S. Geothermal Power Production and Development Update. Union of Concerned Scientists; Retrieved: 15 Oct 2013

Global Solar PV installed Capacity crosses 100GW Mark. renewindians.com (11 February 2013).

Goonan, Brian, "Business Transformation: Doing it Right, Part I," CIO Magazine, 9 February 2005

Goonan, Brian, "Business Transformation: Doing it Right, Part I," CIO Magazine, February 9, 2005.

Gore, Al And Blood, David, Wall Street Journal Online | Opinion; A Manifesto for Sustainable Capitalism; December 14, 2011; Retrieved: October 12, 2012

Green Building Standards; http://www.epa.gov

H

Haanaes, Knut; Arthur, David; Balagopal, Balu; Kong, Ming Teck; Reeves, Martin; Velken. Ingrid; Hopkins, Michael S.; and Kruschwitz, Nina; MIT Sloan School of Management and the Boston Consulting Group; Sustainability: The 'Embracers' Seize Advantage; Winter 2011

Hansen, Morten T.; Ibarra, Herminia; and Peyer, Urs; The Best-Performing CEOs in the World, Harvard Business Review; January-February 2013

Hawksworth, John; Vision 2050: Estimating the order of magnitude of sustainability-related business opportunities in key sectors; PricewaterhouseCooper; February 2010

Herman Miller; http://www.hermanmiller.com/about-us/our-values-in-action/environmental-advocacy/our-vision-and-policy.html

Hewson, Merillyn, Chief Executive Officer and President at Lockheed Martin; The First Things a New Leader Should Do to Build Trust; source: LinkedIn - Leadership and Managment; Retrieved: 19 September 2013

History and Impact, Ceres organization; http://www.ceres.org/about-us/our-history/; Retrieved: 15 December 2012

Honeywell; Create, Grow, Sustain; How Companies Are Doing Well by Doing Good; 2013 Report; Business Roundtable; April 2013

Hot Aisle/Cold Aisle Layout; Energy Star; http://www.energystar.gov

I

IBM, Leading Through Connections 2012 - IBM Corporation, p. 8, Retrieved: 11 December 2012

IEA; Energy-Efficient Transport Could Save Cities $70 Trillion; Environment News Service; http://ens-newswire.com/2013/07/15/energy-efficient-transport-could-save-cities-70-trillion/; 15 July 2013

Important to Recognize the Dramatic Improvement in Data Center Efficiency, Uptime Institute, 9/25/12.
blog.uptimeinstitute.com/2012/09/important-to-recognize-the-dramatic-improvement-in-data-center-efficiency/

Information Technology Settings and Strategies

Information Technology Settings and Strategies

Information Technology Settings and Strategies

Infosys, "Defining Business Transformation", Prem. Hema & Mathew, George Eby; May 2006

Ingeroll Rand; Create, Grow, Sustain; How Companies Are Doing Well by Doing Good; 2013 Report; Business Roundtable; April 2013

Intel; Create, Grow, Sustain; How Companies Are Doing Well by Doing Good; 2013 Report; Business Roundtable; April 2013

Interface Global Vision;
http://www.interfaceglobal.com/Company/Mission-Vision.aspx

J

Jacobe, Dennis, Ph.D., is Chief Economist for Gallup;

Jacowski, Tony; Lean Six Sigma - 5 Reasons Your Organization Needs It; ArticlesBase SC #23028, www.articlesbase.com; 17 Apr 2006

Jones, Jeffrey M.; Worry About U.S. Water, Air Pollution at Historical Lows; Gallup Politics, Gallup News, www.gallup.com; 13 April 2012

K

Kaplan, Robert S. and Norton, David P.; Building A Strategy-Focused Organization; Ivey Business Journal; May / June 2001

Kaplan, Robert S. and Norton, David P.; The Strategy-Focused Organization; Harvard Business School Press, 2001, p. 11

Kaye, Leon; The Business Case For Sustainability is Becoming Easier to Make; TriplePundit,http://www.triplepundit.com; 15 mar 2013

Kill Comatose Computers, Forbes, by Ken Brill, 11/19/2008.
www.forbes.com/2008/11/16/cio-comatose-computers-tech-cio-cx_kb_1119computers.html

Kiron, David; Kruschwitz, Nina; Haanaes, Knut; Reeves, Martin and Goh, Eugene; Chapter 3: World Is Tilting Toward Embracers; MIT Sloan Management Review and The Boston Consulting Group, 10 Feb 2011

Kiron, David; Kruschwitz, Nina; Haanaes, Knut; Reeves, Martin and Goh, Eugene; Companies Profit From Embracing Sustainability; MIT Sloan Management Review; March 12, 2013

KMPG; Expect the Unexpected: Building business value in a changing world; KPMG International; 2012

Kotler, Philip; Marketing 3.0: The 10 Credos; Retreived: 12 Nov 13

Kotter, John P.; Leading Change: Why Transformation Efforts Fail (HBR Classic); Harvard Business Review; 11 pages. Publication 01 Jan 2007.

Kuehn, Kurt; Five Reasons the CFO Should Care About Sustainability, pressroom.ups.com, Kuehn stressed five reasons CFOs and financial leaders should consider sustainability a bottom line priority, Retrieved: 14 May 2012

L

LaMonica, Martin; Apple Data Center Does Fuel Cell Industry a Huge Favor; MIT Technology Review; December 6, 2012

Lash, Jonathan and Wellington, Fred; Competitive Advantage on a Warming Planet; Harvard Business Review; March 2007

Lash, Jonathan and Wellington, Fred; Competitive Advantage on a Warming Planet; Harvard Business Review; March 2007

Leading Through Connections 2012 - IBM Corporation, p. 15, Retrieved: 11 December 2012

LEED Rating System; http://www.usgbc.org/leed/rating-systems; Retrieved: 25 Oct 2013

LEED; LEED is driving the green building industry.; http://www.usgbc.org/leed; Retrieved: 30 Oct 2013

Love Canal: Hooker Chemicals and Plastic Corporation (later known as Hooker Chemical Corporation, and more recently as Occidental Chemical Corporation or OxyChem) bought the site after determining it had an impermeable clay substrate, which made it a good location for a chemical waste landfill. ... approximately 21,800 tons of chemical wastes dumped by Hooker until 1952. ... In March 1980 the President Carter declared a state of emergency at Love Canal and funded the permanent evacuation and relocation of an additional 780 families. http://www.encyclopedia.com/topic/Love_Canal.aspx

M

McWilliams, Abagail; Siegel, Donald S. and Wright, Patrick M.; Corporate Social Responsibility: Strategic Implications; Journal of Management Studies 43:1 January 2006

Medtronic; Create, Grow, Sustain; How Companies Are Doing Well by Doing Good; 2013 Report; Business Roundtable; April 2013

Memo-11-730; Corporate Social Responsibility: a new definition, a new agenda for action; European Commission, European Union, Brussels, 25 October 2011

Michelman, Paul; Steve Bishop interview, global lead of sustainability at IDEO; Don't Bother with the Green Consumer; HBR Blog Network; 24 Jan 2008

MIT Sloan Management Review, Sustainability Study: Interactive Exploration, Retrieved: 24 August 2012

MIT Sloan: Sustainability & Innovation Global Executive Study, MIT Sloan Management Review and The Boston Consulting Group, 2010

Mohin, Tim ; Forbes Leadership Forum, Contributor, The Top 10 Trends in CSR for 2012, Forbes, 1 January 2012

Montgomery, David B., and Catherine A. Ramus (2007) Including Corporate Social Responsibility, Environmental Sustainability, and Ethics in Calibrating MBA Job Preferences. Stanford Graduate School of Business, Research Paper No. 1981.

Moore, Geoffrey A.; Crossing the Chasm;; HarperCollinsPublishers, 2002, p.12

Multi-stakeholder Forum on Corporate social responsibility (CSR), http://ec.europa.eu/enterprise/policies/sustainable-business/corporate-social-responsibility/multi-stakeholder-forum/; Retrieved: 23 June 2013

Murphy, Chris; Collaboration Trumps Innovation For CEOs, http://www.informationweek.com; June 04, 2012

N

Natrass, Brian and Altomare, Mary; The Natural Step for Business, Second edition, 2001

P

Parr, Shawn; Culture Eats Strategy For Lunch; Jan 24, 2012

Pfitzer, Marc; Bockstette, Valerie and Stamp, Mike; Innovating for Shared Value, HBR, September 2013; FSG research Note: Nestlé, Mars, Intel, and Becton Dickinson (BD) are FSG clients. Novartis has financially supported FSG's research.

PG&E; Create, Grow, Sustain; How Companies Are Doing Well by Doing Good; 2013 Report; Business Roundtable; April 2013

PickensPlan, http://www.pickensplan.com/theplan/; Retrieved: 24 Oct 2013

Porter, Michael and Kramer, Mark; Creating Shared Value; Harvard Business Review, HBR.org; January–February 2011

Porter, Michael and Kramer, Mark; How to Fix Capitalism and Unleash a New Wave of Growth; Harvard Business Review; January-February 2011

Porter, Michael E. and Kramer, Mark R.; Creating Shared Value; Harvard Business Review; January - February 2011

Porter, Michael E. and Kramer, Mark R.; Harvard Business Review, The Magazine, January 2011, Retrieved: October 15, 2012

Porter, Michael E.; Hills, Greg; Pfitzer, Marc; Patscheke, Sonja and Hawkins, Elizabeth; Measuring Shared Value

Prairie, Patti; Top Corporate Sustainability Trends To Watch In 2012, http://www.scientificamerican.com/article.cfm?id=top-corporate-sustainability-trends-2011-12, Scientific American, a Division of Nature America, Inc. , December 28, 2011. Retrieved: 9 Apr 2012

PricewaterhouseCooper, PwC, Less Can Be More: Better For The Bottom Line And The Environment, 16th Annual Global CEO Survey; PriceWaterhouse; January 2013

Principal Financial Group; Create, Grow, Sustain; How Companies Are Doing Well by Doing Good; 2013 Report; Business Roundtable; April 2013

Purchasing More Energy-Efficient Servers, UPSs, and PDUs; Energy Star; http://www.energystar.gov

PwC; Create, Grow, Sustain; How Companies Are Doing Well by Doing Good; 2013 Report; Business Roundtable; April 2013

R

Research Report Winter 2013, The Innovation Bottom Line; MIT Sloan Management Review • The Boston Consulting Group

Riley, Jim; Strategic Audit; http://www.tutor2u.net/business/strategy/Strategic_audit.htm; 23 Sep 2012

S

Schuler, Dr. A. J.; "Overcoming Resistance to Change: Top Ten Reasons for Change Resistance", 2003

Selected Sustainable Value Chain Research Findings, Copyright © 2012 Deloitte Development LLC. All rights reserved. Member of Deloitte Touche Tohmatsu Limited

Singh, Aman; New Survey: CEOs See Sustainability Shifting From Choice To Corporate Priority, Forbes, 23 June 2010

Spinks, Todd; From a discussion about personnel in today's age. Nov 2013

Stacey, Mary; Taylor, Marilyn and Legge, David; From Resource Managers to Resource Leaders, strategy+business, http://www.strategy-business.com, Published: March 26, 2012

Stewardship Education Best Practices Planning Guide; A Project of the Association of Fish and Wildlife Agencies' North American Conservation Education Strategy; Funded by a Multistate Grant of the Sport Fish and Wildlife Restoration Program; May 2008

Sunny Uplands: Alternative energy will no longer be alternative; The Economist; 21 November 2012. Retrieved 28 December 2012.

Supplier; BusinessDictionary.Com; www.businessdictionary.com/definition/customer.html

Supply chain energy efficiency critical to reducing carbon footprint; Modern Materials Handling; 7 August 2013

Sustainability people profiles; Unilever; http://www.unilever.com/sustainable-living/betterlivelihoods/profiles/index.aspx; Retrieved: 10 Aug 2013

T

Talent Management, Talent Measurement Overhaul Needed for Generational Diversity, 12 March 2013, Retrieved: 17 March 2013

The Man; W. Edwards Deming Institute; www.deming.org; Retrieved: 22 July 2013

The Sustainable Energy in America 2013 Factbook; Business Council for Sustainable Energy (BCSE), http://www.bcse.org

The World Bank, World Development Indicators (Washington, DC: World Bank, 2011); The World Bank, Global Economic Prospects (Washington, DC: World Bank, 2010); The World Bank, Multi-polarity: The New Global Economy (World Bank, 2011).

Transparency Needs to Have Integrity, Event Horizons, jbseventhorizons.wordpress.com; Retrieved: 29 Nov 2012

U

U.S. Green Building Council; www.epa.gov/oaintrnt/projects/; Retrieved: 16 Oct 13

Universal Wastes, EPA, http://www.epa.gov/osw/hazard/wastetypes/universal/; Retrieved: 31 Jul 2013

Uptime Institute, http://upsitetechnologies.com/images/stories/pdf/whitepapers/reducing bypass airflow is essential for eliminating hotspots.pdf

Urlaub, Julie; Cultivating Talent with Sustainability-Based Incentives, www.taigacompany.com; August 5, 2010; Retrieved: 12 November 2012

V

Variable Speed Fan Drives; Energy Star; http://www.energystar.gov

Velasquez, Manuel; Moberg, Dennis; Meyer, Michael J.; Shanks, Thomas; McLean, Margaret R.; DeCosse, David; André, Claire and Hanson, Kirk O.; A Framework for Thinking Ethically, Markkula Center for

Applied Ethics at Santa Clara University, www.scu.edu/ethics/practicing/decision/framework.html, Retrieved: 29 August 2012

Vokoun, Ron; What is Energy Star for Data Centers?; Data Center Knowledge; http://www.datacenterknowledge.com; 27 Aug 2012

W

Walmart Objectives and Actions; http://www.walmartstores.com/Sustainability/10605.aspx?p=9176; Retrieved: 3 May 2012

Walmart web site: http://corporate.walmart.com/global-responsibility/environment-sustainability

Walmart; Create, Grow, Sustain; How Companies Are Doing Well by Doing Good; 2013 Report; Business Roundtable; April 2013

Waste Assessment Approaches, http://www.epa.gov/smm/wastewise/approach.htm; Retrieved: 31 Aug 2013

Water-Side Economizer; Energy Strar; http://www.energystar.gov

Werbach, Adam; Using Transparency to Execute Your Strategy: Open Up Your Business for Scrutiny--Laying the Groundwork for Building Sustainability into Strategy; Harvard Business Press Chapters; 06 Jul 2009

Why Banks Must Rebuild Confidence Now; Gallup, 18 October 2012

Wikipedia-Sustainability, http://en.wikipedia.org/wiki/Sustainability, Retrieved: 26 November 2012

Wikipedia; http://en.wikipedia.org/wiki/Stewardship; Retrieved: 23 March 2103

Willetts, David; DAW Consulting, UK; Retrieved; 12 Aug 2012

Womack, James P. and Jones, Daniel T.; Lean Enterprise Institute, http://www.lean.org; Retreived: 8 Aug 2013

Wurtzel, Marvin; Reasons for Six Sigma Deployment Failures; BPMInstitute.org; Retrieved 4 Jul 2013

End Notes And Comments

[1] **1. A Vision For Sustainability**
[2] KMPG; Expect the Unexpected: Building business value in a changing world; KPMG International; 2012
[3] DNV's Chief Operating Officer Bjørn K. Haugland underlines growing interest in sustainability as business case.
[4] Brewer, Stuart; COO beat sustainability drum; DNV (Det Norske Veritas); http://www.dnv.com; 29 Oct 2010; Retrieved: 6 Aug 2013
[5] Werbach, Adam; Using Transparency to Execute Your Strategy: Open Up Your Business for Scrutiny--Laying the Groundwork for Building Sustainability into Strategy; Harvard Business Press Chapters; 06 Jul 2009
[6] Fiksel, Joseph; Eason, Tarsha; Frederickson, Herbert; A Framework for Sustainability Indicators at EPA; National Risk Management Research Laboratory, Sustainable Technology Division; EPA/600/R/12/687; October 2012
[7] Drucker, Peter; The Five Most Important Questions You Will Ever Ask About Your Organization; Leader to Leader Institute, 2008.
[8] Chevron Way; http://www.chevron.com/about/chevronway/
[9] Herman Miller; http://www.hermanmiller.com/about-us/our-values-in-action/environmental-advocacy/our-vision-and-policy.html
[10] Interface Global Vision; http://www.interfaceglobal.com/Company/Mission-Vision.aspx
[11] Epstein-Reeves, James; The Six Reasons Why Companies Actually Wind Up Embracing CSR, Forbes, The CSR Blog - Corporate Social Responsibility 10/17/2012
[12] Epstein-Reeves, James; Ibid.
[13] Epstein-Reeves, James; Op. cit.
[14] Willetts, David; DAW Consulting, UK; Retrieved; 12 Aug 2012
[15] Willetts, David; Ibid.
[16] Willetts, David; Op. cit.
[17] Willetts, David; Op. cit.
[18] Willetts, David; Op. cit.
[19] BP Goals; http://www.bp.com/en/global/corporate/sustainability/bp-and-sustainability.html;Retrieved: 10 July 2013
[20] Kuehn, Kurt; Five Reasons the CFO Should Care About Sustainability, pressroom.ups.com, Kuehn stressed five reasons CFOs and financial leaders should consider sustainability a bottom line priority, Retrieved: 14 May 2012
[21] De Morsella, Tracey; CEOs See Sustainability As Engine For Growth But Industry Sectors Split On Priorities, FastCompany, 25 May 2011
[22] De Morsella, Tracey; Ibid.
[23] De Morsella, Tracey; Op. cit.
[24] De Morsella, Tracey; Op. cit.
[25] De Morsella, Tracey; Op. cit.
[26] De Morsella, Tracey; Op. cit.
[27] De Morsella, Tracey; Op. cit.
[28] De Morsella, Tracey; Op. cit.
[29] De Morsella, Tracey; Op. cit.
[30] Prairie, Patti; Top Corporate Sustainability Trends To Watch In 2012, http://www.scientificamerican.com/article.cfm?id=top-corporate-sustainability-trends-2011-12, Scientific American, a Division of Nature America, Inc. , December 28, 2011. Retrieved: 9 Apr 2012

[31] Prairie, Ibid.

[32] Prairie, Patti; Op. cit.

[33] Prairie, Op. Cit.

[34] Prairie, Op. Cit.

[35] Prairie, Op. Cit.

[36] The World Bank, World Development Indicators (Washington, DC: World Bank, 2011); The World Bank, Global Economic Prospects (Washington, DC: World Bank, 2010); The World Bank, Multi-polarity: The New Global Economy (World Bank, 2011).

[37] MIT Sloan Management Review, Sustainability Study: Interactive Exploration, Retrieved: 24 August 2012

[38] Biro, Meghan M.; 5 Leadership Behaviors Loyal Employees Trust; Forbes; 4 Jun 2012

[39] Hawksworth, John; Vision 2050: Estimating the order of magnitude of sustainability-related business opportunities in key sectors; PricewaterhouseCooper; February 2010

[40] History and Impact, Ceres organization; http://www.ceres.org/about-us/our-history/; Retrieved: 15 December 2012

[41] Ceres; http://www.ceres.org/about-us/our-history/ceres-principles; Retreived: 10 August 2013

[42] Wikipedia-Sustainability, http://en.wikipedia.org/wiki/Sustainability, Retrieved: 26 November 2012

[43] Intel; Create, Grow, Sustain; How Companies Are Doing Well by Doing Good; 2013 Report; Business Roundtable; April 2013

[44] Ingeroll Rand; Create, Grow, Sustain; How Companies Are Doing Well by Doing Good; 2013 Report; Business Roundtable; April 2013

[45] Anadarko; Create, Grow, Sustain; How Companies Are Doing Well by Doing Good; 2013 Report; Business Roundtable; April 2013

[46] **2. Executive Commitment And Vision**

[47] This may have been motivated by uncertainty and ensuring short term liquidation. Long-term, however; those investments could have had significant impact on their position with respect to their competitive landscape.

[48] Singh, Aman; New Survey: CEOs See Sustainability Shifting From Choice To Corporate Priority, Forbes, 23 June 2010

[49] MIT Sloan Management Review, Sustainability Study: Interactive Exploration, Retrieved: 24 August 2012

[50] MIT Sloan Management Review, Ibid.

[51] Kuehn, Kurt; Five Reasons the CFO Should Care About Sustainability, pressroom.ups.com, Kuehn stressed five reasons CFOs and financial leaders should consider sustainability a bottom line priority, Retrieved: 14 May 2012

[52] Selected Sustainable Value Chain Research Findings, Copyright © 2012 Deloitte Development LLC. All rights reserved. Member of Deloitte Touche Tohmatsu Limited

[53] Anderson, Ray C.; Mid-Course Correction, Chelsea Green publishing Company, White River Junction, Vermont, 3rd printing September 2005, Page 12

[54] Collins, Jim; Great by Choice, HarperCollinsPublisher, 2011, Page 45

[55] Goonan, Brian, "Business Transformation: Doing it Right, Part I," CIO Magazine, February 9, 2005.

[56] Collins, Jim; Op. Cit.

[57] Infosys, "Defining Business Transformation", Prem. Hema & Mathew, George Eby; May 2006

[58] Dow Jones Sustainability Indexes, http://www.sustainability-index.com/dow-jones-sustainability indexes/; Retrieved: 11 September 2011

[59] Fun Facts - Energy and Water; UCLA Sustainability; http://www.sustain.ucla.edu; Retrieved 12 July 2013

[60] The Sustainable Energy in America 2013 Factbook; Business Council for Sustainable Energy (BCSE), http://www.bcse.org

[61] Externalities; BusinessDictionary.com; http://www.businessdictionary.com
[62] Externalities; Ibid.
[63] Customer; BusinessDictionary.Com;
www.businessdictionary.com/definition/customer.html
[64] Supplier; BusinessDictionary.Com;
www.businessdictionary.com/definition/customer.html
[65] BusinessDictionary;
http://www.businessdictionary.com/definition/competitor.html#ixzz2h4VfVjnn
[66] KMPG; Expect the Unexpected: Building business value in a changing world; KPMG International; 2012
[67] Corporate Social Responsibility, Reference for Business; Encyclopedia of Small Business; Retrieved: 12 Sep 2011
[68] Porter, Michael E. and Kramer, Mark R.; Harvard Business Review, The Magazine, January 2011, Retrieved: October 15, 2012
[69] European Multi-stakeholder Forum On CSR; Ibid; p. 9
[70] European Multi-stakeholder Forum On CSR; Final Report; 29 June 2004; p. 8
[71] Douglass, Keith and DeCosse, David; The Ethical Dimension of Sustainability, Markkula Center for Applied Ethics at Santa Clara University, May 2009
[72] Douglass and DeCosse; Ibid.
[73] Porter, Michael E., and Kramer , Mark R.; Harvard Business Review, The Magazine, January 2011, Retrieved: October 15, 2012
[74] Deming, W. Edwards; Out of the Crisis, 1986, page 8
[75] Deming, W. Edwards; Ibid.
[76] 100 Top Hospitals - CEO INSIGHTS:
Keys To Success And Future Challenges; CEO Insights Research Paper; August 2011
[77] Capozucca. Peter and Sarni, William; Sustainability 2.0 - Using sustainability to drive business innovation and growth., Deloitte Review, Retrieved: 23 Nov 2012
[78] PG&E; Create, Grow, Sustain; How Companies Are Doing Well by Doing Good; 2013 Report; Business Roundtable; April 2013
[79] Walmart; Create, Grow, Sustain; How Companies Are Doing Well by Doing Good; 2013 Report; Business Roundtable; April 2013

[80] **3. Corporate Social Responsibility**
[81] Kiron, David; Kruschwitz, Nina; Haanaes, Knut; Reeves, Martin and Goh, Eugene; Ibid.
[82] Sustainable and responsible business
Multi-stakeholder Forum on Corporate social responsibility (CSR),
http://ec.europa.eu/enterprise/policies/sustainable-business/corporate-social-responsibility/multi-stakeholder-forum/; Retrieved: 23 June 2013
[83] European Commission, Final EU CSR Forum Report; http://ec.europa.eu; June 2004
[84] Corporate Social Responsibility: a new definition, a new agenda for action; European Commission, MEMO/11/730, Brussels, 25 October 2011
[85] Memo-11-730; Corporate Social Responsibility: a new definition, a new agenda for action; European Commission, European Union, Brussels, 25 October 2011
[86] MIT Sloan Management Review, Sustainability Study: Interactive Exploration, Retrieved: 24 August 2012
[87] Kaye, Leon; The Business Case For Sustainability is Becoming Easier to Make; TriplePundit,http://www.triplepundit.com; 15 mar 2013
[88] PricewaterhouseCooper, PwC, Less Can Be More: Better For The Bottom Line And The Environment, 16th Annual Global CEO Survey; PriceWaterhouse; January 2013
[89] PwC, Ibid.
[90] PwC, Op. cit.
[91] PwC, Op. cit.

[92] Kiron, David; Kruschwitz, Nina; Haanaes, Knut; Reeves, Martin and Goh, Eugene; Companies Profit From Embracing Sustainability; MIT Sloan Management Review; March 12, 2013

[93] Lash, Jonathan and Wellington, Fred; Competitive Advantage on a Warming Planet; Harvard Business Review; March 2007

[94] Lash, Jonathan and Wellington, Fred; Ibid.

[95] Dow; Create, Grow, Sustain; How Companies Are Doing Well by Doing Good; 2013 Report; Business Roundtable; April 2013

[96] First Solar; Create, Grow, Sustain; How Companies Are Doing Well by Doing Good; 2013 Report; Business Roundtable; April 2013

[97] **4. Corporate Planning and CSR**

[98] McWilliams, Abagail; Siegel, Donald S. and Wright, Patrick M.; Corporate Social Responsibility: Strategic Implications; Journal of Management Studies 43:1 January 2006

[99] Corporate Social Responsibility, Reference for Business; Encyclopedia of Small Business; Retrieved: 12 Sep 2011

[100] Kaplan, Robert S. and Norton, David P.; Building A Strategy-Focused Organization; Ivey Business Journal; May / June 2001

[101] Kaplan, Robert S. and Norton, David P.; Ibid.

[102] Kaplan, Robert S. and Norton, David P.; The Strategy-Focused Organization; Harvard Business School Press, 2001, p. 11

[103] Kaplan, Robert S. and Norton, David P.; Ibid.

[104] Kaplan, Robert S. and Norton, David P.; Op. cit.

[105] Kaplan, Robert S. and Norton, David P.; Op. cit.

[106] Porter, Michael E. and Kramer, Mark R.; Creating Shared Value; HBR January–February 2011

[107] Hansen, Morten T.; Ibarra, Herminia; and Peyer, Urs; The Best-Performing CEOs in the World, Harvard Business Review; January-February 2013

[108] Moore, Geoffrey A.; Crossing the Chasm;; HarperCollinsPublishers, 2002, pg.12

[109] Moore, Geoffrey A.; Ibid.

[110] Moore, Geoffrey A.; Op. cit.

[111] Moore, Geoffrey A.; Op. cit.

[112] Moore, Geoffrey A.; Op. cit.

[113] Kiron, David; Kruschwitz, Nina; Haanaes, Knut; Reeves, Martin and Goh, Eugene; Chapter 3: World Is Tilting Toward Embracers; MIT Sloan Management Review and The Boston Consulting Group, 10 Feb 2011

[114] MIT Sloan: Sustainability & Innovation Global Executive Study, MIT Sloan Management Review and The Boston Consulting Group, 2010

[115] Kiron, David; Et al. Chapter 3: World Is Tilting Toward Embracers; Op. cit.

[116] MIT Sloan: Sustainability & Innovation Global Executive Study, Ibid.

[117] Kiron, David; Kruschwitz, Nina; Haanaes, Knut; Reeves, Martin and Goh, Eugene; Companies Profit From Embracing Sustainability; MIT Sloan Management Review; March 12, 2013

[118] McKeon, Andrew; Op. cit.

[119] Source: of Innovator's Dilemma by Prof. Clayton Christensen

[120] Porter, Michael and Kramer, Mark; How to fix Capitalism; Harvard Business Review, HBR.org; January–February 2011

[121] Porter, Michael and Kramer, Mark; Ibid.

[122] Porter, Michael and Kramer, Mark; Creating Shared Value; Harvard Business Review, HBR.org; January–February 2011

[123] Porter, Michael and Kramer, Mark; Ibid.

[124] Bockstette, Valerie and Stamp, Mike; Creating Shared Value: A How-to Guide for the New Corporate (R)evolution; FSG at www.fsg.org; Sponsored by Hewlett-Packard Company

[125] Porter, Michael E. and Kramer, Mark R.; Creating Shared Value; Harvard Business Review; January - February 2011

[126] McKeon, Andrew; Ibid.

[127] McKeon, Andrew; Op. cit.

[128] Porter, Michael E. and Kramer, Mark R.; Harvard Business Review, The Magazine, January 2011, Retrieved: October 15, 2012

[129] Porter, Michael E. and Kramer, Mark R.; Ibid.

[130] Porter, Michael E. and Kramer, Mark R.; Op. Cit.

[131] Porter, Michael E. and Kramer, Mark R.; Op. Cit.

[132] Porter, Michael E. and Kramer, Mark R.; Op. Cit.

[133] Gore, Al And Blood, David, Wall Street Journal Online | Opinion; A Manifesto for Sustainable Capitalism; December 14, 2011; Retrieved: October 12, 2012

[134] Gore, Al And Blood, David, Ibid.

[135] Ceres; http://www.ceres.org/roadmap-assessment/company-performance/governance-for-sustainability

[136] Ceres; http://www.ceres.org/roadmap-assessment/company-performance/stakeholder-engagement

[137] Ceres; http://www.ceres.org/roadmap-assessment/company-performance/disclosure

[138] Ceres; http://www.ceres.org/roadmap-assessment/company-performance/performance-operations

[139] Ceres; http://www.ceres.org/roadmap-assessment/company-performance/supply-chain

[140] Ceres; http://www.ceres.org/roadmap-assessment/company-performance/transportation-and-logistics

[141] Ceres; http://www.ceres.org/roadmap-assessment/company-performance/products-and-services

[142] Ceres; http://www.ceres.org/roadmap-assessment/company-performance/performance-employees

[143] Campbell's, Grow, Sustain; How Companies Are Doing Well by Doing Good; 2013 Report; Business Roundtable; April 2013

[144] Ernst & Young; Create, Grow, Sustain; How Companies Are Doing Well by Doing Good; 2013 Report; Business Roundtable; April 2013

[145] Collins, Jim; Great by Choice, HarperCollinsPublisher, 2011, p. 136

[146] 5. Sustainability's Engagement Strategy

[147] Brito, Michael; 8 Cultural Indicators of Social Business Transformation; Social Business News; http://www.socialbusinessnews.com; 14 May 2012

[148] Michelman, Paul; Steve Bishop interview, global lead of sustainability at IDEO; Don't Bother with the Green Consumer; HBR Blog Network; 24 Jan 2008

[149] Barwise, Patrick and Meehan, Sean; Is Your Company As Customer-Focused As You Think? MIT Sloan Management Review; 10 Apr 2010. Prod. #: SMR348-PDF-ENG; pgs 1-8

[150] Kotler, Philip; Marketing 3.0: The 10 Credos; Retreived: 12 Nov 13

[151] Deming, W.Edwards; Out of the Crisis, 1986

[152] Conceptual Issues, Ibid.

[153] Ceres Principles, a ten-point code of corporate environmental conduct to be publicly endorsed by companies as an environmental mission statement or ethic. UN Global Compact includes ten widely recognized humanitarian rights. GRI's 11 principles, covering the economic, environmental and ethical indicators of a company's performance.

[154] EPA, Everyday Choices: Opportunities For Environmental Stewardship, United States Environmental Protection Agency , Washington, D.C. 20460 , November 9, 2005, pg. 1

[155] Wikipedia; http://en.wikipedia.org/wiki/Stewardship; Retrieved: 23 March 2103

[156] Stewardship Education Best Practices Planning Guide; A Project of the Association of Fish and Wildlife Agencies' North American Conservation Education Strategy; Funded by a Multistate Grant of the Sport Fish and Wildlife Restoration Program; May 2008

[157] Stewardship Education Best Practices Planning Guide; Ibid.

[158] Kotter, John P.; Leading Change: Why Transformation Efforts Fail (HBR Classic); Harvard Business Review; 11 pages. Publication 01 Jan 2007.

[159] "Creating a Workable Company Code of Conduct," 2003, Ethics Resource Center

[160] Porter, Michael and Kramer, Mark; How to Fix Capitalism and Unleash a New Wave of Growth; Harvard Business Review; January-February 2011

[161] Porter, Michael and Kramer, Mark; Ibid.

[162] Anderson, Ray C.; Mid-Course Correction, Chelsea Green Publishing Company, copyright 1998, pgs. 78

[163] IBM, Leading Through Connections 2012 - IBM Corporation, pg. 8, Retrieved: 11 December 2012

[164] IBM, Ibid.

[165] Avery Dennison; Create, Grow, Sustain; How Companies Are Doing Well by Doing Good; 2013 Report; Business Roundtable; April 2013

[166] Bausch + Lomb; Create, Grow, Sustain; How Companies Are Doing Well by Doing Good; 2013 Report; Business Roundtable; April 2013

[167] Alcoa; Create, Grow, Sustain; How Companies Are Doing Well by Doing Good; 2013 Report; Business Roundtable; April 2013

[168] Boeing; Create, Grow, Sustain; How Companies Are Doing Well by Doing Good; 2013 Report; Business Roundtable; April 2013

[169] AKSteel; Create, Grow, Sustain; How Companies Are Doing Well by Doing Good; 2013 Report; Business Roundtable; April 2013

[170] ABB; Create, Grow, Sustain; How Companies Are Doing Well by Doing Good; 2013 Report; Business Roundtable; April 2013

[171] Bayer; Create, Grow, Sustain; How Companies Are Doing Well by Doing Good; 2013 Report; Business Roundtable; April 2013

[172] FMC; Create, Grow, Sustain; How Companies Are Doing Well by Doing Good; 2013 Report; Business Roundtable; April 2013

[173] Medtronic; Create, Grow, Sustain; How Companies Are Doing Well by Doing Good; 2013 Report; Business Roundtable; April 2013

[174] **6. All Employees Own The Vision**

[175] Hewson, Merillyn, Chief Executive Officer and President at Lockheed Martin; The First Things a New Leader Should Do to Build Trust; source: LinkedIn - Leadership and Managment; Retrieved: 19 September 2013

[176] Hewson, Merillyn, Ibid.

[177] Hewson, Mcrillyn, Op. Cit.

[178] Hewson, Merillyn, Op. Cit.

[179] Hewson, Merillyn, Op. Cit.

[180] Parr, Shawn; Culture Eats Strategy For Lunch; Jan 24, 2012

[181] Parr, Shawn; Ibid.

[182] Stacey, Mary; Taylor, Marilyn and Legge, David; From Resource Managers to Resource Leaders, strategy+business, http://www.strategy-business.com, Published: March 26, 2012

[183] Stacey, Mary; Taylor, Marilyn and Legge, David; Ibid.,

[184] Urlaub, Julie; Cultivating Talent with Sustainability-Based Incentives, www.taigacompany.com; August 5, 2010; Retrieved: 12 November 2012

[185] Porter, Michael and Kramer, Mark; How to Fix Capitalism and Unleash a New Wave of Growth; Harvard Business Review; January-February 2011

[186] Porter, Michael and Kramer, Mark; Ibid.

[187] Anderson, Ray C.; Mid-Course Correction, Chelsea Green Publishing Company, copyright 1998, pgs. 78

[188] Pfitzer, Marc; Bockstette, Valerie and Stamp, Mike; Innovating for Shared Value, HBR, September 2013; FSG research Note: Nestlé, Mars, Intel, and Becton Dickinson (BD) are FSG clients. Novartis has financially supported FSG's research.

[189] **7. Ethics And Stewardship**
[190] Leading Through Connections 2012 - IBM Corporation, pg. 15, Retrieved: 11 December 2012
[191] Jacobe, Dennis, Ph.D., is Chief Economist for Gallup;
Why Banks Must Rebuild Confidence Now; Gallup, 18 October 2012
[192] Montgomery, David B., and Catherine A. Ramus (2007) Including Corporate Social Responsibility, Environmental Sustainability, and Ethics in Calibrating MBA Job Preferences. Stanford Graduate School of Business, Research Paper No. 1981.
[193] Wikipedia; http://en.wikipedia.org/wiki/Stewardship; Retrieved: 23 March 2103
[194] Love Canal: Hooker Chemicals and Plastic Corporation (later known as Hooker Chemical Corporation, and more recently as Occidental Chemical Corporation or Oxy-Chem) bought the site after determining it had an impermeable clay substrate, which made it a good location for a chemical waste landfill. ... approximately 21,800 tons of chemical wastes dumped by Hooker until 1952. ... In March 1980 the President Carter declared a state of emergency at Love Canal and funded the permanent evacuation and relocation of an additional 780 families.
http://www.encyclopedia.com/topic/Love_Canal.aspx
[195] Berkshire Hathaway Inc. Code Of Business Conduct And Ethics, http://english6.net/c/code-of-ethics---berkshire-hathaway-inc.-w11208.html, Berkshire Hathaway Inc.. Retrieved: 29 Nov 2012
[196] Velasquez, Manuel; Moberg, Dennis; Meyer, Michael J.; Shanks, Thomas; McLean, Margaret R.; DeCosse, David; André, Claire and Hanson, Kirk O.; A Framework for Thinking Ethically, Markkula Center for Applied Ethics at Santa Clara University, www.scu.edu/ethics/practicing/decision/framework.html, Retrieved: 29 August 2012
[197] Velasquez, Manuel; et. al.; Ibid.
[198] Velasquez, Manuel; et. al.; Op. Cit.
[199] Velasquez, Manuel; et. al.; Op. Cit.
[200] Velasquez, Manuel; et. al.; Op. Cit.
[201] Velasquez, Manuel; et. al.; Op. Cit.
[202] Stewardship Education Best Practices Planning Guide; Op cit;
[203] Wikipedia; http://en.wikipedia.org/wiki/Stewardship; Retrieved: 23 March 2103
[204] Stewardship Education Best Practices Planning Guide; Op cit;
[205] EPA, Everyday Choices: Opportunities For Environmental Stewardship, United States Environmental Protection Agency , Washington, D.C. 20460 , November 9, 2005, pg. 1
[206] Wikipedia; http://en.wikipedia.org/wiki/Stewardship; Retrieved: 23 March 2103
[207] Conceptual Issues, The Sustainability Report, Affiliated with the Institute for Research and Innovation in Sustainability; http://www.sustreport.org/; Retrieved: 27 July 2011
[208] Transparency Needs to Have Integrity, Event Horizons, jbseventhorizons.wordpress.com; Retrieved: 29 Nov 2012
[209] Murphy, Chris; Collaboration Trumps Innovation For CEOs, http://www.informationweek.com; June 04, 2012
[210] Coc-Cola Vision; http://www.coca-cola.co.uk/about-us/coca-cola-mission-vision-statement.html
[211] General Mills; Create, Grow, Sustain; How Companies Are Doing Well by Doing Good; 2013 Report; Business Roundtable; April 2013
[212] Honeywell; Create, Grow, Sustain; How Companies Are Doing Well by Doing Good; 2013 Report; Business Roundtable; April 2013

[213] **8. Good People And New Talent**
[214] Sustainability people profiles; Unilever; http://www.unilever.com/sustainable-living/betterlivelihoods/profiles/index.aspx; Retrieved: 10 Aug 2013
[215] Eastman, Business Roundtable 2012, www.eastman.com/sustainability
[216] Campbell's, Business Roundtable 2012, wwcampbellsoupcompany.com
[217] Fluor, Business Roundtable 2012, www.flour.com
[218] Barclays, Business Roundtable 2012, www.barclays.com/citizenship
[219] Talent Management, Talent Measurement Overhaul Needed for Generational Diversity, 12 March 2013, Retrieved: 17 March 2013
[220] Spinks, Todd; From a discussion about personnel in today's age. Nov 2013
[221] Capozucca. Peter and Sarni, William; Sustainability 2.0 - Using sustainability to drive business innovation and growth., Deloitte Review, Retrieved: 23 Nov 2012
[222] Capozucca. Peter and Sarni, William; Ibid.
[223] Capozucca. Peter and Sarni, William; Op. cit.
[224] Capozucca. Peter and Sarni, William; Op. cit.
[225] Schuler, Dr. A. J.; "Overcoming Resistance to Change: Top Ten Reasons for Change Resistance", 2003
[226] Schuler, Dr. A. J.; Ibid.
[227] Schuler, Dr. A. J.; Op. cit.
[228] Schuler, Dr. A. J.; Op. cit.
[229] Schuler, Dr. A. J.; Op. cit.
[230] Schuler, Dr. A. J.; Op. cit.
[231] Schuler, Dr. A. J.; Op. cit.
[232] Schuler, Dr. A. J.; Op. cit.
[233] Schuler, Dr. A. J.; Op. cit.
[234] Schuler, Dr. A. J.; Op. cit.
[235] Schuler, Dr. A. J.; Op. cit.
[236] PwC; Create, Grow, Sustain; How Companies Are Doing Well by Doing Good; 2013 Report; Business Roundtable; April 2013
[237] P&G; Create, Grow, Sustain; How Companies Are Doing Well by Doing Good; 2013 Report; Business Roundtable; April 2013

[238] **9. Sustainability and Quality Crossroads**
[239] A New Era of Sustainability, UN Global Compact – Accenture CEO Study 2010
[240] Porter, Michael E.; Hills, Greg; Pfitzer, Marc; Patscheke, Sonja and Hawkins, Elizabeth; Measuring Shared Value
How to Unlock Value by Linking Social and Business Results; June 2011, p. 9
[241] Lash, Jonathan and Wellington, Fred; Ibid.
[242] Lash, Jonathan and Wellington, Fred; Op. cit.
[243] Lash, Jonathan and Wellington, Fred; Competitive Advantage on a Warming Planet; Harvard Business Review; March 2007
[244] Jones, Jeffrey M.; Worry About U.S. Water, Air Pollution at Historical Lows; Gallup Politics, Gallup News, www.gallup.com; 13 April 2012
[245] Consumers Demand Sustainability Results, Survey Says; Environmental Leader; 24 Oct 2012; Retrieved: 7 Aug 2013
[246] Deming, W. Edwards; Out of the Crisis; 1986, p. 76
[247] Deming, W. Edwards; Ch.2 Principles for Transformation; Out of the Crisis; 1982; p. 20
[248] Deming's 14 Points; American Society of Quality; https://asq.org/; Retrieved: 31 Oct 2013
[249] Natrass, Brian and Altomare, Mary; The Natural Step for Business, Second edition, 2001
[250] Capozucca. Peter and Sarni, William; Sustainability 2.0 - Using sustainability to drive business innovation and growth., Deloitte Review, Retrieved: 23 Nov 2012

[251] Capozucca and Sarni, Ibid.

[252] Capozucca and Sarni, Op. cit.

[253] Capozucca and Sarni, Op. cit.

[254] Cawein, Jenni; Et.al.; The Environmental Professional's Guide to Lean and Six Sigma; U.S. Environmental Protection Agency (EPA); Aug 2009

[255] Cawein, Jenni; Et.al.; Ibid.

[256] Cawein, Jenni; Et.al.; Op. cit.

[257] CardinalHealth; Create, Grow, Sustain; How Companies Are Doing Well by Doing Good; 2013 Report; Business Roundtable; April 2013

[258] Convergys; Create, Grow, Sustain; How Companies Are Doing Well by Doing Good; 2013 Report; Business Roundtable; April 2013

[259] **10. Identifying Inefficiencies and Waste**

[260] Kiron, David; Kruschwitz, Nina; Haanaes, Knut; Reeves, Martin and Goh, Eugene; Companies Profit From Embracing Sustainability; MIT Sloan Management Review; March 12, 2013

[261] Kiron, David; Kruschwitz, Nina; Haanaes, Knut; Reeves, Martin and Goh, Eugene; Ibid.

[262] Anderson, Ray C.; Mid-Course Correction, Chelsea Green publishing Company, White River Junction, Vermont, 3rd printing September 2005

[263] Womack, James P. and Jones, Daniel T.; Lean Enterprise Institute, http://www.lean.org; Retrieved: 8 Aug 2013

[264] Cawein, Jenni; Et.al.; The Environmental Professional's Guide to Lean and Six Sigma; U.S. Environmental Protection Agency (EPA); Aug 2009

[265] Cawein, Jenni; Et.al.; Ibid.

[266] Cawein, Jenni; Et.al.; Op. cit.

[267] Cawein, Jenni; Et.al.; Op. cit.

[268] Cawein, Jenni; Et.al.; Op. cit.

[269] Cawein, Jenni; Et.al.; Op. cit.

[270] Cawein, Jenni; Et.al.; Op. cit.

[271] Cawein, Jenni; Et.al.; Ibid.

[272] Jacowski, Tony; Lean Six Sigma - 5 Reasons Your Organization Needs It; ArticlesBase SC #23028, www.articlesbase.com; 17 Apr 2006

[273] Cawein, Jenni; Et.al.; Op. cit.

[274] U.S. Green Building Council; www.epa.gov/oaintrnt/projects/; Retrieved: 16 Oct 13

[275] LEED; LEED is driving the green building industry.; http://www.usgbc.org/leed; Retrieved: 30 Oct 2013

[276] U.S. Green Building Council; Ibid.

[277] U.S. Green Building Council; Op. cit.

[278] LEED Rating System; http://www.usgbc.org/leed/rating-systems; Retrieved: 25 Oct 2013

[279] Green Building Standards; http://www.epa.gov

[280] LEED Rating System; Op. cit.

[281] LEED Rating System; Op. cit.

[282] U.S. Green Building Council; Op. cit.

[283] LEED Rating System; Op. cit.

[284] Information Technology Settings and Strategies for Energy Savings in Commercial Buildings; National Renewable Energy Laboratory; www.nrel.gov; December 2011

[285] Vokoun, Ron; What is Energy Star for Data Centers?; Data Center Knowledge; http://www.datacenterknowledge.com; 27 Aug 2012

[286] *Finding the Green in Green Computing*, by Mark A. Monroe, Director, Sustainable Computing, Sun Microsystems, Inc. Sep, 2009. Slide 34.

[287] Kill Comatose Computers, Forbes, by Ken Brill, 11/19/2008. www.forbes.com/2008/11/16/cio-comatose-computers-tech-cio-cx_kb_1119computers.html

[288] Important to Recognize the Dramatic Improvement in Data Center Efficiency, Uptime Institute, 9/25/12. blog.uptimeinstitute.com/2012/09/important-to-recognize-the-dramatic-improvement-in-data-center-efficiency/

[289] Purchasing More Energy-Efficient Servers, UPSs, and PDUs; Energy Star; http://www.energystar.gov

[290] Hot Aisle/Cold Aisle Layout; Energy Star; http://www.energystar.gov

[291] Containment/Enclosures; Energy Star; http://www.energystar.gov

[292] http://www.klingstubbins.com/about/pdfs_articles/071001_Fan_Energy_Reduction.pdf

[293] Variable Speed Fan Drives; Energy Star; http://www.energystar.gov

[294] Uptime Institute, http://upsitetechnologies.com/images/stories/pdf/whitepapers/reducing bypass airflow is essential for eliminating hotspots.pdf

[295] Information Technology Settings and Strategies for Energy Savings in Commercial Buildings; Op. cit.

[296] Evans, Tony; Humidification Strategies for Data Centers and Network Rooms; http://www.ptsdcs.com/whitepapers/47.pdf

[297] Air-Side Economizer; Energy Star; http://www.energystar.gov

[298] Water-Side Economizer; Energy Strar; http://www.energystar.gov

[299] IEA; Energy-Efficient Transport Could Save Cities $70 Trillion; Environment News Service; http://ens-newswire.com/2013/07/15/energy-efficient-transport-could-save-cities-70-trillion/; 15 July 2013

[300] LaMonica, Martin; Apple Data Center Does Fuel Cell Industry a Huge Favor; MIT Technology Review; December 6, 2012

[301] LaMonica, Martin; Ibid.

[302] Bouton, Shannon; Creyts, Jon; Kiely, Tom; Livingston, John ; Nauclér; Tomas; McKinsey Sustainability & Resource Productivity Energy efficiency: A compelling global resource;

[303] Information Technology Settings and Strategies for Energy Savings in Commercial Buildings; Op. cit.

[304] Biomass Energy; EPA; www.epa.gov; Retrieved: 15 Oct 2013

[305] Bloomenergy; www.bloomenergy.com/; Retrieved: 15 Oct 2013

[306] Geothermal Energy Association (GEA) 2009. U.S. Geothermal Power Production and Development Update. Union of Concerned Scientists; Retrieved: 15 Oct 2013

[307] EMEC. "Tidal Energy Devices". 5 October 2008, Retrieved: 15 Oct 2013

[308] Global Solar PV installed Capacity crosses 100GW Mark. renewindians.com (11 February 2013).

[309] "Sunny Uplands: Alternative energy will no longer be alternative"; The Economist; 21 November 2012. Retrieved 28 December 2012.

[310] Supply chain energy efficiency critical to reducing carbon footprint; Modern Materials Handling; 7 August 2013

[311] Kuehn, Kurt; Five Reasons the CFO Should Care About Sustainability, pressroom.ups.com, Kuehn stressed five reasons CFOs and financial leaders should consider sustainability a bottom line priority, Retrieved: 14 May 2012

[312] PickensPlan, http://www.pickensplan.com/theplan/; Retrieved: 24 Oct 2013

[313] Waste Assessment Approaches, http://www.epa.gov/smm/wastewise/approach.htm; Retrieved: 31 Aug 2013

[314] WalMart web site: http://corporate.walmart.com/global-responsibility/environment-sustainability

[315] WalMart web site; Ibid.

[316] WalMart web site; Op. Cit.

[317] WalMart web site; Op. Cit.

[318] WalMart Objectives and Actions; http://www.walmartstores.com/Sustainability/10605.aspx?p=9176; Retrieved: 3 May 2012

[319] Universal Wastes, EPA, http://www.epa.gov/osw/hazard/wastetypes/universal/; Retrieved: 31 Jul 2013

[320] Cawein, Jenni; Et.al.; Op. cit.

[321] EPA source: Source: http://water.epa.gov/polwaste/nps/chap3.cfm

[322] EPA source: http://water.epa.gov/polwaste/nps/chap3.cfm

[323] Cawein, Jenni; Et.al.; Op. cit.

[324] EPA source: http://water.epa.gov/polwaste/nps/chap3.cfm

[325] Abbott; Create, Grow, Sustain; How Companies Are Doing Well by Doing Good; 2013 Report; Business Roundtable; April 2013

[326] Accenture; Create, Grow, Sustain; How Companies Are Doing Well by Doing Good; 2013 Report; Business Roundtable; April 2013

[327] The Man; W. Edwards Deming Institute; www.deming.org; Retrieved: 22 July 2013

[328] **11. Transformation's Four Phases**

[329] Goonan, Brian, "Business Transformation: Doing it Right, Part I," CIO Magazine, 9 February 2005

[330] Research Report Winter 2013, The Innovation Bottom Line; MIT Sloan Management Review • The Boston Consulting Group

[331] De Morsella, Tracey; CEOs See Sustainability As Engine For Growth But Industry Sectors Split On Priorities, FastCompany, 25 May 2011

[332] De Morsella, Tracey; Ibid.

[333] De Morsella, Tracey; Op. cit.

[334] Kuehn, Kurt; Five Reasons the CFO Should Care About Sustainability, pressroom.ups.com, Kuehn stressed five reasons CFOs and financial leaders should consider sustainability a bottom line priority, Retrieved: 14 May 2012

[335] Bottom-line benefits of sustainable business practices, Six growing trends in corporate sustainability:an Ernst & Young survey in cooperation with GreenBiz Group; based on over 1,600 online participants; 2012

[336] Bottom-line benefits of sustainable business practices, Ernst & Young; Ibid.

[337] Bottom-line benefits of sustainable business practices, Ernst & Young; Op. cit.

[338] Bottom-line benefits of sustainable business practices, Ernst & Young; Op. cit.

[339] Bottom-line benefits of sustainable business practices, Ernst & Young; Op. cit.

[340] Bottom-line benefits of sustainable business practices, Ernst & Young; Op. cit.

[341] Capozucca. Peter and Sarni, William; Sustainability 2.0 - Using sustainability to drive business innovation and growth., Deloitte Review, Retrieved: 23 Nov 2012

[342] Schuler, Dr. A. J.; "Overcoming Resistance to Change: Top Ten Reasons for Change Resistance", 2003

[343] Wurtzel, Marvin; Reasons for Six Sigma Deployment Failures; BPMInstitute.org; Retrieved 4 Jul 2013

[344] Capozucca and Sarni, Ibid.

[345] Capozucca and Sarni, Op. cit.

[346] Schuler, Dr. A. J.; Ibid.

[347] Capozucca and Sarni, Op. cit.

[348] Schuler, Dr. A. J.; Op. cit.

[349] Schuler, Dr. A. J.; Op. cit.

[350] Schuler, Dr. A. J.; Op. cit.

[351] Schuler, Dr. A. J.; Op. cit.

[352] Research Report Winter 2013, The Innovation Bottom Line; Ibid.

[353] BNSF; Create, Grow, Sustain; How Companies Are Doing Well by Doing Good; 2013 Report; Business Roundtable; April 2013

[354] **12. Realization - Audit and Validation**
[355] Haanaes, Knut; Arthur, David; Balagopal, Balu; Kong, Ming Teck; Reeves, Martin; Velken. Ingrid; Hopkins, Michael S.; and Kruschwitz, Nina; MIT Sloan School of Management and the Boston Consulting Group; Sustainability: The 'Embracers' Seize Advantage; Winter 2011
[356] Capozucca. Peter and Sarni, William; Sustainability 2.0 - Using sustainability to drive business innovation and growth., Deloitte Review, Retrieved: 23 Nov 2012
[357] Schuler, Dr. A. J.; Ibid.
[358] Capozucca and Sarni, Op. cit.
[359] Riley, Jim; Strategic Audit;
http://www.tutor2u.net/business/strategy/Strategic_audit.htm; 23 Sep 2012
[360] Riley, Jim; Ibid.
[361] Riley, Jim; Op. cit.
[362] Riley, Jim; Op. cit.
[363] Riley, Jim; Op. cit.
[364] Riley, Jim; Op. cit.
[365] Bredenberg, Al; Energy and Carbon Management Are Increasingly on Manufacturers' Radar; ThomasNet http://news.thomasnet.com/green_clean/2012/08/27/energy-and-carbon-management-are-increasingly-on-manufacturers-radar/; August 27th, 2012
[366] Mohin, Tim ; Forbes Leadership Forum, Contributor, The Top 10 Trends in CSR for 2012, Forbes, 1 January 2012
[367] Disclosures & Rankings; Annual Report & Sustainability Report; Eaton.
http://www.eaton.com/Eaton/OurCompany/Sustainability/AccountabilityTransparency/index.htm
[368] ConocoPhillips; Create, Grow, Sustain; How Companies Are Doing Well by Doing Good; 2013 Report; Business Roundtable; April 2013
[369] Avery Dennison; Create, Grow, Sustain; How Companies Are Doing Well by Doing Good; 2013 Report; Business Roundtable; April 2013
[370] Principal Financial Group; Create, Grow, Sustain; How Companies Are Doing Well by Doing Good; 2013 Report; Business Roundtable; April 2013
[371] Anderson, Ray C. with White, Robin; Forward, Business Lessons from a Radical Industrialist; St. Martin's Griffin, March 2011; ISBN: 978-0-312-54455-3, ISBN10: 0-312-54455-3,
[372] *Lexicon*
[373] Definitions extracted from the Energy STAR program, http://www.energystar.gov.
[374] Resources: For more information: Biomimicry Institute. (n.d.). What is Biomimicry?. In Biomimicry Institute. Retrieved March 14, 2011 from www.biomimicryinstitute.org
[375] Resources: For more information: BusinessDictionary; www.businessdictionary.com
[376] Resources: For more information: www.ceres.org
[377] Resources: For more information: BusinessDictionary;
http://www.businessdictionary.com/definition/competitor.html#ixzz2h4VfVjnn
[378] Definitions extracted from the Energy STAR program, http://www.energystar.gov.
[379] Resources: For more information: Dictionary.com;
http://dictionary.reference.com/browse/Greenhouse_gases
[380] Resources: For more information: www.globalreporting.org
[381] Resources: For more information: BusinessDictionary.com;
www.businessdictionary.com
[382] Resources: For more information: BusinessDictionary.com; Read more:
http://www.businessdictionary.com/definition/multinational-corporation-MNC.html#ixzz2eWsWevrp
[383] Definitions extracted from the Energy STAR program, http://www.energystar.gov.
[384] Resources: For more information: As defined by the International Union of Pure and Applied Chemistry (IUPAC)

[385] Definitions extracted from the Energy STAR program, http://www.energystar.gov.
[386] Definitions extracted from the Energy STAR program, http://www.energystar.gov.
[387] Definitions extracted from the Energy STAR program, http://www.energystar.gov.
[388] Resources: For more information: UN Global Compact; www.unglobalcompact.org

Made in the USA
Charleston, SC
13 December 2013